PENGUIN BOOKS

Single Mother on the Verge

Single Mother on the Verge

MARIA ROBERTS

PENGUIN BOOKS

PENGUIN BOOKS

Published by the Penguin Group
Penguin Books Ltd, 80 Strand, London WC2R ORL, England
Penguin Group (USA) Inc., 375 Hudson Street, New York, New York 10014, USA
Penguin Group (Canada), 90 Eglinton Avenue East, Suite 700, Toronto, Ontario, Canada M4P 2Y3
(a division of Pearson Penguin Canada Inc.)
Penguin Ireland, 25 St Stephen's Green, Dublin 2, Ireland (a division of Penguin Books Ltd)
Penguin Group (Australia), 250 Camberwell Road, Camberwell, Victoria 3124, Australia
(a division of Pearson Australia Group Pty Ltd)
Penguin Books India Pvt Ltd, 11 Community Centre, Panchsheel Park, New Delhi – 110 017, India
Penguin Group (NZ), 67 Apollo Drive, Rosedale, North Shore 0632, New Zealand
(a division of Pearson New Zealand Ltd)
Penguin Books (South Africa) (Pty) Ltd, 24 Sturdee Avenue, Rosebank,
Johannesburg 2196, South Africa

Penguin Books Ltd, Registered Offices: 80 Strand, London WC2R ORL, England

www.penguin.com

First published 2009

1

Set in 12.5/14.75 pt Garamond MT
Typeset by Palimpsest Book Production Limited, Grangemouth, Stirlingshire
Printed in England by Clays Ltd, St Ives plc

978–0–141–03777–6

www.greenpenguin.co.uk

Penguin Books is committed to a sustainable future
for our business, our readers and our planet.
The book in your hands is made from paper
certified by the Forest Stewardship Council.

For
Scratch T
(a.k.a. my son)

Prologue

Manchester, 29 December

It is snowing very lightly. Damien and I sit by the window in a bar watching snowflakes fall from the sky and disappear into the dark water of the canal. Outside, crowds hurry along Great Bridgewater Street, past the Bridgewater Hall, perhaps on their way to meet friends or heading home from the sales. I sense something might happen. There are subtle signs that no one else notices. Damien is cunning like that. He is able to control my fear like the conductor of an orchestra: one look, a grip of my wrist that feels menacing rather than loving.

We leave the bar at closing time and head towards Oxford Road in search of a cab. I step inside a phone box just outside the Ritz nightclub. Damien's friends are in a takeaway across the road, ordering kebabs and fries. They are laughing. Look over this way. Please look over this way: tell me I can go home with you, not him. Damien glares at me, then takes a step back and runs at the phone box. He kicks the door fiercely, and as his foot hits the glass pane I am willing it not to break.

'It's my birthday, Damien,' I mouth to him through the window. 'Don't.'

Twenty-four today.

'Taxi,' I say into the receiver. 'I'm outside the Ritz, Whitworth Street, Manchester. How long?'

The operator says ten minutes. I replace the receiver on the cradle and look towards the queue of people snaking along the pavement waiting for black cabs. They can see what Damien is doing – they're watching. Don't just watch – intervene. They must think him mad. Me, I'm just lost in all of this.

'When we get home,' he hisses through the glass, 'I'm going to carve your fucking eyes out.'

I can't understand why Damien wants to harm me. I haven't done anything wrong.

Stop shouting at me, Damien. Stop shouting.

Hours ago, I dropped my son Jack off at my mother's house. 'Look after yourself this evening,' Mum said gravely. She stood on the garden path for a long time, waving me off. I should have stayed with her. If I had, I wouldn't be stuck here with him.

I didn't want to celebrate my birthday with Damien. Now I want to be somewhere else, somewhere warm, with someone kind. But where can I go? Nowhere. It's past midnight. My friends and family will all be in bed. Not that they would welcome me in. They're worn down by my trouble with Damien. I should just stroll out of the phone box and walk over to the takeaway. If I pretend that none of this is happening, then maybe it won't.

After I dropped Jack off I collected Damien from the pub. He swaggered drunkenly out onto the road and towards the car. Our drive home was spiked with nasty remarks, so when we arrived at Sunnyside I walked ahead of him through the communal gardens and down our path. Then I unlocked the front door, gesturing for Damien to pass ahead of me so I could bolt back to the car.

I should have been quicker because Damien darted out of the house, grabbed me roughly by the arm and pulled me indoors. 'Get in the fucking house,' he said, squaring up to me against the wall, his nose touching mine, so close his beery breath warmed my lips. 'You're not going anywhere.'

While I soaked in the bath, he ironed the skirt I'm wearing now. He ironed the hem nicely and everything. He poured me a glass of wine before we left the house. And he kissed me. Damien isn't always a monster.

Please stop kicking the phone box, Damien. Stop yelling. People are watching and I'm ashamed to be here, such a silly young girl, a caged spectacle.

The taxi driver drops us off at the edge of the communal gardens just by our front door. I want to ask him to take me away from Damien, but he drives off too quickly. Back in the house, I make my way upstairs.

If I lie very still on the bed in my nightdress, curled up into a ball against the wall, and pretend to be asleep, when Damien comes to bed he may slide in next to me. If he does that, I can pretend to forget about his rants outside the phone box. I hold my breath listening to him stamp up the stairs. He thumps through the bedroom door making me jolt with fear. Then the room bursts bright with white light so I blink and groan as if he's woken me. 'Are you getting into bed?' I ask.

'You're not going to sleep,' Damien snaps from the doorway.

If I can make it out of the house I could hide behind a fence at the end of our street, but I'm not strong enough to get past him – I know I'm not – so I curl back into a ball and cover my head with the duvet.

Damien grips a tight fistful of my hair.

'That hurts.' I wince.

He drags me upright. 'Get out of fucking bed,' he shouts hoarsely.

'Let go, Damien.' I stagger across the bedroom trying to keep step with him, fearful that he will rip my hair from my scalp. He draws me across the landing and throws me to the floor. I tense waiting for the kick. Damien stands above me with a murderous look in his eyes. He places his hands around my neck and squeezes until my skin stings.

'Get off the fucking floor and walk downstairs,' he says.

Suddenly I feel very cold. A chill sweeps across the landing as if a window has swung open. Damien yells and curses at me as I rub my hands over the goose-bumps on my arms to generate heat. Standing up, I tug my night-dress over my knees, then walk down the stairs and into the living room.

Damien leaves the room for a moment, but there isn't time to escape so, hurriedly, I dial 999 and, in a hushed voice, ask for the police. I have barely begun to speak when he walks back in. I shield the phone with my body and secretly put it down. Then it rings. He picks it up. I can't hear what is said exactly but I know that the police are asking if everything is okay because Damien replies very calmly, 'Everything's fine – the call was a mistake, Officer. Sorry to bother you.'

Slowly he turns to me and, exaggerating, replaces the receiver before ripping the cable from the socket. I watch as he crashes his foot down hard on the phone until it smashes into little pieces. 'Did you call the police?'

I don't answer.

'You called the police, didn't you?'

What counts as provocation in a court of law? Have I provoked Damien in some way? The police will come soon. We'll hear sirens. They'll bang on the front door and cart him away. Just as they have many times before.

'Sit there. Sit still.'

I sit on the sofa.

Damien takes the chair opposite. 'I am going to kill you,' he says coolly. 'In a moment I am going to go into the kitchen and get a knife.'

Shivering, I pull my legs up to my chest in an attempt to keep warm. I mustn't let him see that I'm scared. Same old script, Damien, same old –

He lurches up and kicks my leg. 'I said *SIT STILL.*'

I feel faint. Why haven't the police arrived? Josie next door must have heard his shouts. Please, I beg silently, if you can hear, then call for help. Damien leaps up to throttle me again but this time he strangles me for longer than before. His fingers push hard against my throat, and when I look into his eyes, he seems so very sad.

His grip loosens. I rasp for air. My only chance is to wait until he tires of his terrorism. I must mentally disconnect myself from him and do my best not to antagonize him further. I swing my legs down over the sofa, then sit as upright as I can. I will try not to flinch when he kicks me. I cannot retaliate: if I do, he may well go and grab a knife. If he stabs me, who will care for Jack? I wish I could fight back.

Damien leaps up to strangle me again, so tightly that this must surely be the end of me. I don't care if I die, truly I don't, because I'm exhausted with my life. Jack will be better off without me. He's so young – not yet four – he'll forget me quickly.

Damien, if you want to take my life, then get on with it. Don't let's make this last all night. I'm tired. I have a better place to be.

Then the mood changes. He slumps into a chair opposite me. 'I can't do it,' he sobs. 'I'm sorry . . . I love you.'

It's all over.

Thank God for that.

PART ONE

I

'It needs another coat of paint,' I say to Rhodri. 'Look.' I point to the streaks where the matt blue emulsion has dried in uneven stripes across the wallpaper. Each time the clouds move, sunbeams hit the walls, showing up the patchy paint job. It is mid-October and we're sitting cross-legged on bits of cardboard in my son's bedroom. All around us, strewn over the bare floorboards, are empty tins of Tardis-blue paint. I am dunking Digestives into my tea and fishing out lost chunks with paint-stained fingers.

'But I've given it four coats already,' says Rhodri. 'Not another – please.'

We're dappled with blue and white paint, like a pair of strange-looking cheetahs. It's such a beautiful autumn day, too nice to be stuck indoors. Jack is away for the weekend with his grandparents. He has recently turned eight, an age worthy of a more grown-up bedroom with Daleks and *Gorillaz* posters, not *A Bug's Life* characters and matchstick men scrawlings from when he was a tot.

Rhodri and I paint through the night then fall into bed happily. Now it is Saturday morning and we have two whole days of decorating ahead of us. At some point I must go out to deal with the girlie part of the job: soft furnishings.

'I shall go to get more paint, and pick up some bedding

and curtains,' I tell Rhodri. 'We need to measure the windows.'

He scowls at me affectionately: '*Shopping?*'

'Yes, shopping.' I laugh.

We lean into one another across our mugs of tea and kiss. Perfect. This is all so perfect. I search in his pockets for the tape measure and, before I know it, he's undressing me again.

I'm picking up cushions from the shelves in the department store, plumping them, setting them down again, winding through the aisles until I arrive in the bedding section where I find the perfect duvet cover for Jack's bed: navy, printed with orange and gold planets and much cheaper than official *Doctor Who* merchandise. It definitely has an outer-space feel to it. I head off to the reduced section at the back of the store for some curtains and – what d'you know? – find the exact size I want in the exact colour. From the reduced trolley I pull out navy ones with tie-backs, all for the wonderful price of six pounds. It's my lucky day. Lucky year. Lucky two years?

For the first time in ages I feel happy and optimistic. It's been almost five years since Damien left after that awful night when he tried to strangle me. And now my Welsh boyfriend of two years, Rhodri, has joined me, my two white rabbits and my son Jack in our (not very) delightful house on a council estate in Manchester.

Rhodri looks like James Dean. From the day our eyes locked across a film set in Blackburn, he showed amazing potential to match my perfect-boyfriend specification beautifully (see Figure 1).

Figure 1:
My Perfect-boyfriend Specification

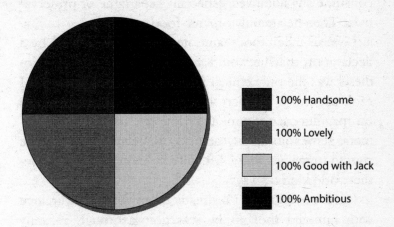

100% Handsome

100% Lovely

100% Good with Jack

100% Ambitious

Within weeks, Rhodri had surpassed my perfect-boyfriend specification. No more so than when, on one of our early dates, he spoke enthusiastically of his ambition To Buy a Van. A Man with a Van is invaluable to a single mother like me and I visualized a new world of home improvements, furniture removals and trips out to the local waste-disposal site. That was until Rhodri said, 'I'm giving up work. I don't want to work in the media. I want to live on the dole. Work is ugly and capitalist. I don't believe in it.' Which was miles away from what he'd said three months previously: 'In five years' time I could be earning eighty thousand pounds a year.' After much begging on my part, he came off the dole and recently found employment as a part-time home help.

A few months after we met he said, 'I don't want a monogamous relationship. We should be free to sleep with who we like.' So I took up with a former lover called

Toga. It wasn't long after this that Rhodri changed from vegetarian to vegan, stopped eating wheat and wouldn't consume any additives, especially aspartame or preservatives. Then he ate only organic food.

Low air-miles food came next, quickly followed by a declaration that he would *never* fly abroad and that biodiesel was the only ethical fuel after vegetable oil. Now I can't use those fun petroleum-based lubricants to bring on magnificent orgasms that you can buy at Ann Summers. It was about a year into our relationship that he started to make my life difficult in a thoughtful let's-save-the-world kind of way.

But it was too late. I'd already fallen completely in love with him. I'd thought he was going through a funny phase, but now that he's moved in with us I'm starting to think – Actually, forget that. The worst thing I can do is think.

'Hello,' I call, going into the house.

Rhodri pops his head around the door, then strolls over to greet me with a passionate and full-on tonsil-tickling kiss. 'I'd love a cup of tea,' I say.

This has got to be *the* major bonus of cohabiting: someone else to make cups of tea for you. I fling myself onto the sofa, throw my legs up over the arm, and puff out my chest so that my breasts look bigger.

'Thank you, darling,' I say to Rhodri, as he hands me a mug. 'How's the decorating going?'

'Just having a rest.'

I can see that.

'Small accident,' continues Rhodri.

I don't like that word, 'accident'. Accidents cost money. The last 'accident' was when Rhodri destroyed Jack's bedroom ceiling. Then there was the other 'accident' when he pulled, rather than carefully removed, the radiator from the wall, leaving a well-like hole that cost me hundreds of pounds to repair. I don't have hundreds of spare pounds. I work as a low-paid freelance journalist, PR girl, website administrator, and more. My executive title is 'Dog's Body' – I'll do anything to bring the money in. I don't even have a study. I run my own little empire from our poky kitchen-diner, except two days a week when I use a desk at an office in Manchester, where I kind of have a boss, Athens.

We're broke, but I can usually fit my working life around caring for Jack, which is the sole perk of being self-employed.

'When I was moving Jack's bed . . .'

'Yes . . .'

'When I was moving Jack's bed . . .'

'Yes . . .'

We're not getting far here are we?

'What's happened to Jack's bed, Rhodri?'

'When I was moving Jack's bed the leg snapped off it.'

'How?'

'I pushed it and it snapped.'

'Did you not think to lift it and shuffle?'

'I was in a rush. I wasn't thinking.'

Jack's bed was an expensive gift from my mother and her husband Rufus. It's one of those cabin beds with a ladder and a desk, and a chest of drawers. It is not a cheap melamine job from a catalogue. It is solid wood.

'It's okay,' I say cheerfully, because after the earlier home-improvement disasters I've only just managed to get Rhodri back into DIY and don't want to discourage him so soon. 'We can solve this.'

We trudge upstairs. The bed looks wonky to me.

'Here,' says Rhodri, showing me the fracture on the bed leg.

Nasty, and it doesn't look repairable either. There's nothing for it: all the legs on the bed will have to be amputated. 'Jack wanted a low bed. We'll just saw the legs off. No problem.'

By 'we' I mean 'he'. Rhodri will have to saw the legs off because I have no idea what to do with a saw – except put it back into its case. Though I'm impressed by my project-management skills: I identified the problem and found the solution. 'While you do that, I'll put the dinner on,' I say, as I back out of the bedroom.

Rhodri glowers at me. 'You're bowing out of this, aren't you?'

'We need to eat,' I explain.

'What are you making?'

'Braised lentils and dumplings.'

Enhanced with lashings of red wine, braised lentils taste meaty, thus satisfying Rhodri, a non-wheat-eating vegan, and me, a bread-munching omnivore. So, I'll be making the dumplings with what? Rice flour, or barley flour . . . I go down to the kitchen to take a look in the cupboards and see what we have.

Cooking for Rhodri can be a very long and complicated process. His mother, Margaret No. 3 (so-called because Jack's dead grandmother on Damien's side is Margaret

No. 1, and her replacement, Damien's stepmother, is Margaret No. 2) is American and an amazing cook. I am English and extremely competitive. Margaret No. 3 creates beautiful homemade meals: fish chowder, venison meatloaf, dhal, stuffed field mushrooms, you name it; even the simplest ingredients, like boiled vegetables, take on some otherworldly quality. This is because Margaret No. 3 marinates her food in motherly love.

Also, Rhodri will eat no processed food, no commercially produced sauces and nothing tinned (unless the contents are organic), no microwave meals, no pre-washed salads or ready-peeled vegetables so I have to scrub and cook everything from scratch. I have to check the ingredients on *everything* because Rhodri will not eat any chemicals – you'd be surprised how many products contain anti-caking agents or sweeteners. Recently we signed up for an allotment and have been trying to grow our own vegetables.

I need to be at least as good a cook as Margaret No. 3 (if not better) so that one day Rhodri will worship not just his mother but me too. Initially this was difficult, because the only meal I could put together was ham sandwiches with salad and crisps, which is no good to a non-wheat-eating vegan.

Our romance improved greatly after I enrolled on a Cordon Vert School of Cookery course at the Vegetarian Society in Cheshire, where a tutor provided me with the basic skills to manage our kitchen . . . I can't help but think that living with a vegetarian would be much easier than it is living with a vegan. As for living with a meat-eater, the very idea is becoming a full-blown fetish.

The sawing has come to an abrupt stop. Under the guise

of helpfulness, I take myself upstairs to see how things are progressing.

The bed looks like a futon. 'I didn't think you were going to cut the legs quite so short.'

'No choice,' says Rhodri.

It looks skewed to me. Perhaps he should have used a spirit level. 'Fantastic,' I say. 'Jack will love it. Like a sofa.' I scatter some cushions over it. 'See?'

What an inspired idea it was to convince Rhodri that the only way to finish decorating Jack's bedroom was to work all through the evening again. We stop at midnight and take ourselves off to the Bombay Balti down the road, a rough-shod establishment that does itself no justice with its blue neon sign and chintz wallpaper. It is, however, the friendli-est, tastiest Indian restaurant I have ever been to. Rhodri is impressed because even the poppadoms are homemade, wheat-free and vegan, as are the onion bhajiis. Two glasses of wine later, we decide that this is 'our' place. Of course we don't say that, but I know we'll come back with Jack.

Then it's home for more sex because tomorrow I need Rhodri to lay the carpet and help me hang curtains, tidy up and replace toys in time for Jack's return. If we carry on like this, I'll be slim but knackered in no time.

It's now Sunday morning and we need to finish Jack's bedroom. I'm driving Rhodri mad. He says I'm grumpy when Jack's with his grandparents, and when he's at home I'm giddy. I enjoy spending time alone with Rhodri but life feels sparkly with a child; you never know in which direction a day will go. One minute you're thinking about bills and work, and the next, an elbow-high quizmaster is challenging you to rapid-fire 'name that line' from the back catalogue of films he's memorized verbatim.

I have never met a small boy as grateful as Jack, which is wonderful, but also sad. During the Dark Years, when things turned bad with Damien, a period much shorter than the Ice Age but just as cold, Jack would open the fridge door and thank me for buying food. He would hug me tightly around the waist and say, 'Thank you, Mummy,' just for buying six tiny pots of *fromage frais*. He went crazy when I bought crisps or biscuits or an ice lolly. So, now that I have redecorated his room, with new curtains, a funky duvet cover, a rug, a beanbag chair and some *Futurama* posters, he may explode.

I was right.

Later, the three of us are sitting on Jack's bed, wearing pyjamas because Jack insisted on a pyjama party to celebrate his new bedroom. When he saw it he gasped and threw himself onto the beanbag. 'Oh, thank you,' he said. 'Thank you.' He loves it all. I knew he would. Three walls are matt blue, one is metallic blue, and we've painted big silver circles on his white wardrobe doors at the far end of the room. We used chalkboard paint on the wardrobe so that Jack can draw on it if he wants to. His toys are lined up on the windowsill and his favourite bears are slouched over the pillows. The short-legs bed seems to have worked wonders too, so the accident was a blessing.

Now we're cuddled up beneath the lamplight, drinking cocoa, biting into toast, and waiting for Rhodri to sit down and read to us. When he opens Ted Hughes's *The Iron Man*, Jack and I applaud, then settle into the pillows and wait for the story to begin.

2

In the weeks since Rhodri and I became cohabitants our home life has been a *teensy* bit tricky. For example, this evening I return home from my office job in town, working for Athens on his literature website, and fall onto my favourite chair – leather, high-backed, used to belong to my father – *fully* expecting a cup of tea, a snog and a fanfare ... only to discover that MY BOOKSHELF IS BEING REARRANGED.

'What are you doing?' I blurt out.

'Putting my books on the shelf,' replies Rhodri, taken aback.

The bookshelves double as soundproofing and are lined up against the wall to muffle Kirsty's singing next door. There is a system to the bookshelves. It may not be the Dewey decimal system but it's mine: non-fiction, cookery, literary fiction, commercial fiction, translation, poetry, Spanish language, feminist theory, drama, children's fiction. There is a system within these categories. Loosely, they are ordered by size, then by favourite. It's so random that only I understand it. And as I used to be the only inhabitant here, other than Jack, it wasn't a problem. Now Rhodri is moving the books and shoving them all over the place.

'There is an aesthetic to the system,' I tell him. Scream at him. 'An *aesthetic*.'

'Don't be ridiculous,' he scoffs.

'There is.' I point it out to him. 'I can't believe I've come *home* to this.'

In retrospect I can't believe *I've* come to this: too many years living on my own, commanding my own space, and I behave like a teenager. I upset Rhodri. We could have rearranged the books together.

Later, to make amends for my bad behaviour and to bond us back together again, I suggest that the three of us go on a bike ride tomorrow from Jackson, the town where we live, to Skelton a few miles away, stopping to drop Jack with Damien's stepmother (that's Margaret No. 2) and going on to see my father, who also lives in Skelton, as does my big sister, Josephine. If we're lucky we'll cadge lunch at my father's house, and dinner at Josephine's.

Jack and I never did anything like this before Rhodri came along because I was just too petrified to go out alone. Even taking Jack to the park was a drama after what Damien had done to me.

The first leg of the journey was a breeze. Now we're resting in Margaret No. 2's kitchen. Jack is slurping orange juice, I'm flicking through the *Mirror*, feigning horror at the latest celebrity gossip, and Rhodri is chatting to Margaret, who's standing by the window, about the merits of non-chemical washing-up liquid and how the ordinary variety pollutes the waterways. At least I think that's what they're talking about. I'm distracted, though, because Margaret has gone quiet, her spectacles have slipped down her nose, and she's wafting her arms back and forth.

'What?' I mouth. 'What?'

She places a finger to her lips to indicate that we shouldn't speak.

Is this a game?

Suddenly she rushes into the hall and I hear her say loudly and clearly, 'Hello, DAMIEN. Your dad isn't here, DAMIEN. He's just gone to the pub, DAMIEN. You'll find him there.'

Then I hear Damien's voice. It's been years, almost five now, but he sounds exactly the same. We can't just sit here – can't just wait for him to find us. Think . . . think . . . I look out to the garden where bath towels are hanging on the washing line. Grabbing Jack's arm I lead him out through the back door.

'What are we doing?' asks Jack.

'Just going into the garden.'

'Why?'

'It's a secret.'

I make eye instructions to Rhodri, who follows. Amazing how once you get to know someone you no longer need words to communicate, just grunts and gestures.

We stand on the lawn, hiding behind the towels flapping in the breeze, no doubt revealing our legs. Rhodri is bent double because he's so tall.

'Why are we hiding behind the washing?' asks Jack, over and over again. His bottom lip quivers. 'You're making me feel scared.'

'There's nothing to be scared of,' I soothe. 'I'm here, Rhodri is here, and Nana Margaret is here.'

'I feel stupid,' says Rhodri.

So do I.

But then Jack's voice fills with excitement: 'It's my dad, isn't it?'

I'm going to lie. It's a horrible thing to do. 'No. It's only a man,' I say uncertainly. 'Just a man, Jack.'

'Then why are we hiding behind Nana's towels?'

Margaret calls to us from the patio, 'He's gone. Maria, what *are* you doing?'

Sheepishly I shuffle out from behind the washing line. Jack follows, persistent in his inquiries: 'That was my dad, and you made me hide behind a towel?'

'Yes.'

Jack has only recently figured out that Eddie, Margaret's husband, is Damien's father. There are no pictures of Damien in their house. In all these years Damien has never appeared at their house unannounced when Jack and I have been there. He vanished from our lives. I was beginning to enjoy his absence.

'It was the bikes,' says Margaret. 'He was walking past and he saw them. That's what made him come in. Next time,' she adds, 'bring the bikes through to the back of the house.'

'Where has my dad gone?' demands Jack.

'I've no idea,' I say.

'He was in the house and you made me *hide* behind the *washing line*?'

Mothers do peculiar things, and I do more peculiar things than most: like refusing to open windows in the mad hot heat of summer, sleeping with the light on, refusing to put the bins out at night or even to step into the garden after dark.

'I panicked,' I explain. 'I heard his voice and wanted to

hide. It's all I could think of doing. My body did it, not me.'

I'm not superhuman.

Margaret is miffed. She knows that Damien's appearance at her house could jeopardize her special day with Jack, her gold-plated shining star of a grandson. She has no children of her own, but does have two Shih Tzus, Pixi and Fifi, that rank almost but not quite as highly as Jack: she feeds them fillet steak, they sleep on her king-size bed and she takes them to the park in Jack's old pushchair because they're too lazy to walk. Jack has his own room at Margaret's complete with toys, PlayStation 2, DVD player, flat-screen TV, CDs – he even has a stash of clothes, all far better than I can afford to buy.

Reluctantly, I leave him with Margaret on the promise that should Damien return – which seems unlikely: he will probably bag a couple of pints from his father and go wandering – I'm to be called immediately. I'll be just down the road at my father's house.

My mobile will be switched on. If Damien appears, Rhodri and I will race back to the house, retrieve Jack and off we'll go, full speed on our bicycles. I may need to rethink our choice of getaway vehicle. And route.

Rhodri and I have just sat down at my father's, when, as I'm relaying the story of what has just happened to my stepmother, Eleanor, my phone rings.

'He's here,' whispers Margaret.

'Where's Jack?' I whisper back.

'I pushed him over the fence into Michael's garden.'

Michael lives next door to Margaret. He's a caring single

dad to three young boys, who spend much of their time bouncing up and down on a trampoline. When Jack stays with Margaret he bounds between Michael's house and hers. Before Rhodri and I became serious, I used to think about asking Michael out, but maybe I couldn't have coped with so many lost boys.

'Damien is demanding to see Jack,' says Margaret.

'I'll be there in five minutes. Do *not* let Damien see Jack. I'll sort this out when I get there.'

I don't want Rhodri to witness any of this. If it hadn't been for Damien's arrival, our bike ride would have been perfect: the sky is blue, the sun's shining, there's a sharp chill in the air, the birds are thinking about migrating, then changing their minds and resting on bare branches. I'm wearing a fluorescent yellow cycling jacket – not sexy at all. Poor Rhodri. What if Damien tries to fight him? He'll think Jack and I are too much bother to live with so he'll pack up and leave. Then Jack will feel abandoned again. I wish I had a happy history, really I do. I wish I could say, 'I fell in love with my childhood sweetheart, we married young. He died. He loved us very much.' I wish I had the kind of past that speaks of romance and passion, not violence and trauma.

'Are you going to let Jack see him?' asks Rhodri.

'I don't know.'

'Do you want me to sit with you when you talk to him?'

'I should do this on my own.'

'Shall I stay close by?'

'If you could.'

I knock on Michael's door. He shows us in, shakes

Rhodri's hand, and encourages me to step into the hall-way. 'Jack is upstairs playing with the boys,' he says, with a smile. 'He's fine.'

I feel awkward that Michael has wound up in this. 'Can Rhodri stay here while I go next door to speak to Damien?' I ask.

'Certainly.' He turns to Rhodri. 'Families can be so complicated.'

I remember all the times when Damien turned up at my old house in the early hours of the morning, banging and shouting for me to open the door.

Hearing my voice, Jack bolts down the stairs. 'My dad's next door,' he stammers.

'I know.'

'So, can I see him?'

Rhodri kisses my cheek. 'Sit by the window,' he says. 'I'll watch you from here. At the first sign of trouble I'll come and get you. How are you feeling?'

'Nervous.'

But as Jack takes my hand and we leave Michael's house, I'm frightened. We walk steadily down the driveway and to Margaret's. Jack holds his breath, his little fingers tip-tap between mine. The front door has been left open for us so we walk straight into the kitchen. We gaze out of the window to the garden, where Damien stands. From his mouth a drooping cigarette casts swirls of smoke into the air. We watch as he bends down to tie his shoelace. Upright, he stares blankly ahead of him. Not at the house, or the roses, or the pear tree. He just stands there. Empty.

Jack looks up at me, bursting with expectation.

'Would you like to speak to him, Jack?' I ask.

'Yes.'

I had thought I could walk with Jack to join Damien, but I can't. How weak. I can't even stroll with my son to meet his father so he's left to do it alone. Jack looks so tiny, so hopeful. I watch sadly as Damien scoops him into his arms. I try not to cry when Jack clings to him and burrows his head into the warm space on his shoulder, trying to breathe in his daddy's smell.

'Hello, mate,' says Damien.

When he attempts to set his son back on the ground, Jack will not let go. His little hands grip Damien's as he gazes up into his face, nodding solemnly and replying in brief but well-formed sentences, eager to impress, eager to be the best little boy he can. Jack is wonderstruck by his very own hero standing right before him.

When Damien catches sight of me in the kitchen, he heads indoors with Jack. We sit opposite each other at the dining-table, while Jack takes the big chair at the head: he's sitting between his mum and dad – all three of us together for the first time in years.

Damien attempts time and again to get me to talk but I have nothing to say. Whenever I had imagined this moment, it was with fear, but now when I look at him I am filled with regret. He may be dressed smartly, but his clothes appear dirty from a heavy night out. He struggles to talk to us, repeating the same few words over and over again. Jack will remember none of this. He will only remember the wonder of seeing him again, hearing him say, 'I think about you every day, son. I love you, son.'

After twenty minutes, Jack unhappily collects his shoes to go. When I leave the table to gather my keys from the kitchen, Damien follows me.

'When can I see my dad again?' calls Jack, from the hall. 'He says you'll arrange it with him. You will, won't you, Mum?'

'We'll see.'

I don't like being alone in the kitchen with Damien: he leans in too close, until my back is pushed against the wall, his body blocking me. 'You and me,' he mutters. 'You know what I'm talking about.'

I'd rather not be loved than be loved by Damien. But there's something. He has this look, always had it, that makes me want to love him. I see that look in Jack too.

'It won't happen,' I say. 'Ever.'

That evening, as I lie on my bed, I feel weightless. I'm happier, and relieved: I understand now that I wasn't to blame. After all this time Damien is the same as he ever was. It wasn't my fault that he did what he did to me.

'You need to come downstairs,' calls Rhodri.

'A minute.'

'You need to come downstairs now,' he says steadily.

Rhodri is sitting with his legs stretched out on the kitchen floor, Jack flopped over his lap, sobbing. 'He was talking to me about Damien.'

But I'm not listening to Rhodri: seeing Jack cry has filled me with panic. We still live in the same house as we did all those years ago. I still sleep in the same bedroom where I was attacked. I wouldn't move house after what Damien did that night because we had already given up one home to move into a refuge. I didn't want to feel like a victim all my life, I wanted to feel strong, so we stayed put. Ever since, I've been plagued with nightmares. Now that Rhodri has moved in I feel safer, but I still live in fear that Damien will turn up.

'I need you to pack us a bag,' I interrupt. 'Damien may come round. I don't want us to stay here tonight.'

'I'll call my mother, tell her that we'll be driving over to Liverpool. We can stay there for the night. Talk about all this in the morning.'

I crouch down to them and slowly uncoil my boy from Rhodri. We encourage Jack to walk to the living room, but he won't stand, won't talk. I carry him awkwardly and lay him on the sofa, where he curls up into the cushions. I sit by him, stroking his hair humming a melody, like I did when he was a baby and he shrilled through the night. His cries echo through the house. I'd never known he was so full of sorrow.

3

Jack cannot understand why a whole week has passed and no arrangements have been made for him to meet his father. Seeing Damien again after all those years wasn't good enough for him: he wants to spend time with him and talk to him on the telephone. That's why today I'm standing on the path leading to the safe-house for women. Jack and I lived here when I was in my second year at university. A year before the night Damien strangled me. A simple argument had turned into weeks of turmoil. It seems naïve now, but I didn't know back then that I was experiencing domestic violence. It was only after a number of police visits, when a woman handed me a leaflet with a helpline number, that the gravity of our situation struck me. That was when I packed our bags and abandoned our lovely terraced house on a quiet family road because of Damien's constant threats.

He had never harmed Jack and I believed he never would, but the workers at the refuge told me that my life and Jack's were at risk. I was only twenty-two and suddenly I was being told how not to be murdered. I was terrified.

We shared our living space with other women escaping violent partners. Mothers stood in the kitchen drinking tea and swapping distressing stories. Some afternoons we sat in the playroom making crafts with the kids. I cried choked tears, like Jack's are now, and he became a difficult, demanding toddler. He must have been a very confused little boy.

I want us never to go through that again. I must do the right thing because if I don't, and things turn bad, Social Services might take Jack away.

When we lived at the refuge there was a large white-board in the office listing the names of women using the service. Each day a member of staff mapped out which refuges had beds, and how many women needed them. There were never enough to go around. I learned that nineteen-year-old girls were hit by their husbands or boy-friends, and women of eighty too. Domestic violence, said the workers, happens regardless of age.

Looking at the safe-house now I feel sad that its inhabitants are shielded from the outside world. Heavy blinds block out each window, and a high wall protects the back garden. When we lived there, the garden reminded me of the lonely castle grounds in Oscar Wilde's *The Selfish Giant*. It should have rung with the sound of children's laughter.

I look up to the room where Jack and I stayed. I'd lie on the bed frightened that Damien would discover where we were. It was about this time of year when we moved here and it seemed perpetually dark. The workers warned me never to return to Damien: they said it was only a matter of time before he tried to kill me. He displayed all the traits of a dangerous man. They feared not just for my safety but for their own and the other women's, so two days before Christmas we were moved to another refuge. I lost my friends, my family, my job, my home. When my self-esteem lay flat on the floor, I returned to Damien because I was lonely. He left messages on my phone saying he loved me, he wanted to be a good father, and he promised he would change. A year later, just days after he'd tried to strangle me, I landed back on this refuge's doorstep, desperate for advice.

What a stupid, stupid girl.

Looking up into the CCTV camera guarding the entrance I take a deep breath, press the buzzer, and wait. A young woman with dark hair opens the door. She looks distant and afraid. I imagine she saw my face on the CCTV screen and assumed I wasn't a threat. To open the door or not? I remember that dilemma. For a moment I'm not looking at her, I'm looking at me. Not me now but as I used to be.

I watch the girl walk back to the kitchen, then a serious-looking woman strides out from the office. 'You do not open the door to anyone,' she says harshly to the girl, 'unless you know who it is.' Then she turns to me. 'Can I help you?'

'I used to live here.'

'I don't remember you. When was that?'

I tell her the name of the worker who looked after me. I explain about Jack wanting to see Damien and about my fear of Social Services. 'I don't want my son to be taken away from me.' I hesitate. 'I don't know what to do.' I stand in the corridor and gaze around me, shocked by how bleak and unhappy the house feels.

'It must have been very hard for you to come back here,' she says softly. 'It must have been terrible for you to have been carrying that worry with you for all these years.'

'Horrible,' I say, and before I can stop myself I begin to cry.

'If Damien wants to see a solicitor, in order to gain access through the courts,' she explains, 'maybe he can see Jack.'

'Good day?' asks Rhodri, kicking off his muddy boots in the kitchen. His trousers are dirty and wet up to the knees. He has spent the day at the allotment and smells of freshly dug soil. 'Hey, what's happened?' He drops his rucksack to the floor, then sits down at the kitchen table with me. 'You're shivering,' he says, wrapping an arm around me and pulling me towards him. He hands me his cotton handkerchief and smiles reassuringly. I move closer to him until my knees are wedged comfortably between his.

'I can't do it,' I tell Rhodri.

'What?'

'I went to the refuge today to speak to a worker. I don't ever want to end up back there.'

'He'll be upset.'

'I don't want to take the risk. I can't let Jack see Damien,' I tell Rhodri. 'Not now, and probably not for a long time.'

4

Today the plan is for us to spend hours digging at the allotment to distract Jack. Last night I told him that I will not allow him to see Damien until he is at least fifteen and able to get out of tricky situations by calling a cab or catching a bus. Now Jack sees me as the enemy standing between him and his dad. In the meantime, I have issued my own safety measure: Damien needs to stay out of trouble for twelve consecutive months before I will even consider contact. If he can do that, I may relent.

I open the front door to our house to water the plants before we leave for the allotment. Jack is in the back garden, trying to chase the rabbits back into their hutch. As I step outside my neighbour, Josie, shakes her head at me wearily. She is standing beneath her porch unspooling string that has been tied across a bush to her doorknob, through the knocker, over the letterbox and back. 'That Scarlet's a little madam,' she says. 'It was the milk last week. Someone needs to take her in hand.'

'What about the milk?' I ask. I'm trying to figure out what's happened to my hanging basket. All the flowers are standing to attention rather than falling over the edge in a colourful cascade. I think Rhodri has put geraniums in it and I'm sure you're not supposed to put them in hanging baskets. 'What happened with the milk?' I ask again.

Rhodri is in the kitchen spreading peanut butter on oatcakes – I wish he wouldn't do that: it gives him dreadful wind. I need to talk to him about the aesthetic of the hanging basket. It's all wrong. Now he's chopping a banana, arranging the slices on rye bread and eating spoonfuls of tahini. You have to watch vegans: if they don't combine food thoughtfully they'll blow you into outer space.

'Last Sunday,' Josie is saying, 'I caught her hiding the milk, and when I went over to tell her mother, the boyfriend insulted me.'

This is typical of the council estate where we live. Tiny wars over things like milk, bins and pizza deliveries. It's like living among school bullies.

'That's dreadful, Josie,' I say.

'If they needed milk, they could have just asked.'

Josie would help anybody if they asked but nobody does around here: they just take. I've lost count of the times Jack and I've returned from the shops or the park to find the local kids whizzing up and down the street on his trucks, or his bike, or kicking his ball at the window of another house. And the mothers just stood there, daring me to challenge them. Of course I didn't because they scare me. I had a high fence installed instead.

'It's not Scarlet's fault,' I say. 'She's always good for me. You need to be friends with her, and then she's great.'

I pause to wave at Albert across the communal garden. He waves back, shakes his walking-stick at me, then begins to unravel string from his front door. Elsie, who lives next door to him, steps out from her door and shouts, 'She's a little devil, that one, and you can't tell her mother anything because you'll end up with a skateboard through your window.'

Scarlet, the love, has booby-trapped half the street. Unfortunately it's the retired half with poor eyesight and walking difficulties.

'The youngest one,' another neighbour calls, 'fell over the other week.' She's referring to Scarlet's sister, Anna. She's just a toddler and is frequently seen trotting about in the car park, her bottom, in a nappy, sticking into the air as she bends down to pick up stones to throw at passers-by. 'And she just bounced back. Those children are made of rubber. If something happens to those girls,' she adds, 'they'll say the neighbours did nothing. It'll be all over the papers,'

'I know,' I say. 'But it wouldn't be true.' Something terrible could happen to those children and then we'll all be sorry.

Scarlet's my favourite little girl on the planet. She also happens to be the naughtiest little girl on the estate, or perhaps even in Jackson. I'll have to commission a survey to find out. She's nine, feckless and bossy. She and Jack used to spend hours barking like dogs – I'm glad they've grown out of that. Scarlet has had such a difficult time. I think of the years she lived next door to us and I heard her screaming in the night . . .

'It's not her fault,' I tell Josie. I always say this. Many mothers on these streets won't allow their children to play with Scarlet and wonder why I let her into our house to play with Jack, who adores her. 'I wouldn't have her in my house,' they say. 'Nowhere near my children.' Sometimes they say worse. But you shouldn't write a child off at nine or, in Anna's case, two, just because her mother put us through hell with noisy parties.

Josie heads indoors and I go to the kitchen in search of a cup of tea. Rhodri has made one already. It's sitting on the counter waiting for me. It doesn't look like tea. '*Pwuh!* What's that?'

'Organic Fairtrade rooibos tea, with rice milk,' says Rhodri. 'You'll get used to it. What was Josie saying?'

'Scarlet's making mischief again.' I give the tea another go, and by the third sip it's not so bad.

'A good day for the allotment,' says Rhodri. 'Why don't we invite Scarlet? She'll keep Jack company.'

'Great idea. I'll send him over to ask her.'

I packed a lunchbox for Jack and Scarlet, and a football, and they took their bikes to speed ahead of us along the paths that lead into and around the allotments. I told them they can climb trees and explore the plots close by, but Jack is hiding behind the compost heap, beneath the elder tree, sulking. He said he wanted to dig deep holes, which was fine, but now we need to fill them in to make seed-beds. Scarlet has been a great help all morning so I've been praising her, and now Jack is jealous.

'I want to go home,' he moans.

'We need to plant the garlic and onions!' I say enthusiastically, as though he's a very lucky boy to be toiling on an allotment.

Scarlet tears the weeds from the soil and chucks them into a big bucket over by Rhodri.

'Do you like digging?' I ask Scarlet.

'I love it,' she shouts.

Jack mooches over. 'I want a spade,' he says.

'Can you dig up some weeds?' I ask.

'No,' he says, cramming his mouth with banana. 'I want to dig holes.' Bored, he heads towards the brambles and begins to build a den out of fallen branches.

When he's out of earshot, Scarlet purses her lips and casts her eyes to the ground. 'Mum's back with him, in't she?' she says quietly, kicking the soil. 'So we can't live with her.'

I pat her head gently. I want to hug her, but you can't just hug other people's children nowadays, even if they need affection. What a stupid world. Scarlet doesn't cry when she tells me she can't go back to live with her mother, Tanya. She doesn't even cry when she tells me that Tanya is pregnant again. Scarlet is such a little trooper she deserves a trophy.

'You'll still see your mum,' I say brightly. 'And she'll get things sorted. You'll be living at your nana's. You can play at our house whenever you want . . .' I try to think of something cheerful '. . . and *soon* you'll have a new baby brother or sister.'

'Yeah,' sighs Scarlet, completely unimpressed.

'Let's see if we can pull this one out.' I point to an enormous weed with a stalk as thick as my arm. We yelp and shout as we yank it from the ground.

When we tire of digging, I lay my coat on the grass and sit down to hunt for crisps in Rhodri's pannier, pour orange juice for the kids, and get out some apples. 'Why don't you take the bikes and ride around the allotment? Show Scarlet the giant vegetables,' I say to Jack. There's a plot by the gate where a man grows huge pumpkins. I watch Scarlet race Jack down the path. That bike is too small for her. She needs a new one. Not for the first time, I wish I could help her more.

36

I scan the allotment: the other plots are picture perfect. The couple next to us have a main pathway covered with polyurethane and wood chippings. If you walk to the far end of the plot, there's a cute pond, with log seats placed randomly around the water and a barbecue.

'Their allotment's looking beautiful. Look what they've done,' I say to Rhodri. He looms over me, all sweaty and dirty. There's something about men, spades and soil that is so . . . 'Ours is a mess.'

'Yes, but you don't want wood chippings, do you?' he says, taking a seat next to me. 'They're very bad for the environment.'

I do want wood chippings, I think. I want a pretty allotment with flowers, a blue seaside-type hut, a lawn and a swing in the elder tree. But Rhodri insists we use nothing but reclaimed materials.

'Can't we use a Rotavator?' I ask, for the thousandth time. 'Do we have to dig all sixty-five feet of it by hand?'

'Yes.'

'This allotment's been abandoned for five years and the weeds have grown as tall as me. Why can't we just get a machine to do it?'

'Because it'll make the weeds worse,' says Rhodri. He pinches my thigh, then bites into his apple.

'Tanya's pregnant again,' I tell him. 'And Scarlet and Anna are being taken away from her.'

The girls had been living temporarily with their grandmother, Philomena. It wasn't supposed to be for long. Last summer Scarlet told me that Tanya had promised her that she'd be home with her for the winter.

'Where are they going to live?'

'At Philomena's'

'Is Scarlet okay about that?'

'I think so.' I tell him that Tanya's back with Cain. Rhodri grimaces. That man is horrible. What he has done to Tanya is far worse than anything I've experienced. If only Jack knew how the violence has affected Scarlet, he'd understand why I won't let him see his dad.

'I wish we could foster her,' I say to Rhodri, 'but we'd have to take Anna too. And we've no room.' Our home is the size of a Wendy house and Rhodri and I just about manage to feed and clothe the three of us.

'She'll be with Philomena,' says Rhodri. 'She'll be fine with her, and she can come over and play with Jack.'

Philomena lives nearby. That's something.

It's dusk when we drop Scarlet off at her grandmother's. She is covered with mud from head to foot but excited and tired. Minutes later she knocks on our door and proudly holds out a tray of seedlings Philomena has prepared for us. This happens a lot. We take Scarlet out, and Philomena sends over little gifts, which is how we ended up with rabbits.

'Tell your nana thank you very much,' I say. Scarlet grins, and runs off. I close the door and take the tray of seedlings into the kitchen. Jack is splashing about in the bath singing 'American Idiot'; the transition from Bob the Builder to Green Day fan has come too soon. Jack always sings when he's happy. Which means our excursion to the allotment has worked. He has forgotten about Damien, for now at least.

'Let's have a living-room disco,' I suggest, when he's in his pyjamas and snuggled next to me on the sofa. I'm determined to keep him in a good mood. We sit by the record player, which is the best thing Rhodri moved in, except for himself, and sift through his vinyl collection for something appropriate. This quickly proves difficult because most of what Rhodri owns is anarchist punk rock, which rants about the perils of the world and the destruction of the earth. I settle for Pink Floyd, and Jack and I begin what could be described as a fusion of waltz, jive and street dance.

I can't keep the entertainment up for ever. At the dinner table an unhappy silence mixes with the beetroot and chickpea soup Rhodri has made. He has chopped and cooked for hours – it looks like a crime scene in the kitchen – but Jack doesn't want to eat it. No surprise. He hates soup and has never eaten chickpeas. Neither does he understand beetroot, which stains like paint and looks like blood. 'I'm not a Vulcan like you,' Jack says to Rhodri.

'Vegan,' I correct.

'I'm not a vegan,' Jack cries. 'You like this food, I don't.'

I'm not certain I like it either but, frankly, at this time of night, I'll put anything into my mouth. 'It's good to try new food,' I plead. 'This'll make you strong and Rhodri has worked so hard to make dinner for us. We should eat it.'

Jack is upset, and now Rhodri is upset, making me the hungry piggy in the middle.

'We didn't have a choice about what we ate when we were your age,' Rhodri says grumpily. I can't imagine his mother ever made him eat such a strange concoction as chickpea and beetroot soup. He's told me he ate sausages as a child.

I smile at Jack persuasively. 'If you eat all your dinner, I'll give you a gold star. How's that? We'll get a star chart going and when you have twenty stars you can have a treat. What do you think?'

'Okay,' he concedes. He takes a gulp of soup, but with the spoon still in his mouth he begins to bawl, 'I can't believe my own mother is *trying to kill me.*' He splutters the soup back onto his spoon. 'My mother is *trying to kill me.*' He leaps off his chair and runs upstairs to his room.

A storm's brewing. I can feel it.

5

Jack wanted to stay the night at my mother's, and I needed to escape, so I arranged a last-minute trip to London. It's a break, but it's also research as I'd like to write a play or a film one day, though I don't know when I'll get the time. I sit on a high stool in the café at the National Film Theatre, swinging my legs nervously as I pick at a sandwich. I gaze out of the window, watching arty types saunter by the river Thames, pausing to rummage through boxes crammed with second-hand books at the makeshift market. Zelda, my best friend from my postgraduate days at university, is sitting next to me drinking a bucket-sized coffee and running her hands through her curly hair, regaling me with tales of unrequited love. She has recently returned from travelling around Italy where romance followed every sunset. She lives in Manchester, but is in London today for an academic conference. 'You're so lucky,' she says, over the clatter of plates and the chuff-chuff of the coffee machine.

'It's a different climate down here,' I say, pretending not to have heard her comment. 'Always so warm.' As far as I'm concerned London may as well be on a faraway continent: people speak a different language, live in apartments, not houses, are spoiled with more sunshine, and eat artichokes.

Jack would love London. He'd like the galleries and the

theatres and the parks, although he'd hate walking up and down all those steps to the Tube, or getting squashed on a bus. Rhodri will only visit London for an anti-Trident or disarmament protest, not something flimsy like a *play* at a *theatre*.

'Rhodri is such a fantastic guy,' she continues. 'You've got it made.'

'I haven't got it "made" at all.'

'You have.' She laughs, sipping her coffee. 'You have Rhodri, and you have this other man, Toga. And Rhodri is totally fine about it.'

Oh, yes. That.

My old flame Toga lives in London so I asked him to accompany me to the theatre this evening. We haven't met up in months. I wonder if I still fancy him, or if he's changed. Zelda is intrigued by the arrangement Rhodri and I have. I suppose you wouldn't call it a normal relationship, but it feels quite normal to us. 'Perhaps you're suited to an open relationship,' I suggest.

Zelda shakes her head, as though to say, 'Are you mad? What kind of person suggests to their partner that they have an open relationship?'

A swinger, or an enviro-anti-establishment vegan, that's who.

'You look so good together. When I saw you last summer. . .' she's referring to when Rhodri and I cycled over the river from Jackson to Boho to meet her and our friend Prince for a drink, then trundled back in the dark '. . . on your bikes . . .' she's going to say 'romantic' '. . . it was so romantic.'

'I was pissed,' I say. 'I fell off my bike. That wasn't

romantic.' Anxious to change the subject, I ask, 'When are you heading back to Manchester?'

'Tonight. What time are you meeting Toga?'

I check the time on my mobile. Six o'clock. He'll be finishing work about now.

'That was delicious,' I murmur, wiping my mouth on my sleeve and regaining my balance. I feel quite dizzy, must be the – 'Easy, Tiger-bear.'

Toga is diving in for more kisses. He's doing that thing he does with my hair, gathering it in tight fistfuls while he nibbles me. His hands are roaming too. I pull back from him. 'What's wrong?'

'You know.' I make a sweeping gesture with my arm in the direction of the crowds of people swarming past us into the theatre, most of them aged fifty-plus and signed up members of Saga. 'The public.' Saucy behaviour is *de rigueur* in Madrid, but in England we call it dogging. Oh, forget the play, we should just go shagging. Only there's nowhere to have sex, unless we rent a room for the hour, and I've just paid for the theatre tickets so that would be a terrible waste of money.

We make our way into the Cottesloe Theatre to find our seats. Fortunately they're located at the back, very close to the exit. Handy, should we wish to leave early and make illicit use of the toilets. When the lights go down and the play begins, I fidget uncomfortably in an attempt to get closer to Toga. He looks sternly ahead. Then, catching my lascivious stare, he points to my eyes with a chastening finger, then to the stage. I huff and watch the drama unfolding before us. Minutes pass, then my fingers tiptoe along Toga's thigh. I lean into his shoulder. I remove my shoes and rest my feet between his legs. He grabs my hand. I stroke his fingers.

During the interval, I browse in the theatre bookshop while Toga jostles for the drinks at the bar. Then I tuck myself into a corner where I steal short kisses from him between sips of red wine.

'Like it?' he asks, removing his glasses and rubbing the tail end of his scarf over the lenses. He gazes at me, waiting for an answer, but I just rock on the sides of my feet in my patent ballet pumps, my dress swishing against my knees, fascinated by this lens-cleansing ritual of his. Toga is one of those media-savvy Londoners; he's as exotic to me as a foreign holiday.

'Do *you* like it?'

'It's all right,' he says. 'A little slow.'

By the time the play is over, I'm tipsy and starving. We have an endless discussion about where to dine. 'Well, what type of food do you want to eat?' Toga asks finally.

'I'm not bothered,' I reply.

And so, because it's late, we end up outside Strada.

'I've already eaten here this week, and I probably will again tomorrow,' says Toga.

'Let's just go in,' I reply. 'I've never been to Strada.' Any more dithering and there'll be no time for smooching after dinner because, come midnight, lover-boy will be running off to catch the Tube home.

An hour later, we've finished our food and sunk our last glass of wine. When the waiter brings the bill, and Toga pays, he says, 'You're very lucky to have such a generous husband.'

Boy, has he got it wrong.

We start walking over the river across Hungerford Bridge in the direction of Embankment station. Toga strides quickly, I loiter and dally, stopping every so often to look out at the view across the Thames, each time grasping for his hand. I'm bewitched by the colour of London at night, the chatter of trains as they clatter past, the austere silhouette of the Houses of Parliament, and the bulbous dome of St Paul's Cathedral. Beneath the bridge a quartet plays rhumba on makeshift instruments, while a group of young girls dance. I love how strangers rush from place to place, that they behave carelessly and arrogantly towards one another as they try to get across the city, but in the theatre they laugh together.

Toga points out landmarks to me. I look at the lights reflected on the river like little dreams. I wrap my arms around Toga's waist and beg him to kiss me.

When we have reached the far side of the bridge, Toga sits on a bench and I sit on his lap. I love that I'm in London with him, far from all the difficulties at home.

'Did you have sex, then?' asks Rhodri. He is bent over the cooker, shaking the kettle to see if there's enough water to make a cup of tea. He runs the cold-water tap, fills it and slams it on the hob. Then he turns the dial, and presses the ignition until the hob snaps alight. 'Well?' he insists. 'Did you?' He smiles at me encouragingly. 'Let's get it out of the way. So I'm not wondering.'

'No,' I say truthfully. 'There was nowhere to have sex. I stayed at a backpackers' hostel and shared a room with strangers. The rest of the time I was in a theatre surrounded by senior citizens.'

Rhodri laughs at me, rather than with me. Modern technology, I think, has a lot to answer for. Its pros: text-sex while grocery shopping; e-seduction while working. Its cons (with particular reference to CCTV, video mobile phones, and YouTube): you can't have sex in the street, in pub toilets, in the park. Modern technology is therefore a passion killer. Which is why Rhodri is laughing *at* me: he considers me a frustrated pint-sized nymphomaniac, a pornographic hobbit.

Rhodri and Jack picked me up from the station. Jack ran at me almost knocking me to the ground. The short break seems to have been good for both of us. Rhodri didn't even kiss me. Or hold me. Or welcome me back. Sometimes I doubt that he's pleased to see me at all. Sometimes I think he regards me as a full-time nuisance: I eat meat, I want to clean the house with chemical products and spend, spend, spend. He does, however, seem pleased that I didn't have sex. I'd almost say he's relieved. Rhodri is such an odd fish: he flies into a raging debate when I use Fairy Liquid, and asks me if I've enjoyed myself when I spend time with other men. Damien would become jealous when I took a shower and wore skimpy knickers to university.

Rhodri is an anomaly to me.

He doesn't know anything about Toga, other than that I have a 'close' friend who lives in London. From time to time, when I visit London, I see this 'close' friend. Which Rhodri is fine about, because it means I'm not wandering across the capital on my own like a tourist: someone else, someone who isn't a threat, is looking after me. As Rhodri hates London, this makes logistical and practical sense. Rhodri knows that Toga has other girlfriends and, because of that, I'm not going anywhere. Even if I did, I'd boomerang back. And I do love Rhodri: Toga, he's just a bit of fun. At least, I think he is.

I plan to cook Rhodri a lovely dinner: the only vegan meal I do really well: banana and leek curry. When Jack's in bed, we'll sneak upstairs for an early night and I'll try to forget about the weird arrangement I have with Toga until the next time. There's too much going on already with Damien and Jack for me to start worrying about anything else.

6

So much for trying to be calm and positive. Nothing *ever* goes to plan. I hate this house. The heating's broken down again and we have no hot water. I must have an icy body wash because it takes fifteen minutes to boil the kettle on the gas hob. It's so cold that my toes sting, my fingers are numb and my head hurts. A gale blows through the windows, pushing beneath the door and through the hall. I'm standing on the landing wearing my mother's tent-like knickers, which I stole from her when I stayed over one night. Meanwhile, Rhodri is wrapped up beneath the bedcovers: socks on, pyjamas on, sweatshirt on, hat on. Jack has the spare blankets, a quilt, a sleeping-bag, and the only hot-water bottle. We own an electric blanket but Rhodri would never agree to use it because it's such a waste of resources. So, our only option is to pile on the layers. In addition to the big knickers, I pull on jogging pants, a T-shirt, a fleece, socks, a hat and gloves. My choice of sleepwear is a 100-per-cent-effective contraceptive. I dive into bed, where Rhodri and I paw at one another affectionately, grinding our legs up and down as though shunting up a fireman's pole. Nothing sexual. The sole intention is for the friction to create heat. Once warm, we'd be crazy to get undressed.

If only we had money to buy clothes or shoes or furniture or a new boiler to keep us warm. I know Rhodri and

I will start to argue. In my eyes, everything is wrong, and everything is unfair. The house isn't big enough for the three of us. Rhodri piles his things in a corner and stacks bin-bag after bin-bag of his old clothes on cardboard boxes. We share one small wardrobe, which is held together with gaffer tape. It was a hand-me-down from some friends who live in a big house and own a villa in Spain. Before it arrived with us it had spent two years in their garage. Under the bed is a toolbox, and next to it an old fax machine my stepfather gave me. On the dressing-table is the breadmaker Margaret No. 2 passed on to me, while dirty clothes from our day on the allotment are thrown on the floor, and clean clothes, because we don't have any-where to put them, are in the laundry basket. Odd socks lie on the windowsill like dead rats. Only last week Marga-ret No. 2 walked into the bedroom and immediately walked out, shaking her head. 'I can't see you get up to much in here,' she said. 'You need a boudoir.'

And she's right. We don't get up to much in here. A boudoir is just one of the many things I need.

When we've warmed each other, Rhodri slants towards the light. In one hand he picks up a Welsh novel, in the other a Welsh dictionary.

'Any good?' I inquire.

'Not bad,' he says.

'Will you be reading for long?' I probe.

'A bit longer,' replies Rhodri, pulling me to him. He tucks me under his arm, then struggles to turn the pages. I wriggle up the pillows so I can kiss his cheek, before moving over to my side of the bed where I curl up into the duvet to stay warm.

Eventually, he switches off the bedside lamp and spoons into me; his arms crisscross over my chest, his long thin legs intertwine with mine. '*Da nos, cariad,*' he whispers.

'*Da nos,*' I reply.

Many hours later, when Rhodri is asleep, I slip out of his arms and make my way downstairs. It has been weeks since I've slept easily until morning. Too many things are troubling me: Jack, and what I should do about Damien, not to mention the guilt of meeting up with Toga.

Tonight I make a chamomile tea, then flick on the television. As I sit on the big leather armchair, feet tucked under my bottom, watching a crazy documentary about a man who married a donkey, I wonder why I can't ever do the right thing.

I should not have met Toga in London because now I feel desolate. I resolve never to email him again. I will delete his number from my phone. Instead I will throw myself into my relationship with Rhodri – it squeaks and jars at the moment because I'm distracted. Then the pangs begin low in my stomach: I yearn for another child, which strikes me as madness, given our circumstances.

Wearily, and despite the cold, I move to the sofa and lie down. I drape my dressing-gown over myself as a makeshift blanket and form a pillow out of a pile of cushions. I will sleep here until morning.

Today I should be working from home but I have other plans. After the cold snap of the last few weeks, I have decided that we must sort out the house. It's freezing, but also the rooms are decorated in exactly the same way as they were when Damien lived here. His presence is embedded in the walls. No wonder I feel so jittery all the time. As I can't afford to move, we should paint away all of those memories and start anew.

It's not right for Jack to live like this so I've taken drastic measures. This morning I went secretly to the building society and applied for a home-improvement loan. Then I arranged for double glazing to be fitted, a new kitchen, a new bathroom *and*, most exciting of all, I've found an eco-company that will draught-proof the house for *free* and install an energy-efficient boiler for *free*. All this work will be done in time for Christmas, which gives me seven weeks. No problem.

Or small problem: Rhodri.

He is seated comfortably with his rooibos tea and peanut-butter-covered rice cakes. He worked a four-hour shift this morning for a homecare agency and is exhausted. It's past noon. Jack is at school.

'We need to rip the kitchen out this weekend,' I say.

'What?' demands Rhodri.

'The kitchen fitter is coming in twelve days.'

'Pardon?' he says, this time with eyebrow intonation to match his stormy eyes.

'Double-glazing in two and a half weeks.'

'What?'

'New bathroom suite arrives in ten days.'

'What?'

Stop saying 'What?' and start saying, 'How wonderful.' Rhodri has that startled stance, the one that means he wants to run away, and his voice has that don't-involve-me-in-this tone.

'Best of all . . .' Rhodri emits a very loud groan '. . . we have a new boiler being fitted, an *energy-efficient* boiler, and draught-proofing in three weeks!'

This makes Rhodri smile.

'And even better than that—'

'Stop screeching!' shouts Rhodri. 'You're hurting my ears.'

'Eleanor and my dad are going to spend the whole weekend with us stripping and emptying the kitchen and bathroom.'

I've arranged it all with such ease that I'm starting to think I should apply for a new job with a housing developer rather than working in the woolly arts, in woolly literature, arranging training seminars for independent publishers. For a fleeting moment, I see myself wearing a hard-hat, walkie-talkie in hand, barking orders to a fleet of work-men. Brilliant. I'm brilliant. Hm . . . Something about Rhodri's demeanour suggests that he doesn't consider me brilliant. 'Don't do this,' I say.

'Do what?'

'This. Whenever something's urgent, you do *this*.' In the face of something requiring immediate action, Rhodri backs off. He retreats gently, then quickly. He doesn't say 'no' exactly, but he does become very difficult.

'You said to me,' I remind him, '"The house is a mess." You said it was shabby and that we needed to do some-thing about it. And I need to think about Jack's wellbeing. So I'm doing something about it.'

My tough-cookie voice isn't working so I try a different approach. 'It'll be a few weeks of disruption and then, sweetheart, the house will look great.'

My creepy-girlfriend voice isn't working either because Rhodri escapes upstairs to the bedroom to change out of his work clothes. Meanwhile I email my boss, Athens, to tell him I'll be in tomorrow, and the day after, then sit down at my computer for my latest assignment: I need to figure out how to promote an Asian lesbian, bisexual and transgender performing arts company to the regional press.

'What would you like to eat?' I ask Jack. 'What do you want to eat?' I ask Rhodri, peering up at the menu in the chip shop.

My lucky, lucky family: a Friday night out on me. I'd rather go to a seafood restaurant for monkfish, but we'll have to make do with a sit-down chip shop where we can get three meals, with drinks, for under ten pounds.

Back home, much of the kitchenware has been packed away. This evening when Jack returned from school he saw all the boxes packed chock-a-block into the living room and scrambled over them as though he was climbing Ben Nevis.

At the Formica table I pull out a notepad and biro to keep him amused. I write down a couple of sums, then put together a quick crossword and a wordsearch. Rhodri and I gulp tea from cracked old mugs as Jack swigs from a can of Coke oblivious to Rhodri's disapproval.

'It's really very good of Eleanor and my dad to offer to help us prepare the kitchen,' I say. 'Don't you think?'

Rhodri shrugs his shoulders. Makes some comment about no free time. Not his choice.

'We'll have to get up early tomorrow. They're arriving at nine.'

'I know,' he says. 'You said.'

The waitress brings us three plates of chips. We tuck into them silently. Behind us an eager young woman is chatting into her mobile phone about her move to a new flat.

'During the week we'll have to lay the laminate flooring,' I say.

'It's too much of a rush.'

'It's the only way we could do it. Then the bathroom suite's arriving.'

'Where will we put it?'

'In the living room and Jack's room.'

'We'll have the new kitchen in boxes in the hallway,' says Rhodri, 'the contents of the old kitchen, with your office stuff, in the living room and our bedroom, the contents of the back room in there too, the new bathroom in Jack's bedroom and the lounge. Where will Jack sleep?'

'With us?'

'Where will we eat?'

'On the bed?'

Annoyed, Rhodri turns away from me.

'It's the only way,' I urge. I explain to Rhodri that there are complicated conditions linked to the loan. He scowls all the more. The building society won't release the money until the work is done, so to save on charges and so forth, much of the work has to be completed at the same time. And the house is *freezing* and *draughty*. We haven't had heating or hot water for more than a month. Winter is taking grip. Jack has asthma. There's no point in having a new boiler with rubbish old windows.

'Think of how much energy we'll save,' I encourage him. 'The carbon footprint. The money.'

'But I planned on doing some activism,' retorts Rhodri. 'When will I have time for that?'

I don't know. Living in a warm house and paying the bills are more important to me than environmental activism.

'Stop arguing,' says Jack.

'We're not arguing,' I clarify. 'We're simply having a discussion.' Then I turn to Rhodri. 'You always do this,' I say to him, a comment that instantly catapults our 'discussion' into full-blown-argument territory. I eat my chips hurriedly, then stalk out of the chip shop. Jack plugs his MP3 into his ears and runs ahead of me towards the car.

Rhodri storms down the road after us. 'Your keys,' he shouts, hurling them at me.

They clank onto the pavement so I have to bend down to retrieve them. How humiliating.

'I'll make my own way home,' he bellows. He turns on his heels and stamps round the corner, past the station and down the high street.

At first I smile. Then I grin, and soon I'm laughing naughtily to myself. I shouldn't, but I can't help it.

'Where's Rhodri going?' asks Jack.

'I don't know,' I answer.

'What are you laughing at?'

We climb into the car and wait for a few moments. Sure enough, Rhodri comes round the corner. At first he strides fiercely, but as he nears us he lollops boyishly. When he reaches the passenger side of the car, I press the fob to unlock the doors.

'I don't know which bus to catch home from here,' he says, sliding onto the seat.

'Fancy a lift, then?'

'Go on,' he says, clipping the seatbelt over him and switching on the car stereo.

7

'Where's Rhodri?' asks my dad. 'And where's my cup of tea?'

'Cup of tea right here,' I say, handing him a mug.

My stepmother Eleanor is amusing Jack with a red balloon in the hallway, bouncing it on his head until he yelps, 'No, no, no! Do it again! Again – again!'

'Any biscuits?' asks my dad.

'Coming right up,' I chirrup. Rhodri doesn't get this, that when people – my family to be precise – come to the house to carry out odd jobs, they expect to be waited on.

'So, where's Rhodri?'

'In the garden,' calls Jack. 'Pretending to be a bird.'

On your average day this comment would swoop over my head. Today, with an audience, it's bizarre. Cringing, I look out of the kitchen window to see if what Jack has said is true. Sure enough, Rhodri is on the grass, flapping his arms up and down as he strides the length of the garden, our two fat white rabbits hopping at his feet. My father is standing behind me. 'What *is* he doing?' he mutters in disbelief.

'*Qigong* exercises. That,' I point out to my father, 'is the Flying Bird.'

'But we're supposed to be ripping out the kitchen.'

'I know,' I say, picking up a hammer and walloping the kitchen cabinets. 'You tell Rhodri that.'

*

The old kitchen cabinets are out and lying in broken bits by the back gate. Rhodri sloped off at various points to do more flying exercises around the garden. 'I have a sore back,' he insisted, 'from that very bad car accident I had four years ago. Remember?'

I'd forgotten about it. 'I have a sore back too,' I replied petulantly.

Other times he said he needed a rest and took himself off to the cluttered living room to lounge on the sofa and sift through the Review section of the *Guardian*. I smouldered a bit but I didn't burst into flames.

This evening Rhodri and I have been laying the laminate floor. I can honestly say it has brought us closer together: I held the planks in place as he banged energetically. This joint effort brought with it many curses, accompanied by deep satisfaction. If it weren't for the fact that Jack is sleeping in our bed, there's a bath on his bed, a flat-pack kitchen in the hall, no carpet on the stairs, nowhere to move in the living room, and no curtains in the kitchen, this would have been Rhodri's lucky night. I'll keep his gold stars for extra-good behaviour in his sexual-favours savings account. If he accumulates ten, I'll treat him.

He's doing a wonderful job. When he's warm and obliging like this, I adore him. I forget all my other frustrations: his acute environmentalism, the never-ending lectures on the evils of Persil . . .

The next phase, even though the kitchen is still in progress, is the bathroom. Damien's father, Eddie, has been hauled in for that job. I'm going to pay him with cans of Boddington's bitter. I've estimated that eight cans should do it, approximate value nine pounds (a professional wanted to charge me a thousand to fit a bathroom – what was he thinking?).

According to Eddie, we have problems with the soil pipe, which runs from the toilet into the kitchen. For some reason he's had to cut a section out of it, and says he can't get a replacement fitted until tomorrow so he's bunged it up with a rag. Now he's gone off to play a round of golf. We're without a kitchen and have no bath, no wash-basin, and an unusable toilet.

'Whatever you do,' said Eddie, 'do *not* flush the toilet.'

So, there's a bucket in the bathroom to pee in, and if we need a number two we'll have to go to Philomena's house. She won't mind. We can take our own toilet roll. That would be polite.

My dad's arriving in an hour to finish the last of the flooring and fit new taps ready for our brand new kitchen sink. I've had to switch my mobile to silent and stop answering it. I have loads of freelance jobs on but I can't work and oversee renovations in the house at the same time. Paid employment and the Asian-lesbian performing troupe will have to wait.

Father and I are admiring the copper piping ready for the new kitchen sink. Before Dad went bankrupt during the recession in the 1980s, and lost his home, his business, wife and kids, he was a plumber. Now he's a gas engineer. A good copper-piping job is, to my father, the plumber's equivalent of a Rembrandt. Rhodri is upstairs changing into his DIY clothes.

'That's quite something,' I say.

'It is, isn't it?' agrees my father, rubbing his hand over his baldy patch. 'See how I've curved the pipes there?'

I lean in closer. 'Beautiful. You've done an amazing job, thank you.' I kiss his forehead lightly. But Dad isn't satisfied with just a few compliments so I go *on and on* about the piping. 'Look at those parallel lines,' I try.

'Hmm . . .' he says.

'Brilliant, beautiful,' I say again. 'A work of art.'

He's happy with that: a work of art.

Just then the rag fires out of the soil pipe, we hear a heavy thud, and water shoots all over the new laminate floor.

'Is that what I think it is?' I shriek, horrified. '*I told him not to flush the toilet!*' My *brand new* kitchen floor is now covered with sewage.

'What?' says Rhodri walking into the kitchen, munching a bag of sunflower seeds. 'What are you looking at me like that for?'

'The soil pipe,' I shriek, holding my nose.

Fucking hell.

I want to cry.

'You're doing a fabulous job,' I tell the fitter. I couldn't persuade any friends or family to install the kitchen in exchange for beer so I've had to pay someone. I'm trying not to think about the cost.

Everything is marvellous. It's taken less than a week for the new kitchen units to be assembled and placed *in situ*. I watch the man shaping a worktop with his circular saw and play with the wicker baskets, sliding them in and out. Oh, *yes*, we have wicker baskets for vegetables and fruit, a stainless-steel oven, and a chimney extractor-hood thing. At last we're middle class.

'I'll be finished by the end of the day,' the kitchen fitter shouts, over the loud grinding of his power tool.

'That's fantastic,' I yell back.

I hand him yet more tea and biscuits, remove myself to the living room and, on a small corner of the sofa, squashed between boxes, get back to work.

A week has passed since the double-glazing arrived. Rhodri and I admired the shiny new windows. I kissed the glass and thanked God for the man at the mortgage company. 'Stop stroking the windows,' Jack shouted. 'Anyone would think you love them.'

'I do love my windows.'

'They're *just* windows.'

They are not *just* windows. The woman who lives at the end of our terrace thinks she has the nicest windows, but actually I have – by miles. All week I've enjoyed endless hours on the sofa gazing at my beautiful double-glazing with complete adoration because the house is less draughty and wondrously quiet. I can't even hear the hum of the motorway.

Rhodri didn't agree with the uPVC element because it doesn't biodegrade, but what can I do? Hardwood from sustainable UK forests is just too expensive. The alternative would be cheap wooden imports. The trouble with globalization is that, although prices go down, your carbon footprint goes up.

Today will see another triumph: our new boiler is being fitted. Far too many men are trampling through the house swearing and moaning as they install it. In the meantime I sit at the kitchen table, wrapped up warm and wearing red-leather gloves as I type a feature for a magazine. They must think me some sort of leather fetishist.

At last we're blessed with warmth and comfort. Jack won't need to sleep with his jumper on top of his pyjamas. As for me, I'd almost forgotten how it felt to be stripped naked. It's definitely warmer in the bedroom tonight, and because of the radical change in temperature, Rhodri and I are about to enjoy a jolly good fumble.

8

My phone vibrates. It's a text message from my boss, Athens:

M. Need to know what days you are working this week.

Athens often calls me M, like I'm a Bond girl or something.

Good question. It's a Wednesday afternoon, early December, and I haven't made an appearance in the office since last Friday. I work fifteen hours a week for Athens, administering a literature website and arranging meetings. I work on flexitime, but I may have flexed a step too far. Athens is very understanding: the fifteen hours can be spread over different days, and different times. Occasionally I get to work from home: Athens is very rational about my single-mother status – I can have time off for school assemblies, school holidays, and sickness.

I text back – best to be cheery: it'll quell any suspicion that I may be skiving.

Hi! Working from home today! Be in tomorrow.
Mx

That little 'x' should dampen any dispute. I'll work really hard this evening, I will.

> **Okay, but you must come in on Friday. I'll see you at ten.**

Oooh . . . I consider myself ticked off. I check my work email . . . 2,789 million unread messages. Great. I sift through them. Most offer me hanky-panky with Russian girls, but one is an utter gem of an invitation: tonight, in Manchester, at a world-famous hotel (*cue fanfare*), a literature award dinner is taking place. There are some speeches to sit through but I'll be rewarded with a three-course meal and wine. All I need is to be a member of the press.

My mind is working overtime.

Now then . . . If only I can find someone who will commission a piece about an award dinner *because* I'm bloody starving. All that vegan cuisine I've been cooking just doesn't hit the spot. I call a few contacts, then email my friend Emmeline, who works on the features desk of a newspaper.

Emmeline is going. I definitely want to go now. I telephone a few more regional publications. No luck. I sense they don't want to pay me to have a free meal.

As a last-ditch attempt I call a website – and what do you know? I can write about the event for no cash remuneration. A small exchange for delightful food and lashings of free wine. A quick telephone call to the PR firm and all is arranged. I won't be eating mung beans tonight; instead I shall have a medium-rare steak.

I need to make an effort to look good, but there's

nowhere in the house to have a thorough wash because Eddie has ripped the entire bathroom suite out, and we're waiting for him to plumb in the new one. Last time I had a shower was two days ago, or was it three?

There isn't enough time for me to shower. Unless . . . I'll shower at the local leisure centre. While Jack's enjoying his swimming lesson, I'll dart into the changing rooms, don my bikini and wash my hair.

A couple of hours later, I arrive at the hotel. The black dress I'm wearing delivers quite a cleavage, and it only cost me four pounds on the reduced rail at Asda.

Emmeline should be around somewhere. I pick up a glass of red wine . . . then another. Lots of men in penguin suits are sauntering around the foyer to the dining area, prattling and guffawing about one thing or another, mostly literature. A quick glance around the room reveals that approximately 70 per cent of the attendees are silver foxes – that is to say, attractive men who are well and truly over the hill. They'd be lucky still to have their own teeth.

'Good evening,' a silver fox says, prowling straight past me.

'Good evening,' I purr.

And another silver fox: 'Good evening.'

'Good evening.'

And another silver fox: 'Good evening.'

'Good evening.'

I could keep this up all night but time's getting on and my stomach's rumbling. Rhodri was a little peeved to discover that he was babysitting while I headed out for a posh dinner but, being the peacemaker that I am, I bought him a packet of organic smoked tofu.

I nip outside for a social cigarette. I don't often smoke, but 'Have you got a light?' works well as an opening gambit when I find myself alone at an event, which frequently I do. If I give up smoking completely, what will I say then? Something inviting, such as 'Hello, my name is Kitty Luscious, and you are?'

A few minutes later I'm standing by the seating plan, looking for my name, when I realize I know the silver fox standing next to me. He was my ever-lovable tutor at university. He gave me endless essay extensions when I landed in his office looking a fright, with excuses such as 'My boyfriend says he's going to kill me, so I can't finish this essay on Byron until next Friday,' or 'I nearly died the other day so I'm a bit behind on this presentation.' He never snarled at me but reached into his heart for a metaphorical prop and shoved it up my back so I didn't collapse. A year later, I walked out of there upright.

'Hello, Professor,' I say. 'It's me.'

'Oh, hello,' he says.

'Do you remember me?'

'Of course I do. How are you?'

'I'm really well, thanks.'

'And your son?'

'He's great too. He's eight now.'

The professor makes a sound commonly used to acknowledge that children grow up quickly. I pull a facial expression in agreement. If I'm drunk enough at the end of the night, I'll hug him and thank him for the support he lavished on me. 'Are you still teaching?' I ask.

'No. I'm retired.'

'Enjoying your retirement?'

'Yes. Very much.'

'Where are you sitting?'

He points to a table. I look at the names around his, all notable academics. Mine isn't there. I scan the seating plans for tables towards the back of the dining room. My name isn't there either. Perhaps the PR firm didn't put it on the list. This might prove embarrassing. I'll be all dressed up with nowhere to sit.

'I don't know where I'm supposed to be,' I say, with a nervous laugh.

'There.' He points. 'The table at the front.'

'Oh.' In my head this is followed by 'Crap. Oh, crap. Oh, crap. Oh, crap. Oh, crap.'

'Fantastic,' I say. 'Thanks. Enjoy your meal.' *Why, oh, why* have I been seated on one of the front tables with the head of the Literature and Philosophical Society, and a multi-millionaire aristocratic couple, plus other luminaries? I wanted a table at the back with some boys, getting drunk, cracking jokes and eating steak. I'm going to have to be clever and polite and sober. I look for Emmeline's name. Thankfully, she's at the table next to mine.

I step off the last tram home and zigzag along the pavement, soaking up the silence of the winter's night. The road is beginning to ice over. A wagon rumbles past, spitting out grit. The lights seem brighter and the dark feels darker. I should have worn a thick coat and a scarf. If I'm not careful, I'll slip and land on my arse.

In Jackson village up ahead I can make out the sparkle

of Christmas lights. As I walk in that direction a knot of anxiety tightens in my stomach. As I curve the road leading to our estate the panic rises. I'm hard-wired to expect trouble. I expect Rhodri to hit me because he's the man I live with. I know absolutely that he won't, but even so, it's what I expect. And so, when I turn the key to my house and drop my things in the hall, hang my coat up, part of me is waiting for him to appear slyly around a doorway and frighten me like Damien did. I expect him to pin me to the floor or push me up against a wall.

'You look sober,' Rhodri says, hurrying me through the door, and into the kitchen, where he wraps his arms around me. 'You're so cold.' He rubs my hands between his. 'Good evening . . . good food?'

'Food was okay,' I say. 'I could have done with a thicker piece of steak.' It'd been so long since I'd eaten good meat that I'd have happily eaten an entire cow.

'I thought you'd be well and truly pissed by now.' He laughs. 'Hot drink?'

'What is it?' I quiz. 'It smells funny.'

'Valerian tea,' says Rhodri. 'Helps you sleep.'

The pre-Rhodri me would have thought valerian was a tropical disease.

The following morning I begin work on a new freelance PR assignment. All this DIY is expensive, and I've got to earn some cash to pay off the loan. I'm at a meeting, trying hard to think about Asian lesbian, bisexual and transgender performing artists. One of whom is sitting directly opposite me, in a bar in Leeds.

'. . . so what I really *don't* want . . .' says Narinder.

Concentrate, I tell myself. Concentrate. We awoke to discover that the bath pipes Eddie had sealed are leaking. All night, as we slept, water dripped through the floorboards, causing the paint on the kitchen ceiling to break out in angry blisters.

'. . . is . . .' continues Narinder, sternly.

I twirl my hair around my index finger while chewing a pen. I'm trying not to imagine that the bulging ceiling will burst and wreck my lovely new floor and kitchen cabinets. What if the ceiling collapses? How much will that cost me?

'. . . for the group to be *exoticized* in any way.'

I'm not getting this: *exoticized* how, exactly? Narinder is wearing biker boots, combats, a black T-shirt, has a boyish crop and looks as if she wants to beat the life out of me. I write it down anyway, in capital letters for effect. DO NOT EXOTICIZE.

'Okay,' I say, 'could you explain?'

'You know,' she snaps, 'the *Asian-lesbian* thing.'

'We could approach women's pages,' I say. I've worn my cutest dress for this meeting, red ballet-style shoes, and a smudge of make-up. The look I aspired to was 'approachable', but I'm sensing I come across as a homophobic fairy. 'If you tell me what you do,' I encourage, 'we can go from there.'

That afternoon, on the train back to Manchester, I call Rhodri. I expect him to ask me how my morning has been, or to reveal something about his, or Jack's, but no conversation is forthcoming.

'Have you had a good day?' I ask, wondering if I can

push him to do more overtime. I'm baffled by how we're going to pay for Christmas presents this year.

'Eddie is here,' he says, 'fixing the leak. When is he planning to fit the bathroom?'

'Tomorrow.'

Rhodri sighs unhappily. 'I'm going,' he says. 'What time are you back?'

'Around six,' I say.

'So you want me to collect Jack from after-school club?'

'That would be great,' I say. 'Thanks.'

'See you later, then.'

'Can't we chat?'

'You know I don't like to talk to you on your mobile.'

We've argued about this for years. I'd hoped that when we lived together Rhodri would relent and use a mobile phone for convenience. But he's resolute. Because he doesn't approve of mobile phones, he therefore discourages me from using one. Mobile-phone masts allegedly cause children to contract leukaemia and die. Mobile phones are made on the breaking backs of underpaid workers in developing countries. Everything about the mobile-phone industry is bad, except they keep you in touch with loved ones when you're far from home. But I don't want children to contract leukaemia and brain tumours just so that I can have a telephone conversation about my lesbian encounter. I don't want to add to the already catastrophic CO_2 emissions depleting the ozone layer to the point at which one day my future grandchildren will drown. Not to mention those families across the world who are being torn apart by melting polar caps, so I blow Rhodri a kiss and hang up. Then I feel dreadful for making him talk to me on my mobile phone in the first place.

When I finally arrive home it's much later than I'd expected. I cycled from Piccadilly to Jackson against a biting headwind that slammed against me causing my nose to bleed. The usual forty-minute bike ride took well over an hour. Whatever there is for dinner I'll eat it, even if it's roasted rabbit shit. Not that that would happen: no one cleans out the hutch but me, and roasted rabbit shit isn't vegan.

I drop my bag on the kitchen floor and pull off my cycling gear while I admire my shiny new oven. Something's simmering on the hob, voices are bubbling away in the living room, and my stomach is craving something tasty. 'Hi, love!' I call cheerily.

Jack runs into the hall to greet me, throwing his little body at mine, so I lift him up, balance him on my hips like a toddler and kiss him. 'You look like you're having lots of fun, what are you doing?'

'Making posters,' says Jack, showing me something that looks suspiciously like a protest placard.

'Let me see,' I say.

Just then a gangly, bearded lad I've never seen before walks into the kitchen to check the pan. He murmurs a gruff hello, then heads back into the living room. I follow him. 'Evening,' I call to Rhodri from the doorway. 'What's cooking?'

'Nothing. Where have you been? I called you on your mobile loads of times, and you didn't answer. I was worried.'

'I was cycling. It was windy. I didn't hear it.'

'I called *three* times.'

This, I think, is the point of mobile phones. 'So, what's on the hob?'

'Vegan glue.'

Silly me. Of course it's vegan glue, rather than a pan of soup on a freezing cold day when I've been out working since eight thirty this morning.

'So, there's no dinner?'

'No, didn't have time.'

'What are you doing?'

'Making subvertising posters.'

Subvertising posters are witticisms that are pasted over advertisements to subvert their money-grabbing consumer messages.

'Can I have a word?' I say, motioning to Rhodri that this 'word' should be in private. The bearded lad looks worried – and so he should be because I'm starving and there's no dinner on the table. 'Who's that in the living room?'

'Joel.'

'Where do you know him from?'

'Activist meetings.'

'How old is he?'

'Twenty-two.'

Now, at twenty-nine Rhodri and I aren't exactly ancient, but I do feel uncomfortable that this young lad is being drawn into subversive activity in my house. One thing could lead to another and, before you know it, I'll be playing Simone de Beauvoir to Rhodri's Jean-Paul Sartre, and I haven't enough energy or time for another lover; especially one with a beard.

'Not appropriate, Rhodri,' I say pointedly. 'The house is a tip. We've a bath being fitted tomorrow. We need to move furniture around so Eddie can get to things.' I can feel myself becoming more and more irate. 'Too much on. Not appropriate to be making subvertising posters tonight. No. Not happy.' The angrier I become, the less able I am to speak in full sentences.

'This is very important,' Rhodri says sternly. 'Christmas is approaching and there is already a deluge of advertisements. People will be spending on credit cards, and think of all the waste that will end up in landfills, not to mention the appalling working conditions suffered so that we can buy cheap goods. Mass consumerism is bad for the environment. The corporations are plunging people into debt, making us think we need to buy things. No one is concerned about climate change, you *know* that. If things carry on as they are, we may not have a future.'

This is just what I need after an afternoon of mollycoddling an Asian lesbian with the temperament of Jaws – a lecture on the end of the world being nigh.

'Another night, but not tonight,' I sing.

'It'll always be a bad time. We're going out after midnight to paste the subverts up on billboards.'

'What's that?' I say, pointing to a jar.

'I had to empty the bottle of washing-up liquid for the glue.'

'What's that?' I say, pointing to the pan.

'Flour and water.'

'What am I supposed to eat?'

'Make something.'

'Please not tonight. Do this another night,' I whine,

motioning to the boxes and stacks of furniture. 'I need you to help me with all of this.'

But Rhodri refuses. He glowers at me, disgusted that I would prevent him from taking action against corporate monoliths. I want to throw myself on the floor, arms akimbo and legs kicking up a storm, wailing, 'No no no no *nooooo*! Think about us. Think about *our* debt. Think about *my* world.'

Oh, what's the point? Rhodri thinks I'm one of them – one of the uneducated in need of eco-conversion, even though I cycle rather than drive, use Ecover rather than Flash, and install energy-saving lightbulbs in the house. Whatever I do, it's never enough.

I go upstairs, piss in the bucket, come down to wash my hands in the kitchen, boil the kettle, wash Jack by the oven, pack him into our bed, then begin to heave boxes from his bedroom to mine to make a path leading to his bed, where the new bathroom suite, still wrapped in cardboard and cellophane, awaits to be plumbed in when Eddie arrives tomorrow.

9

The race is on to restore order in time for Christmas Day. Rhodri's mother, Margaret No. 3, is arriving early tomorrow morning to help us reorganize the house now all the dirty work is finished. This very minute Damien's stepmother, Margaret No. 2, is busy ridding the kitchen of dust left by the workmen. If I could have summoned the army to help, I would have done. Jack has brought the rabbits into the kitchen to keep warm: unable to get a good grip they skate across the laminate floor, leaving poo pebbles behind them.

As Margaret No. 2 and I haul boxes from living room to kitchen and bedroom to kitchen, Rhodri saunters about the house in his dressing-gown, sneezing and blowing his nose. 'You go out strolling the streets of Manchester at midnight in December and you're going to catch a chill.' Of course I don't say that. I'm a woman lacking a spine. Instead I coo: 'Would you like some paracetamol, sweetheart?'

To which Rhodri unsurprisingly says, 'No,' because pharmaceutical companies commit endless bad deeds.

At least we have a toilet now, which no longer leaks into the kitchen.

I don't understand what's happened: a few months ago Rhodri said, 'Let's spend Christmas together this year. We'll host Christmas dinner.' I had the perfect Christmas planned out for Jack. I even *had a new kitchen fitted* and invited my father over, my stepmother, Eleanor, and my stepbrother, Luke, to spend the day with us, but now Christmas Day is rapidly approaching, Rhodri is spouting ridiculous things like: 'I don't see why you have to spend money.' What am I supposed to feed everyone on Christmas Day? Deep-fried dandelion leaves?

'How much can you give me towards Christmas?' I asked him last night. Three hundred pounds seemed a reasonable amount.

'I haven't any money.'

That's just perfect. Neither have I. What fun we'll all have. Fortunately, my stepmother is lending us her plastic Christmas tree. Christmas trees are, of course, another bone of contention. I can't win on any level. Unless I make my entire Christmas decoration collection out of discarded cardboard boxes and I haven't got the time.

As I mull this over while making a hot toddy for Rhodri, Margaret comes into the kitchen and closes the door behind her. 'Where is Rhodri?' she whispers.

'Gone back to bed,' I whisper back.

'Good. Tell me if he's coming.'

Margaret digs into her bag, pulls out some rubber gloves and a bottle of bleach. Then she pours it over the work-tops and kettle, scowling as she scrubs away turmeric and cayenne-pepper stains. 'See?' she says. 'Just a little bleach, and it all comes off.' A look of pleasure creeps over her face: 'I've been dying to do this for days,' she says. 'A brand new kitchen worktop ruined because you won't use bleach.'

'But it's bad for the waterways,' I begin, 'and all those

chemicals . . . our lungs . . .' Lord help me, I'm starting to sound like Rhodri.

I loiter about the kitchen anxiously. If Rhodri catches a whiff of this cleansing orgy he'll go berserk. I open the door, no sign of him. In which case I can polish the bookshelves.

Okay, I'm going in.

I pull a tin of Pledge from Margaret's secret supply, spray it on the wood and begin to polish. Usually this is done with warm water and washing-up liquid. The effect just isn't as good. I'm having such a wonderful time, singing along, admiring the wood and feeling free. Margaret is making contented sounds from the kitchen as she washes the dishes. It's akin to a scene from *Snow White*, minus the birds, when Rhodri stumbles down the stairs and catches me red-handed. 'It stinks,' he says.

Uh-oh, now I'm in trouble.

'I can't sit in here.'

Oh, bother.

'It smells *clean*,' Margaret calls from the kitchen.

'It smells *chemical*,' argues Rhodri.

'Where's he going?' asks Margaret, staring at Rhodri as he strides into the garden.

'I'm not going to return to the house while you spray that stuff,' he says, and then begins a half-hour protest in the back garden, wearing his dressing-gown, in the middle of a freezing afternoon in December.

Margaret turns to me. 'If he was my man, I wouldn't let him get away with that.'

But he's not her man, I think, he's mine, and I do feel a little fondness then for Rhodri and his insane ways.

*

The following morning I find myself wondering what kind of lunatics wrap Christmas presents in brown-paper bags they've lifted from the vegetable aisles in supermarkets. Eco-lunatics like us, that's who. It's not stealing, exactly. The bags are free and there are no customer notices saying, 'One bag per purchase'. Our so-called gift situation is like this: I take a book from my bookshelf (a nice hardback I received as a review copy or bought from a charity shop on a whim) scrawl 'Happy Christmas Mum/Dad/Nana xxx' in my poshest handwriting, slot it into a paper bag, Sellotape the ends down, then draw a quirky festive picture on the front, *et voilà*, Christmas presents sorted out. Horror! This reminds me of when Jack was a baby and I wrapped up some of his old toys to go with the new toys to make it look like I'd bought him lots of presents: we were *nouveau pauvre*.

It's the thought that counts, yes? And we don't want to contribute to this evil eco-disaster that masquerades as 'a celebration'.

The Christmas-card situation is thus: no Christmas cards for immediate family, a kiss and smile should do the trick. For those people I do need to write a Christmas card to I have one of two options: pull out a used card from the dozens I've hoarded in a box over the years, snip the greetings section off, and I have a Christmas postcard! Another option is to get an A4 piece of paper, fold it in half, cut a festive picture out of a magazine, stick it on the paper and write '*Happy Christmas!!!!*' inside. If I get Jack to do this we'll look creative, not skint, and recipients will think I'm one of those mums with heaps of spare time for crafts and baking with my talented child. Little will they know that I oversee a strict PVA glue factory line.

Small thought: am I making Christmas cards off the broken backs of knackered horses? Better hide the glue just in case.

Today I'm feeling good because I've just found out that the Asian lesbian, bisexual and transgender performing artists are happy with my PR work. I didn't exoticize them. 'That's great,' I said. Some producer is going to make a non-pornographic documentary about their experiences so my work is done.

Jack, on the other hand, is not happy: 'A plastic Christmas tree?' he yelps, as if someone had trodden on his foot. 'Why can't we have a real one?'

'Because . . .' I don't know what comes next. Because giant rabbits are stamping through the county eating all the real Christmas trees? 'Listen, love.'

'I know,' he mumbles, shuffling his bottom onto my knee. 'You haven't got loads of money for presents this year.'

'Yes, but we'll still have a great time.'

'It's okay,' Jack says. He falters. 'What I really want for Christmas is to see my dad.'

What I really want for Christmas is a whole lot of fun shopping at Harvey Nichols. But that's not going to happen, is it?

'Can I see him over Christmas? You can phone Nana to fix it up.'

'I don't think I can,' I say.

'Why?'

'I don't want you to see him.'

'Why?'

'We're happy right now and I don't want anything to disrupt that.'

From my uncompromising tone, Jack senses that I'm not going to change my mind and removes himself to a chair at the far end of the room. 'Can I buy him a present? I have pocket money in my piggy-bank.'

'If you like.'

'And send him a card?'

'That would be nice, he'd like that.'

What is worse than me taking Jack Christmas shopping for Damien's present? Let me think . . . A hysterectomy without an anaesthetic comes a close second.

'Jack, I'll take you.' Rhodri has seen the blood drain from my face. 'I've got to go into town, so I'll take you to buy a present for your dad.'

'Thanks.' Jack stomps upstairs to pull out cash from his piggy-bank.

'That's very generous of you,' I say to Rhodri.

'Well, I didn't think you'd want to go shopping for Damien. And we can buy you a present while we're there.'

I hand Rhodri ten pounds, 'Give this to Jack,' I tell him, 'to spend on presents.'

Rhodri puts the note in his pocket, expecting me to explain further.

'I don't mind if he spends *some* of it on his dad.' By which I mean, not a lot.

When Jack and Rhodri have left for the shops, I call Margaret No. 2. 'Jack's off to buy Damien a Christmas present,' I huff. 'Has Damien bought Jack a present? If he hasn't,' I add bitterly, '*he'd better* because Jack will be *very* upset.'

'I don't know,' she says.

'I doubt it,' I add. 'He's never bought Jack a present in his life.' Which is almost true. Damien has bought Jack very few presents over the last eight years. 'I'll get Eddie to call him and then I'll call you back.'

A few minutes pass before Margaret calls back: 'He's assured Eddie he's bought Jack a present, so we'll see.'

The boys are back just in time for Margaret No. 3's arrival. I bargained with Rhodri's mother that if she helps me to rearrange the house I will cook dinner. Unfortunately, she has been instructed to cook for us because I'm too busy finding odd shoes in odd places and Rhodri is again semi-horizontal with man-flu.

'I'm sorry you've been invited for dinner then had to make it yourself,' I say to Rhodri's mother.

We really should treat her better. She spends all her time cooking for other people. This is her first visit to our house and she's been enlisted to wash dishes, fold clothes and slave over the cooker. She said, 'I don't mind, I love to help.'

But as I point out to Rhodri, 'It's a bit cheeky of us.'

Christmas Eve – Lord, give me strength. I'm whizzing down the aisles in the supermarket in a festive stupor throwing all sorts into the trolley and wondering why this Christmas will be as desperately skint as all the others, even though Rhodri and I hold university degrees. Benefit claimants on the estate seem richer than us. Education has made me an articulate, debt-ridden pauper. Joy to the world!

Jack is scooting about in front of and behind me, generally being a bit of a pest, but full of excitement, chanting: *'Can I have this? Can I have this? Can I have this?'* Meanwhile I lob bright green bottles of pop into the trolley.

Rhodri is far, far behind us; so distant I'd have to set off a flare for him to find us. He's checking the ingredients on the labels of everything we've hurled or plan to hurl into the shopping trolley. I sped off because he was snickering and dragging his feet. The moment he started with 'Do you know what this contains?' I hissed, 'Shut up, Rhodri.' But still he went on to tell me how I was going to contract breast cancer, or stomach cancer, or some other cancer. Which may well be true, but it's not practical to check the ingredients of every product in a store the size of a small town when I just want to stock up on sugary crap and party food and get my sorry arse out of there. I don't want to be told that some time in the future I may have a mastectomy because of a cancerous lump caused by spraying chemicals onto my armpit skin. It's *Christmas Eve*: I simply want to buy a can of fragrant body spray so I don't stink to high heaven on Christmas Day.

Oh, bugger. Rhodri is closing in on us. 'Don't,' I warn.

'I don't know why we had to shop at a supermarket,' he protests.

'Because it's easy, and I'm short of time and it's cheap and you wanted me to cook Christmas dinner this year.'

'This is depressing,' he moans, flopping against shelves piled high with crisps and nuts.

'What's depressing?'

I look around us. A toddler has thrown himself on the

floor, his mother is screaming at him. We're at the big out-of-town place near one of Europe's largest council estates; you don't get a high-class shopper here – many people have tattoos and facial piercings, and most of the trolleys are loaded with high-fat snacks, frozen food and multi-packs of beer. That's where I need to go, the wine aisle, and soon.

'It makes me feel sad, all these people buying things they don't need, all the waste. All the cars in the car park, and no thought for climate change. Or a thought that supermarkets are exploiting workers in other countries.'

'Don't feel depressed, feel happy. It's a special time to spend with the ones you love.'

'I can't help it, I hate Christmas,' he insists.

Well, why the hell didn't he say that before he elected to spend time with us over Christmas? A small boy's future jolliness is at stake here. One miserable Christmas and he could hate me for life. 'You're being unfair,' I say sternly, my mind set on the booze aisle. 'Think of Jack.'

'It's his future I'm thinking of,' says Rhodri. 'He won't have one if we carry on like this.'

'You're being ungrateful,' I say. 'I'm trying my hardest to make sure we all have a good Christmas, that our home is comfortable, that we have nice food. I'm financing it, and you want to make me feel bad about the environment. That isn't fair.'

And it isn't. My heart is breaking. All I want is to give Jack a fun Christmas.

In the hours since we returned from the supermarket, Rhodri has been on the brink of tears. He is standing behind me, leaning against the cooker. We've opened a bottle of red wine. The radio is belting out festive hits. With my bare hands I'm shoving butter under the skin of a fat, dead, but organic, locally reared and homeopathically treated turkey. I purchased this extravagant bird from an uncharitably expensive independent butcher. Excluding the obvious slaughtered-bird part of this, Rhodri should be proud of me, not despairing. Jack is watching Christmas television, writing his list, checking it twice, and running into the kitchen every few minutes asking, 'Can I pull a cracker?'

We're all wearing Christmas hats and I'm sporting a dashing red apron with laughing reindeers printed all over it. It's not quite one of those scenes you see on the adverts and that I fantasized about. For a start, we're not hysterically chirpy; right now the turkey is the only one getting any attention.

In my ideal world everything would be different. Jack would be tucked up in bed, his Santa sack bulging with gifts. Rhodri would be helping me stuff and baste the turkey. This scene would swiftly morph into the Patrick-Swayze-shags-Demi-Moore pottery sequence in *Ghost* but with Vitalite sunflower spread, not clay.

'Come on, Rhodri,' I exclaim, with a forced smile. 'Cheer up. It's almost *Christmas*!' I jig my hips a little to Slade on the radio in a useless attempt at getting him to boogie with me, or alternatively to bend me over and give me a good seeing-to on the kitchen table. He ignores me. Slade drones on and on about wishing it could be Christmas every day until Mariah Carey swings in to take the baton. I sing along to 'All I Want For Christmas Is

Youuuuuuu', but don't add, 'to fucking well cheer up' at the end. 'It's supposed to be fun,' I say.

'It hasn't been much fun.'

'This is what Christmas is like as an adult with a family. You have to do it all yourself.'

Rhodri looks at me blankly.

'When your mother has all you boys and the girlfriends over for Christmas dinner, she has to do it for you. She has to work hard to make it good for you.'

'But she enjoys waiting on us.'

'And she has to clean and tidy the house beforehand,' I explain, 'and shop, and wrap presents and prepare the table. It's a lot of work, Rhodri.'

'But she likes it.'

Rhodri has proved my suspicions correct: men genuinely are dim if they think women enjoy this preposterous débâcle that is tantamount to slave labour.

'All these years your mother has done it for you, now it's your turn to do it for other people.'

'If that's the way it is, I don't want it. I don't want to do this.'

'*You* said you wanted us to host Christmas dinner. *Not me.*'

'I didn't know it would be like *this*.' He pauses and looks directly at me, 'What's the point?'

'Of what, Rhodri?'

'Christmas – when the earth is . . .' Then Rhodri starts to cry. Not over me. Or Jack. He cries because families all over the world are indulging in the most heinous crime against the planet known to mankind.

Glancing at the opened recipe book I see I need some

fresh rosemary for the potatoes. 'Jack,' I shout, 'go and dress head to foot in black.'

'Why?'

'Because we're going to go and steal some rosemary from that garden around the corner.'

'Why?'

'Because I need it for this recipe and the pre-packed rosemary in the supermarket travelled on a plane from Israel to get here.'

'So we're going to steal it from that old lady's garden instead?'

'Yes. Pretend you're James Bond and this is Mission Rosemary.'

'Sick,' he says, which means 'great' in kidspeak.

Ooooh, I want to kill myself. Seriously, I do. Tomorrow I'm going to take that bubbling roasting tin from the hot oven and shove my head in it.

PART TWO

10

I made as much progress on project 'happy family' at Christmas as I would have done roller-skating up a glacier backwards. That is, I made everyone happy but me. A fortnight later, I'm in a bad mood. The happiness was, in reality, condensed into three hours on Christmas Day when Rhodri ate a vegan haggis, while my omnivorous stepfamily tucked into a three-course meal, taken straight from my Gordon Ramsay cookbook and using vegetables that Rhodri grew on the allotment. As for presents, Rhodri seemed to appreciate the organic and ethically farmed Welsh woollen jumper I'd bought for him until I shrank it in the washing machine.

Jack went back to school today, and Rhodri is at work, so I thought I'd polish the bookshelves with my secret supply of Pledge that Margaret No. 2 left behind for me. I need to open the windows and waft the smell away before Rhodri comes home. I'm neatening the shelves when a book by Janice Galloway called *The Trick Is To Keep Breathing* catches my eye. This inspires me to take a coffee break and compile my own tailor-made list of tricks:

– The Trick is to stop opening bills.

– The Trick is to stop spending.

– The Trick is to stop working.

— The Trick is to stop wanting a married life with three children.

— The Trick is to stop wishing for the magical day when I will leave this bloody awful council estate.

— The Trick is to stop imagining an easier life than this.

While I'm at it, I give myself some New Year resolutions:

1. I am going to be the best mum ever and take on difficulties with a positive attitude, including Jack's reluctance to do homework.

2. I am going to be the best girlfriend ever and not engage in extra-relationship romances, even if my boyfriend encourages me to.

3. I am going to cut down on tedious low-paid work and write a play instead.

I am sick of this place. Ever since Christmas I have had problems with my wheelie-bin. Somebody keeps swiping it, and that someone lives round the corner: Tina. Henceforth, this internationally important political issue shall be known as the Wheelie-bin War. I should add another New Year resolution to my list:

4. I am going to stick up for myself on this estate, and not quiver behind the curtains when someone like Tina upsets me.

Of all my resolutions, this one is the most pressing. Throughout Christmas week I hauled bags of rubbish out to my bin, only to find it wasn't there. Then one day I opened the gate to find piles of rubbish scattered everywhere outside my garden fence. The local council will issue a penalty fine for this, and it isn't even my rubbish.

I opened the bin-bags and rifled through them to discover it was Tina's rubbish. I sneaked down the alley and peered through the gap in Tina's fence to discover she had, once again, taken my wheelie-bin. It has my house number painted on it in huge white figures. It is *my* bin.

Two days ago Tina walked past my house so I opened the front door and called nervously: 'Tina, have you got my bin?'

'No,' she lied.

I said, 'I think you have got my bin. Can you please leave it outside my gate?'

'I will,' she shouted.

I look out today and still no freaking bin. Even more rubbish has accumulated outside my gate.

I'm not being petty. This has been going on for months, years even. And she has her own foul, smelly bin. She doesn't pay someone to clean it like I do with mine.

This very moment Tina is walking through the communal gardens and past my window. Now is as good a time as any to tackle New Year Resolution 4. I take a deep breath, ignore my jitters, and head out of the front door. There's only one way to do this and it's at full volume. That way, if she thumps me, Josie or Philomena can come to my rescue.

'Tina,' I call, striding down the path, swinging my arms in the most aggressive way I know how.

'What?'

'I've called Environmental Health, and if you don't

shift that rubbish this afternoon – it has your name written all over it – you'll get a massive fine. And I'll have my bin back, thank you.' I turn to go.

'I've spoken to the police about you,' she snaps back. 'If you or ya knobhead boyfriend come in me garden again, you'll get arrested.'

She's saying this because for the past two months I have been sending Rhodri on retrieval missions. He scales her fence, grabs the bin and darts out with it, yet the next week it still ends up back in her garden.

'But it's my bin!'

'Yeah, 'n' it's my garden ya trespassin' on.'

'Just put the bin out, Tina.'

'Ya can tell ya boyfriend that if he comes in the garden again, Keano's gonna batter 'im.'

I make a mental note to add that name to the list of people who threaten to batter one or other of us. It's quite long now. I'll speak her language, see if that works: 'Put the fucking bin out, Tina – *okay*?'

'Yur off ya head. Yur fuckin' freaks, the pair of ya. An' my Keano will knock him out, so you can tell him not to step foot in my garden. All right?'

Yes, yes, yes, Tina, that's all very interesting: 'Environmental Health On the Way. Shift It,' I say, then turn on my heels and stamp off, shaking with fright.

'Weirdo,' she hisses, when my back is turned.

As I walk through the gardens back to my house, I feel uneasy. I really don't like confrontation. But if I don't stick up for myself on this estate, I'll just end up getting bullied. On a more practical level, I have nowhere to leave our domestic waste.

When Rhodri returns from work at lunchtime, I inform him of his impending hospital visit. 'Tina said that if we go in her back garden again, Keano's going to batter you.'

'Come on,' Rhodri says, with a will of steel. 'We need to end this.' He strides out to the back garden, and down the alley, dragging me with him. He swings open Tina's gate.

'I don't know if we should.' I wince, thinking of Keano. Then again, the man is a wimp. Rhodri could manage him, easy.

Rhodri doesn't enter the garden. Instead, his feet stay firmly in the alleyway as he stretches his arm into Tina's garden. He yanks the bin out, tips it upside down and shakes the contents into a heap by her fence. Then he collects all the bags of rubbish she has left by our back gate and hurls them outside hers. 'She can clear that up too,' says my wheelie-bin super-hero.

Oh dear. Tina's going to be *so* miffed about that.

A couple of hours later, I open the window to hear Tina cursing and huffing as she sweeps the mess up. War over, I think. We won. Hoorah. And I didn't really call Environmental Health.

Saturday morning, I open the curtains and am relieved to see that Tina has not thrown eggs at the windows all week. There'll be some form of retribution, I'm sure. Hero-of-the-month Rhodri is relaxing in bed, enjoying a weekend lie-in, a good time, I think, to tell him about one of my other New Year resolutions. 'I'm going to give up that job with the newspaper. I'm going to write a play to take to the Edinburgh Fringe this summer.'

'That's great.'

'I'm doing it on Monday.'

'You'll feel better for it.'

'Once I've done it, I can't go back.'

'Good, you'll be more relaxed.'

'Relaxed', 'bankrupt': if I looked these words up in the *Oxford English Dictionary* would they share a definition?

I also thought about giving up Rhodri because he's turning out to be a full-time job and the benefits and working conditions aren't always great. It was almost another of my New Year resolutions but on Tuesday when I wandered into the local estate agent's to daydream about living in a three-bedroom semi-detached in the posh part of Jackson, the man said, 'This is the best time to buy. Couples separate around about now because of a dreadful Christmas together. They want to shift properties quickly.' He rubbed his hands together greedily.

Rhodri and I are not going to be one of those statistics: we are not a couple who cannot stand to be with one another. Christmas may have been rocky, but if I hold on tight through January and stop myself doing anything drastic, like throwing his clothes out of the window or setting fire to his rucksack, I'm certain we'll reach spring intact.

'You might need to get another job,' I tell him. 'We'll be losing four hundred pounds a month.'

'I told you,' he says. 'I don't want to work full time.'

Monday morning, I sit down at my desk to catch up on some freelance work: finishing off a few bits of PR, updating a website and trying to get an interview with some poets for a feature for a magazine.

Rhodri may have said he doesn't want to work full time,

but if I go through with New Year Resolution 3 and give up my job compiling entertainment listings for the what's-on section in a newspaper (the most depressing job for an English graduate, ever, but very easy money), and write my play, we'll be so broke Rhodri will have to work extra hours. Having made this radical decision, I take executive action and speak with the editor: 'I'm going to write a play,' I say uncertainly, 'so I'd like to take a break for a year.'

Camouflaging my resignation as a sabbatical is a safety net: that way I can always ask for my job back.

'No problem,' the editor says. 'When would you like to finish?'

My original plan was to give a month's notice, but I may as well quit now before I change my mind. 'At the end of the day?'

'That's fine. Just let me know when you want your job back. It'll remain open for you.'

Kind words. But, hopefully, I'll never need it back. Little did I know that giving up work would feel so liberating. Suddenly I am transformed into a *decision-maker*. I go back to my desk and twiddle my fingers for an hour, trying to decide what to do next, battling against the desire to resign from all work completely. Now I have fewer assignments, I can devote more time to being a loving girlfriend and mum. Which is what I've always wanted.

I look on curryfrenzy.com, intending to make an impressive vegan curry for Rhodri. This afternoon I will collect Jack from school and take him to a nearby fishmonger to choose a piece of fish. Then I will prepare his all-time favourite meal: baked salmon with pasta and salad.

*

I have collected Jack, baked his salmon, and served it up. He is now sitting happily at the kitchen table, doing his homework and experiencing the benefit of my unerring patience and assistance. Margaret No. 2 has dropped in and is sipping her tea while watching me with utter disbelief. 'What *are* you doing?' she says, scanning the piles of herbs and vegetables on the worktop.

'Making mushroom dhansak.'

'How long have you been making it?'

I look at the clock. 'About three hours now. I had to blanch the tomatoes first and make the curry massala gravy.'

'You could buy it in a jar.'

'Rhodri won't eat those sauces in jars.'

'You're mad,' she says, as I crush yet more garlic to stir into a pan.

I spend the next hour making pillau rice, ten minutes eating, an hour washing the dishes, and am so exhausted from all that cooking I can only manage five minutes of sex at bedtime. I imagine that this is what life as a housewife is all about.

This morning I cycled with Jack to school with the promise that tonight I will read to him in bed. He kissed me in the playground and said, 'I love you, Mum.' New Year Resolution 1 is on course for success. Meanwhile Rhodri enjoyed his curry and his bowels are in top working order this morning. New Year Resolution 2 would also have been well on its way to success – had I not checked my emails this morning and found a message from Toga:

I've just plugged in my old phone and found lots of rude texts I
sent you last year. Ah, the memories . . . How you? How is the
New Year treating you so far? X

So, of course, I had to reply:

Bear, Might visit London next month to see a play. What are you
up to? Busy? I have to book a visit in with you really early.
Anyways, when you coming here and wooing me? Am getting
bored. X

To which Toga replied:

Yes, it's been a while, Baby Bear. [He sent me a link to a
YouTube video of some bears.] When you say 'woo', do
you mean what I think you mean?

Toga thinks 'woo' means 'shag', but I actually mean
'romance'.

I'm up soon for work. I'll be staying at the Hilton Hotel, and you
can visit me in my room on a professional basis if you like. Quite
fancy a play some time, yes, then some slap and tickle. X

What does Toga think I am? An educated hooker?

Can I visit and stay, and when? X

If I were to stick to New Year Resolution 2, I should not
be drawn in by the promise of hot sex at a luxury hotel.
Although, as a firm believer in change for nourishment not
punishment, I don't go in for needless self-denial and, lucky
me, because of this open-relationship business, I don't have
to. Also, I like spending time with Toga. He makes me laugh,
and the sex (when we get that far, and we haven't for about
a year now) is great: none of this romance interspersed with

the it's-your-turn-to-wash-the-dishes-love business. In bed we're like two frustrated animals, caged up together, tearing pieces out of one another. *Grrrr*.

I should start dieting now if I'm signing up for bed Olympics at the Hilton in a few weeks' time. How much weight can I lose in two weeks? About four pounds. I'll still be fatter than I was the last time Toga saw me.

This whole exchange has given me an idea. If Rhodri won't work extra hours in a pub, or sign up for extra shifts at a home care agency, maybe . . . 'Rhodri?' I call, because it's his day off and he's reading the newspaper in the living room.

'Yes?'

'Rhodri?'

'Yes, love?' He wanders into the kitchen and opens the cupboards in search of pumpkin seeds and nuts. He may have been a squirrel in a former life.

'I've come up with a way for us to make some money.' Rhodri groans. He thinks I'm going to suggest a real job. 'You could be a male escort.' As he doesn't object immediately, I carry on: 'You could earn loads of money dating women – you'd be perfect.'

'What would I have to do?'

'Take rich women out, eat meals, put them in a taxi home.'

'What if the women want to have sex?'

'You don't have to say yes.'

Rhodri looks disappointed. In light of this I try a different approach. 'Would you like to have sex with them?'

'I'm not sure.' He shrugs, smiling. 'It would depend on the woman.'

'That's why it's perfect. You go out to posh places for dinner, have sex, don't pay for any of it and earn loads. All our money problems will be solved.'

'How much would I get paid?'

'A couple of hundred pounds per night – even per hour.' Rhodri is a handsome man. He'd easily earn four hundred pounds a night.

'I'd only have to go on one date a month. . .' he begins, while I'm calculating how much we'd rake in if Rhodri went out three times a week: £400 x 3 nights = £1200 per week, approximately £4800+ per month, which is *circa* £57,600 per annum. Then I deduct half that sum for national insurance, income tax, clothes, hairstyling, designer stubble, condoms, etc. I think we're on to a winner here. Rhodri can still do the good thing during the day, looking after elderly people with Alzheimer's and so on, but a very bad thing at night. If I had any spare time, I'd offer to become an escort too.

'How would I go about it?'

'Sign up with an agency.'

I pull up a couple of websites on the computer for Rhodri to look at. He's far handsomer than those jokers. 'You'd get so many more bookings than these men,' I assure him, pointing at the computer screen. Rhodri would make an ideal male escort just as long as he didn't – 'You wouldn't be able to start ranting about veganism and the environment to your paying ladies.'

Come to think of it, he'd be a cheap date. He'd only eat a salad.

'I wouldn't do that.'

'Just be polite, talk about their jobs, kids, et cetera, don't

99

get too drunk and so on.' How exciting – our money worries could soon be over. Oh, but what if Rhodri were to fall in love with one of these women? He might leave me, an eco-barrel-scraping single mother, for a new life as an international playboy financed by a fifty-year-old billionairess. I wouldn't like that.

'As long as you don't fall in love,' I add.

'I won't fall in love with anyone else,' he says, incredulous that I could imagine he might. Not incredulous, though, at my efforts to encourage him into a life of prostitution. 'I don't think I'd have sex with a client.'

'Best to leave these options open,' I say pragmatically. 'You might be on a date with a foxy lady and find you quite fancy her, and that she's prepared to pay a thousand pounds for the pleasure of a night with you. And,' I plead, 'we need the money.'

Rhodri hates it when I beg. When I do he always says, 'No' to whatever it is I want. He needs a motive other than money.

'It might do you good to sleep with someone else,' I say, because if he's going to marry me one day he should have some fun with the ladies first, and if it means we can pay the bills, I'll turn a blind eye to just about anything.

'Hm . . . maybe,' he says, picking up a newspaper. 'Maybe if I fancied her I'd have sex. I have got some catching up to do.'

A few days later we're using the white walls of the living room as a blank canvas for Rhodri's photo-shoot. 'Is this shirt okay?' he asks.

'You look gorgeous,' I oblige.

'With the jumper or without?'

'Let's try both.' I stand on the sofa snapping away with the camera. If I take a picture from above I can capture that 'come hither, wench' look. Rich women out there will love it. 'I think you should wear the dark jumper,' I advise. 'You're vanishing into the walls with that pale shirt.'

Rhodri pulls it on. That's better. He looks more defined now.

'Smile,' I command, snapping away. 'Look sexy. Look moody. Look manly. Now look gentle and caring.'

'I've decided upon an escort agency,' he says, leaning alluringly against the wall. 'I'll need an escort name.'

'Oh, I hadn't thought of that. What name do you fancy? How about Max?'

'Not Max.'

'We can think about it.'

'My mum won't be very happy when she finds out.'

His mother is open-minded. I can't see why she'd complain.

'You wouldn't be doing anything wrong, simply looking after ladies who need some safe male company. Think of yourself as a modern-day knight in shining armour.' There's no one safer than Rhodri. I recommend him personally. If there were a Michelin-star equivalent in the world of male escorts, I'd give him three.

Photo-shoot over, we lean against the wall flicking through the pictures on the digital camera. 'I still fancy you,' I whisper.

'And I still fancy you,' smirks Rhodri.

11

I should give up trying to be the 'best girlfriend ever' because it's hypocritical. The 'best girlfriend ever' probably wouldn't want to pimp her boyfriend to pay the gas bill. I have, however, achieved three out of four New Year resolutions and it's only the last weekend in January. Maybe I'm not doing too badly after all.

Tonight is yet another Friday night when I look around me, thinking, At what point did we move into a potting shed? There are gardening tools and seeds and pots everywhere. I open the cupboard under the stairs to search for my slippers only to find strings of onions dangling between coat sleeves. Potatoes are chitting in Jack's chest of drawers. A trail of dirt runs through the house from the patio doors, across the kitchen and up the stairs. I need help with this. I can't cope. I want to cry. I want to escape somewhere.

'Is anything planned for this weekend?' asks Rhodri, pouring two glasses of red wine.

'No. Why?'

I hope he's going to swoop me off to the Lake District for some adult fun. Or maybe he, Jack and I are going for a weekend activity break. I'd even settle for a drive out for Sunday lunch.

'I've arranged a protest at a supermarket tomorrow.'

'But I'm away next weekend,' I tell him. 'In Yorkshire, on a scriptwriting course. Remember? I told you months ago.'

'That's next weekend,' he says, clearly hoping to end the argument.

'But I'm working all week so we need to wash the clothes and do the food shopping and tidy the house and clean the rabbit hutch *this* weekend.'

'The protest is already arranged. Why don't you come along?'

'What are you protesting about?'

'The introduction of ID cards.'

'I like the idea of ID cards,' I say. 'It'll be handy having all my details in one place.' I'm always losing my personal belongings. ID cards sound a great idea to me.

'*No, Maria!*'

Why does Rhodri have to say my name in that tone, instantly turning me into a four-year-old? He uses the same berating version of 'Maria' my father used when I melted custard creams by the fire.

'ID cards are BAD,' drills Rhodri. 'They are an invasion of our privacy.'

'Some people might agree with ID cards,' I venture. 'It's more practical than carrying a driving licence, passport and bills to prove who you are.'

'Those people don't know what they're talking about.'

Rhodri includes me in the people-who-don't-know-what-they're-talking-about Venn diagram etched in his head.

'I need you at home to help me.'

My argument is pointless: as far as Rhodri is concerned, Britain is one step from becoming a totalitarian state and urgent action is required.

'This is more important. The government plan to

introduce ID cards and people need to know that they are being duped.'

I spend the rest of the evening ironing. I used to go to clubs. I used to have friends. I used to have rampant sex on Friday nights with Rhodri. Now we lie in bed bickering about what shit-hot idea the Labour Party will come up with next.

On Saturday morning I switch on the computer to check my emails. Toga has become reticent about the luxury night in a top hotel. I don't think it's going to happen. Now he's talking about staying at a windmill instead. When do I have time to stay at a windmill? I could do the Hilton – it's only a train ride away. I idly click my way through the links he sent me, one of which leads to a weekend break in Norfolk. And now I'm romanticizing about Thai massages in cornfields, followed by sensual nookie to the tick of a windmill.

An old schoolfriend called me with the news that Damien is likely to go to prison for some petty crime. And nothing's happening on Project SUFFR (Save Us From Financial Ruin) because Rhodri is wrapped up in a greater cause than our income crisis. All he'd have to do is dally with a couple of strangers and our bank accounts would be stable for months. This morning I asked him, 'Have you sent that application form and picture off to the escort agency yet?'

'I will do,' he said, then added guiltily, 'I haven't had the time.'

But he's had heaps of time for concocting plans to disrupt shoppers at the supermarket on a busy Saturday afternoon.

'What do you think?' He parades proudly in his protest gear around the garden. My head is in the rabbit hutch, and I'm scraping out urine-soaked sawdust.

I scowl at him. 'I think you should help me.'

'Do what?' he argues.

'Do things. Grocery shopping and so on.'

'I told you what I'm doing today.'

'What if you get arrested?' I bite back. 'What about us?'

'That's a risk,' he admits. 'But I have to do this.'

'What about . . .' I begin, then stop myself continuing because he'll only say that I'm wrong.

Rhodri has been arrested in the past. He was one of the protesters blockading the road at the G8 summit in Scotland. He didn't catch a train there, or drive, or take a coach: he cycled from Manchester to Wales to meet a friend, then cycled on to Ireland to meet another friend, and then from Ireland he cycled to Scotland where he stayed on a self-erected campsite for protesters. I didn't see him for three months, and we barely spoke on the phone because he demolished his mobile by snapping the sim card with his teeth. During his journey to Scotland and back to Manchester he slept under a sheet of tarpaulin strung between trees in dense woodland, and when he returned to my house he was scabbed from head to toe with bites where midges and tics had feasted on him. His muscles were something to behold, though, and he had a wild and sun-burnished look about him, which was incredibly attractive. I'd thought that that break would get all this eco-antagonism out of his system, but it seems to have spurred him on.

Rhodri points to his chest and the T-shirt he's made for

the protest. Across the front he has drawn a super-sized barcode. If only I had it in me to praise him. 'It's a barcode,' he explains, thinking I haven't got it. 'I'm going to wear it on the protest, climb onto a conveyor-belt at the supermarket with a megaphone and yell, "SCAN ME," at the checkout girl.'

If I were a checkout girl, I'd be scared. 'How many others are taking part?' I ask, imagining a legion of bearded young men, wearing barcode T-shirts, lying on conveyor-belts yelling, 'SCAN ME,' at petrified checkout girls.

'There'll be about ten of us.'

'And will you *all* be lying on the conveyor-belts?'

'No, just me. The others will be handing out leaflets to shoppers warning them of the dangers if we accept the proposed ID cards.'

'I don't get what the link is between supermarkets and ID cards.'

'We're being treated like objects. That's the link,' proclaims Rhodri.

Of course. I should have known that.

'Why don't you come along with Jack and hand out leaflets?' he asks *again*.

As if I have time for that. 'No,' I snap. 'There's too much for me to do here.' Then I propel myself into a full-on rant at him. Why should I be locked in the house weekend after weekend like a housewife? I work long hours. He works part-time. It isn't fair. I'm left to be responsible for everything while he's out with his mates disrupting shoppers. I can't cope with it. I won't cope with it.

Rhodri shouts back, 'Shove the fucking washing-up your fucking arse, you po-faced bitch.'

Yes, I think, I might just shove the *fucking* washing up my *fucking* arse. It'll be more fun than this. 'Oh, fuck off,' I shout back.

Hearing raised voices, Jack runs out of the house to the garden. 'Stop shouting,' he commands. 'And stop swearing. I heard you swear,' he points to Rhodri, 'and *you* swear.' He points at me disapprovingly so I'm forced to apologize to everyone, thus agreeing in principle that, yes, I'm a po-faced bitch and what I need to do is become even more laid-back – to the point where I'm as horizontal as a super-market conveyor-belt.

'We haven't seen Scarlet in months,' I say to Rhodri. He's sitting on our bed watching me cram clean clothes into our wonky wardrobe. My attempt to interrupt his account of what happened at the supermarket is useless: I'd need a Trident missile convention to throw him off track, not an absent ten-year-old.

'So I just lay there, yelling, "Scan me," at the checkout girl, until she took the handheld scanner and whizzed it over my belly. I made beeping noises as she did it – it was great.'

I'm diverted for a moment. 'Yes, but did people listen or did you make them angry by holding the queue up?'

'A lot of people took leaflets and asked what it was all about and were *interested*.'

Unlike me – no, that's unfair. I do enjoy listening. I just don't want to listen right now.

Small thought: if I were to have placed a lonely-hearts advertisement in a newspaper would it have read, 'Large-rumped and impoverished single mother complete with bad attitude and diamond aspirations seeks opinionated activist to lie on conveyor-belt at supermarket with for arguments, twice-monthly sex, and battles over the washing line. Interested? Call this number and yell BEEP BEEP BEEP'?

It has been a testing afternoon. Jack called at Scarlet's house but she wasn't there, so he had no friends to play with all day. It's on weekends like this that I wish I had a brood of children. Enough for two five-a-side football teams – I'd have a nanny, naturally, and ten domestic staff, and an on-hand masseuse, hairdresser, stylist and make-up artist.

I'm worried for Scarlet, and miss her. Families usually stay indoors in winter, but I haven't seen Scarlet since the day we went to the allotment. 'Where do you think Scarlet is?' I ask Rhodri.

'I don't know,' he says, laughing to himself. He's still high from the protest.

If I was anywhere near a decent girlfriend, I'd be basking in his jubilation. But I'm not, I'm a mean ole grumpy bitch of a girlfriend so I pull a cranky face instead.

'Do you think Scarlet's okay?' I try again later when we're in the kitchen.

'She'll be fine. Probably playing with some other kids.'

'I'd really like to go on holiday,' I say, to change the subject. 'It'll be Easter soon, and Jack will be on his spring break. We should arrange something. How about France? We could take Scarlet.'

'I'm not flying,' he scoffs.

'By rail, then,' I suggest. Then I go totally off on a tangent. 'Let's travel the world. We could even take Jack out of school and teach him ourselves.'

This makes Rhodri stop to listen: he thinks I should

home-educate Jack before he's institutionalized and becomes yet another sad victim of 'The State'.

I've no idea how we'd finance a round-the-world trip but it's good to dream. Maybe if Rhodri were in demand as a high-class escort . . . 'I'll get the globe,' I say, sensing an opportunity. I head to Jack's room and unplug the broken lamp that doubles as a globe. I hunt through his bedside drawer for a pencil. When I've found one Jack follows me from his bedroom to ours, then tumbles onto the bed next to me and I begin plotting our journey. 'So, if we start north we can go to Russia, then on to China on the Trans-Siberian Railway, catch a boat to . . .'

This trip could take decades, not months.

'What you doing?' asks Jack.

'Plotting our round-the-world trip.'

'When are we going?'

'September.'

Jack points out all the countries he wants to visit. 'Kenya.' He giggles. 'I want to go to Kenya on safari. See the animals.'

Rhodri joins us, I can feel him disapproving of this suggestion: it reeks of fuel, a plane journey, and many trips in a four-by-four looking at caged animals in compounds, not his thing at all. Still, I'm sure we could swap Kenya for New Zealand and Jack would be happy.

How exciting that we're making plans as a *family*. We're going to travel the world. I can't wait.

12

Because Rhodri is busy again, on Sunday morning Jack and I go for a play date at my friend Lucy's house. Lucy and I met in the refuge. She has two daughters, one of ten and the other of eight. They live in the most splendid semi-detached house with a garden the size of a football pitch filled with toys, swings, a slide and an enormous trampoline. Our children don't remember living in the big safe-house together but they do feel bound to one another. Jack adores Lucy's girls. To him they're princesses.

I ring the bell once. Lucy opens the door and embraces me tightly. 'Hello, little man,' she says, rubbing Jack's head. 'Look how big you've grown.'

Jack puffs out his chest so that he looks macho.

'The girls are in the garden if you want to run and play.' On cue, Jack sprints off and, seconds later, we hear the creak of a swing.

'Come in, come in,' says Lucy. She looks at me. 'Something's happened, hasn't it?' She sweeps her hand over and around my body. 'I can feel it. I'm very spiritual today. I'm going to read your cards and consult the oracle.'

My aura must be a funny colour or something. Usually I don't go in for all this fortune-telling crap. For a start, I don't want to know what the future holds because I've only ever just about got a grip on the past and the present. And, also, Lucy is a conduit for dead people who make an appearance from time to time in her kitchen. During a reading she glazes over, the room feels cool and creepy and I expect the lampshade to shake. Then she'll start a conversation with a spirit. It freaks me out. I saw a ghost once and I was petrified – so no ghosties for me. Not even people I once knew. Dead people should stay dead.

'You're not happy, love. I know you.'

Is there a flashing 'unhappy' sign stuck to my forehead?

I'll never forget what you looked like when you started going out with him.'

Before Lucy was into spiritualism, she was a reflexologist and beauty consultant. She thinks Rhodri isn't the one for me. She'll never forgive him for the summer he convinced me not to depilate any body hair, and I swapped roll-on deodorant for a block of crystallized salts. Then there was the Mooncup he wanted me to use in place of tampons. If you've never seen one, it's a rubber contraption that collects menstrual blood, which you wash at intervals, much like the teat on a baby's bottle. When Rhodri balked at me wearing perfume and make-up, I gave them up too. Lucy watched me turn from Betty Boop to a Scottie dog overnight.

She tuts loudly. 'You're letting yourself go again. I don't like it.'

I know I look a mess. I've seen the photographic evidence. I don't need reminding.

'Take a seat,' she says, handing me a coffee and pulling out a chair. Expertly, she shuffles the cards and sweeps them out across the table. The reading claims I will find myself single, an older man will appear on the scene soon,

I will enter a new career and become stinking rich. Tarot readings always say I'm going to become stinking rich. I wish it would happen this week.

'Well?'

She wants me to tell her that it all sounds possible. 'Maybe.' I shrug.

'Let's consult the oracle,' she says, hauling out a board with weird signs on it. 'Place your hand in the middle and close your eyes.'

I do as I'm told.

'Now ask the oracle a question.'

In my head I whisper, 'Will I stay with Rhodri?' My hand moves up and towards the left.

'Now let your finger settle,' instructs Lucy. She looks at the symbol and searches for the answer in her fortune-telling manual. 'You'll never get the commitment and love you need from this relationship.'

Lucy doesn't know I've asked the oracle about Rhodri.

'Ask another question.'

I ask the same question again to trick her. My finger lands on the same symbol.

'You'll never get the commitment and love you need from this relationship.'

Drat.

'I'll ask another question,' I say, before she has me hooked up to a crystal for some healing.

Lucy looks at me mischievously: 'What did you ask?'

'I'm not telling.'

Jokingly, I whisper in my head, 'Should I pursue Toga?'

Then Lucy begins to pace the kitchen floor. 'Ssh. Something's coming through.'

'Oh, I do hope it's my wisdom tooth and not a dead person.'

'Don't look at me like you don't believe me,' she insists. 'It's a man. He says you know who he is. When you were kids he used to play tricks on you. Do you know who he is?'

'No.'

'He says he's been playing tricks on your mum.'

'It could be anyone.'

'He's holding up a pair of jeans. He's holding them up high because he says you'll know what this means.' Lucy leaves the room to pace the hall. 'You don't believe me, do you?'

I don't want to disappoint her, but neither do I wish to admit she can talk to the recently deceased either. 'I don't know,' I say. 'Maybe.' But I do know who it is. It's my stepbrother who died of a heroin overdose. I have one favourite memory of him. He's in the cellar at my mother's house, aged about sixteen, standing by the washing machine holding up a pair of new Wrangler jeans, grinning.

'Try the oracle again,' says Lucy.

I ask the same question: 'Should I pursue Toga?' My finger moves to a symbol.

Lucy checks her manual. '"If you follow this route," she reads to me, '"it will lead to happiness."'

I ask the oracle out loud, 'Are you tricking me?' Some force moves my hand to a symbol: 'No.'

Lucy looks at me. 'I told you,' she says proudly.

'I've been looking for ways to cut down on my diesel consumption,' remarks Rhodri. 'A co-operative runs a biodiesel station over in Ancoats. I'm heading out there this afternoon. Are you coming?'

I remember my (now almost redundant) New Year resolution to be a better girlfriend and agree. In one of Manchester's seedier areas, we pass a line of prostitutes working the streets.

'Why are those women wearing funny clothes?' asks Jack.

'Read your magazine,' I respond. 'That one must only be about fifteen,' I say to Rhodri. 'If we were truly good people, we'd give a prostitute some money so she didn't have to work the streets tonight.

'They charge twenty pounds,' he says.

'What do you get for that?'

'I think everything.'

'How do you know?'

'Because a prostitute shouted it at me once when I stopped at the traffic lights.'

Rhodri pulls in to the community biodiesel station, which is housed in an abandoned garage. It doesn't look safe to me. One stray match and we could all blow up. He stands talking to a young man with wild curly hair and a stripy knitted jumper. I daren't leave the car because the vegans will see what a pariah I am. I'm wearing a Primark vest top, a supermarket skirt and leather shoes. The lad peers through the window. 'Hello, Jack,' he says.

'This is Blue,' says Rhodri.

'Hello, Blue,' I say.

Jack waves at Blue from the back. He must have met him before.

'I've invited Blue and his girlfriend, Joy, to come over

for dinner next week,' says Rhodri, as we drive home. The sun is slowly setting and all along the red-light district more women are making their way onto the dusky street. Jack is singing along to Johnny Cash on the radio.

'Blue and Joy are vegan and teetotal so you don't need to buy any wine.'

A teetotal dinner party: how novel. 'Is Blue his real name?' I ask.

'Yes,' says Rhodri, as though I have no business questioning why a grown man is named after a primary colour.

Later as I'm washing Jack's hair in the bath, I find myself mulling over what Lucy said. Destiny is such a tricky concept. When I found out that I was expecting Jack I thought it was my destiny. (I'd missed a contraceptive pill, then swallowed half a packet in an attempt to make up for it.) Even when I ended up in the refuge, I thought it was my destiny. When I met Toga I thought it was my destiny. When I first laid eyes on Rhodri I thought it was my destiny. Perhaps destiny isn't kind. But what if the spiritual malarkey was right about Rhodri? What a mess.

'I've soaked some field beans for dinner,' Rhodri shouts up from the kitchen.

'Did you have fun today with the girls, darling?' I ask Jack.

'Yes,' he says, running a small car along the rim of our beautiful new bath. 'Can I have a trampoline?'

'When we have a house with a bigger garden. We've nowhere to put a trampoline right now.' Surely he must see that there's no room in our garden for anything.

'I wish we had a garden like Lucy's.'

'You can play any time you want to at Lucy's.'

'It's not the same.'

'Field beans,' shouts Rhodri, 'and salad.'

'Great,' I yell back. 'Lovely.'

Jack screws up his nose. 'I don't want any of that.'

'I'll make you something else,' I say, to mollify him. 'But try just a little, please, for Rhodri?'

'A tiny bit.'

I hate field beans. There are few foods I truly hate – even sprouts make it down the hatch – but I can't stand field beans.

On Wednesday, keen to rise to the challenge of a teetotal vegan dinner party, I make a lentil dish I find in my vegan cookery book. As Blue, Joy, Rhodri and I sample my pulse mush, we talk about the end of the world, and how nigh it is. It's so nigh that we might as well be dead now. It's so nigh that I should let gas stream out of the cooker and flick on a light switch so we all go BOOM.

Joy and Blue tell us about their plans to go to France and settle in a commune. I should suggest to Rhodri that we move to one of those polyamorous communities that are so hot in the States. Being polyamorous is a 'lovestyle choice', you know, 'not a lifestyle choice', so don't go getting the two things confused.

Polyandry, which is when one woman has many husbands, could be seen as a practical solution to a very modern problem. I read an article on the Internet claiming that men do just eight per cent of domestic chores. If that's true, then a woman needs at least 6.25 husbands before they even begin to fulfil their share of the housework. As

Rhodri does five per cent, I'd need at least ten husbands before I stopped complaining.

When Joy and Blue leave, Rhodri and I trawl upstairs. We make love skittishly to the burr of a helicopter hovering above the house. Flashes of light sweep across the estate in search of a criminal. For a while we carry on following one position with another, but then the helicopter remains over our house for an unfeasibly long time – so long that I suspect the police have given up searching for criminals and are instead tantalized by the thermal-imaging outline of Rhodri and me shagging. So I tumble off Rhodri and lie by his side, listening to the drone of the helicopter as it whirrs away.

13

It's not quite a cross-country trail along the Trans-Siberian Railway, but a bolt up the M62 to Yorkshire. What a bad idea to set off for this scriptwriting course so late in the evening in blizzard conditions. I flick on the windscreen wipers. Useless. Moments later the glass is obscured again. Visibility is so poor that I can barely see the cars in front of me. There is nothing but black sky ahead and black sky behind me. Cats' eyes blink up at me from the tarmac.

I'm breathless with panic. If I continue on the road to Yorkshire, I'll die in a car accident. If I turn back, I'll die. If I pull onto the hard shoulder, I'll be hacked to pieces by a madman. If I pull into a service station, a rapist will be waiting in the toilets. I would book into a motorway motel for the night but then some trucker waiting in the corridor might abduct me, holding me hostage for months in an underground pit before burying me alive.

How will I get out of this simple car journey alive? If I had a suicide pill in my pocket, I'd take it. When fear grips me like this I become hysterical, then utterly defeated. What will Jack do without me? Will he live with Damien? I hope not. Perhaps he could live with Rhodri.

I turn off at a sign for a service station. The road twists and turns until, finally, I pull into a bleak car park. What a cold, desolate and empty place. I turn off the engine, slide back the seat and sob.

The radio switches to a travel report. 'Unless the journey is essential,' says the forecaster, 'you are advised to stay indoors.'

Too late.

I should have checked before setting off.

I search through my bag for my mobile, panic rising at the thought that I've left it at home. My fingers brush against the toy cars, empty sweet wrappers and receipts at the bottom of my handbag. Finally, I locate my phone and call Rhodri.

'Come home,' he says persuasively. 'You can set off early tomorrow morning. The weather should be better, and it'll be daylight and safer.'

'I don't know if I can drive home,' I cry.

'You can.'

'*I can't.*'

'You can. How far away are you?'

'About an hour.'

'Call the hostel you're supposed to be staying at, tell them you'll be there in the morning. I'll have the kettle on ready for you. Think of that hot cup of tea waiting for you when you step through the door.'

'Okay.'

'You'll be fine. Drive safely. I love you.'

'I love you too.' I sniffle. I know I switch from an independent woman into a weak simpering mess because of my past troubles with Damien, and I feel completely ashamed of my weaknesses. Stepmother Eleanor said recently, 'I'll never forget the sight of you when we came round that day after your birthday. You stood in the kitchen like this,' she made a hunched-over motion, 'the heating on full, wearing a long-sleeved polo-neck jumper, jeans and a thick coat. You kept wrapping your arms around yourself as you made us a hot drink. You moved slowly. We knew something had happened because you weren't talking. But we didn't know what. You looked like a terrified little girl and I wanted to hold you.'

I feel like that now: lonely, vulnerable and afraid.

I turn the key in the ignition and the engine shudders to life. I sweep the car around and set off for home.

'Sorry, I'm late.'

Rhodri was right: the drive this morning was much better and safer. I breeze into the classroom, dropping my bags and coat onto the floor. In the four corners pairs of women are role-playing an intimate scene.

'We're just working on a story based around the theme "The Kiss",' says the man who is leading the day's workshop. 'You can be the audience. After each performance, clap loudly.'

'Okay,' I say, then shuffle my bottom onto a desk. 'I'll just sit here.'

I gaze out of the classroom window at snow falling and gathering on the rooftops. Below, stone cottages curve up the hill towards the village in the distance.

'Morton McDonald, film agent,' he says, by way of introduction.

I turn to smile at him. 'Maria. Pleased to meet you.'

As the session goes on, and Morton talks, I find I'm entranced by him: he's much older than me – I place him at around fifty, but he could be more. And what a very fine specimen of a silver fox he is: well dressed, tall, tanned, funny, clever, a face that knows too much, a thick mass of grey hair, twinkling brown eyes, and . . . I scan the rest of the participants, noting vague competition in the form of a mature busty brunette called Janice.

Morton paces the room bellowing intellectual discussion points on love, regret and jealousy, something about Faust, Orpheus and Achilles. I do my best to impress him, like a puppy turning tricks for treats.

We break for lunch. Morton gathers up a copy of the *Guardian,* pops it under his arm and heads towards the door. 'Where's the nearest pub?' he asks, then strides off in search of the Mischievous Monkey.

At lunchtime, I find myself seated with half a dozen chattering women. I nibble half-heartedly at ham sandwiches, drifting in and out of a daydream.

Back in the classroom we sit in a semi-circle. Morton is positioned at the front, posing and setting creative tasks. I find myself playing with my red-leather gloves, teasing them on and off my fingers. My hands are cold because Morton has opened the classroom window and now an icy gale blows across his audience. It must be his age: middle-aged men have an inner boiler system, and the menopausal women aren't complaining, but I'm shivering.

'The audience love people making decisions,' declares Morton. 'What will it lead to?' He tells us that some statements can polarize the audience and polarize a play. He talks about unpalatable truths, such as when a character says, 'I don't love her.' Then he asks, 'What if I were to ask, "Are you happy?"'

Don't ask that question, I think. Don't ask that question.

'If I asked, "Are you happy?" that could cause all sorts of problems.'

Why did he say that? All of a sudden I'm unhappy. I was fine until then.

Hours pass. Morton says, 'Okay, any more questions?'

What are you doing after this? Where are you staying?

'We'll call it a day, then.'

I watch Morton talk to some of the group. He has a good posture, confident and inviting, like Sean Connery. What a tremendous laugh he has, and such golden manners. When he's alone, I get up and take a step towards him. 'Hello,' I say.

'Hello,' he replies.

What can I follow 'hello' with? I could praise him. That's always a good one. 'That was *really, really* very interesting,' I say. 'I *really* enjoyed today.' Overuse of 'really'. I'll come across as too keen.

'What's the plan?' he asks. 'I could do with eating.'

'I don't know,' I reply hopefully.

He shouts over to the organizer: 'Is there somewhere to go for a drink and a bite to eat?'

'The Mischievous Monkey?'

'Would you like to come for a drink?' Morton asks me.

'All right,' I say, then add, 'That would be delightful.'

What bad luck. I didn't expect all those other people to come too. Morton and I walk side by side on a slim pavement. We cross the cobbled road to the pub. I have all his attention and he tells me dirty jokes, some of which I get, some of which I don't, but I laugh all the same because it's like I've known him for years, not just the past eight hours.

When I'm not gazing at my feet, giggling, I gaze at Morton, how he moves his hands, how he walks. I notice that his left hand lacks a wedding ring.

The pub is busy so our group squeezes into a corner. Morton sits at the head of the table. I seat myself at the opposite end. A man squashes himself into a space at my side, and asks for my phone number.

People jostle for drinks and slowly unwind until the corner is filled with ferocious tittle-tattle. Morton rewards his listeners with story after story. If I stretch my legs under the table, I might just be able to touch him. If only I had longer legs. If only these people would go elsewhere. Morton wants to talk to me, I'm sure of it.

Slowly the group drops away one by one as boyfriends, husbands and babysitters beckon them home. Eventually it's just Janice, the busty brunette, Morton and me. He moves his stool closer to me. I move to the bench opposite him. From here my only distraction is his captivating grin. His only distraction is Janice's spectacular cleavage.

I've almost given up hope of having ten minutes alone with Morton when Janice's husband arrives. 'Hello, I'm Andrew,' he reveals, shaking my hand.

'Pleased to meet you, Andrew. Are you a writer too?'

'No, I'm an architect.'

I've always fancied getting to know an architect, in case I should ever wish to convert a barn or some rundown French château.

'Can I get anyone a drink?' he asks.

'Red wine, please.' I may as well get pissed. I've nothing else to do. Morton appears to have had the same idea.

There's talk of ordering food from a chip shop, which ends when Andrew discovers it's closed.

Janice thinks me a pest. Janice thinks I have bad intentions towards Morton, but from where I'm sitting he doesn't look as if he wants protecting: he wants to peer down my shirt. Obligingly, and because it's very hot in the pub, I remove my cardigan.

After closing time, and many glasses of wine later, we're hungry and not yet ready to turn in for the evening. Janice suggests we go to her and Andrew's house for crumpets. I wonder if she's making a dig at me.

Morton struggles to walk up the hill to their mansion. I laugh raucously as he slips and slides on the gravelled driveway.

We're drinking wine in Andrew and Janice's comfortable sitting room when, inspired by Rhodri, I kick off a debate by bleating on and on about the value of independent businesses. Morton studies me as if I'm the hired jester. When I overstep his boredom threshold, he calls, 'Time to go,' and ushers me quickly out of Janice's house and into the heavy rain.

We huddle together at the bottom of the garden path, beneath an umbrella, trying drunkenly to decipher Andrew's hastily drawn map under the sodium glow of a streetlamp. Soon it's drenched, illegible, and hangs in wet ribbons from my fingers.

'You'll have to walk me home,' I croon, screwing what's left of the map into a ball and popping it into my pocket. 'I'm a young woman, out on the street in the early hours of the morning – anything could happen to me.'

Morton translates this as an invitation: 'My bed-and-breakfast is around the corner,' he says quickly.

Hm, maybe I could go for a quick nightcap ... *No* ... definitely *no*.

'I can't stay at your guesthouse. I'm going back to my hostel.'

I'm set on behaving discreetly and respectably when I notice that the village graveyard is looming seductively next to us. I try the gate. It swings open. So I take Morton by the arm and pull him in there after me. Hanging on to one another, we wade through rivulets of mud. I suspect Morton is calculating when, and where, we might get intimate. I'm huddled next to his warm body when a gust of wind causes the umbrella to collapse, washing cold rain over our faces. 'I love graveyards,' I gurgle.

'Have you ever had sex in one?' Morton asks, wiping water from his mouth.

I wrench the torch from him and throw beams of light on gravestone after gravestone. I read out the names of the deceased and when they died, commenting on the design of the inscriptions. 'Oooh, look at this one, Morton,' I call, spotting a large statue of an angel. 'This lady was lov–' I slip, landing bottom first in the mud. Morton laughs, then bends down and pulls me up. We stand face to face, blinking away raindrops, and for a brief moment I think he might kiss me.

'You need to blow hard,' I command. Morton is on his knees at my feet. I'm soaking wet. 'Nothing's happening. You need to blow much harder than that. Put some effort into it.'

'Is that working?' he asks, exasperated.

'At your age, you should be an expert at this.'

For a walkers' hostel, this lounge is surprisingly cosy. There is even a real fire.

'I'm trying.'

Morton must know how to light a coal fire. He's so old that gas fires probably weren't in existence when he was a child. 'Did you light coal fires as a boy?'

'Yes.' Morton groans, throwing more paper onto the embers. He blows into the fireplace, then prods the poker at various spots. 'There, it's going now.'

'You're dripping all over the carpet,' I tease. 'You should take your trousers off and dry them by the fire.'

'Do you think so?' he asks worriedly.

'Yes. Definitely. You'll be ill if you stay in those wet clothes.'

I leave the room to change into my pyjamas. When I return Morton is stretched out, fully clothed, on the rug waiting for me. I hand him a coffee. Wrapping his fingers around the mug, he invites me to sit with him. So I do, and together we watch the flames lick at the kindling.

I return home from my brief sojourn in Yorkshire to discover that in my absence Rhodri has been having a go at some DIY. On past projects, this has stood for destroy-it-yourself. 'Look at this!' he says, leading the way upstairs.

Good grief, I think, how much is this going to cost me? But then I see that Rhodri has retiled the bathroom. He's done an amazing job – he's found his niche. I should find more walls for him to tile. The entire bathroom looks so luxe that for the next hour I stroke it.

Later we share a cuddle together on the sofa and I lavish

affection on him. 'I had a productive weekend,' I tell him. 'I learned so much about scriptwriting, and I met this very interesting man.'

'Did you sleep with him?'

'No.'

'Did you kiss him?'

'*No*. We talked, that's all.' Those London lah-di-dah cheek kisses we exchanged at the door as Morton left hardly count and I wasn't wearing my lucky Janet Reger knickers. They're red silk-satin and rather skimpy. I bought them in the January sales years ago. When I wear those red knickers the world stops turning. Because I'm a considerate girl, I can't wear them all the time or the universe would topple into a right mess. I wear my lucky knickers when: I'm sitting exams; I'm going for a job interview; I have a mad crush on the person I'm due to meet that day. Never in the history of my lucky knickers has their charm failed. My lucky knickers' success rate is 100 per cent.

Still, Morton gave me his business card with his number, email and home address on it so I may write to him. He also said that if I ever wanted to go to the theatre in London I should call him.

'Would you like me to tell you how it went?' I ask Rhodri.

'Not really,' he says.

Hmph. Rhodri is distracted by something other than my return. I wish he'd show even a tiny amount interest in the things I love.

A week after my trip to Yorkshire, I'm sitting opposite my quirky friend Sybil in an arty little bar at the university end of town. Our friend Emmeline is in the room upstairs, preparing to read a story to a crowd of literary punters. We pick at a mezze platter placed on the table between us. I scrape up some hummus with a triangle of pitta bread, wondering if I should make a grab for the last black olive or dive for the last dolma instead.

'So, how are things at work?' she asks, after we've talked about her boyfriend gradually moving himself, unasked, into her flat. Men really should come with a warning attached to them. And an alarm that rings when they leave socks under the bed.

'Good,' I lie, gulping a mouthful of wine. 'I'm looking for more freelance work. Athens and I are always arguing.' Things have been difficult in the office, these past few weeks: I keep saying and doing the wrong thing.

'Rhodri?'

I sigh. 'In a mood because I dyed my hair with a non-organic colour. I couldn't afford an organic colour at the salon so I opted for a normal one. I didn't want to dye my hair at home in case I ruined the new bathroom tiles.' Sybil nods. 'We had a big row when Rhodri insisted he could dye my hair for me by holding my head over a bucket.'

'A bucket?' Sybil shakes her head. 'How's Jack?'

'He's made it as sports monitor. He's very pleased about that.'

'Toga?'

'I don't know. He promised to take me to the Hilton, then to a windmill. I've heard nothing lately.' I know I'm smiling to myself. I take a sip of wine to hide it.

'What?' asks Sybil.

'Nothing.'

'What?' she insists, arching her eyebrows.

'I have a crush on someone.'

'Who?' Sybil is enchanted by my crushes.

'It's very strange.'

'Do I know him?'

'No.'

Sybil looks at her watch. 'We'd better go upstairs. Emmeline will be reading soon.'

As we stand up I reach for the last dolma. Sybil pops the olive into her mouth.

'He's called Morton,' I say. 'And he's fifty next week.'

Sybil frowns. 'Is he a George Clooney fifty?'

'No. Not like George Clooney at all.'

'Then what do you like about him?'

'His eyes. His voice. His smile. Everything. I'm in London at the end of the month to attend some seminars for work. Maybe I'll see him then.'

The next afternoon I'm seated in a café in Jackson. Outside, pensioners sit on chairs sucking cigarettes as if they're lollipops. A cup of tea here costs just sixty-five pence. The thick smell of bubbling fat sticks to my skin. Everyone looks greasy. The girl at the counter sways along to Rod Stewart and the Faces on the radio as she rings money through the till and froths milk for cappuccinos. The cook sings over the spitting of frying sausages. Beneath the table my foot bobs along to the music, a waitress clacks across the floor in flat shoes, then slaps two plates on the Formica table opposite mine, calling, 'Full English. Full English.'

Spying a mother from school at a table by the window,

I wave awkwardly, then flick open my writing pad and unscrew the pen lid. I tear out grubby curled pages and on a clean sheet of paper write:

Dear Morton,
Happy birthday! I'm in London at the end of the month if you'd
like to meet for a coffee.
Maria x

In the bottom right-hand corner I print my email address. Nervously, I slide the note with a book into an envelope, lick the edges and seal it. Was my handwriting messy? It usually is. I leave money on the table for the tea, gather my bag and coat, then head quickly to the post office before Jack finishes school.

14

It's a sunny afternoon in early March. Jack and I are cycling home from school together. He's very quiet. He has a secret, I'm sure.

'What's wrong?' I ask.

'Nothing,' he answers sullenly.

'Has something happened at school?'

'No. Just leave it.'

'If something's happened, you can tell me about it. Anything. You can trust me. Promise.'

'Nothing's happened, okay?'

I'll press him after dinner when he's finished his home-work and we've read a story together.

We glide past the enormous houses, which tower over us. The sun is bright and buds are bursting on the blossom trees. Jackson is lush in early spring. I say to Jack, 'That's a nice one, isn't it? We'll live in a house like that one day.'

'When we do can I get a dog?'

Rhodri would say I'm encouraging Jack to be a capital-ist. But I couldn't live without hope. I don't want a man-sion. I don't need stables and vintage cars. All I want is an above-average house. All I want is something other than what we have.

By the time Rhodri returns home, Jack is already asleep. I tried to get him to talk but he wouldn't. Rhodri sits on the leather chair, and I balance on the arm, legs stretched out over him. The curtains are swept back so we can look out of the window onto the street. Together we watch a group of teenagers race around the corner throwing stones at one another, shrieking and drinking.

'To be a teenager –' I stop as a car hurtles around the bend and smacks into the bollards that edge the communal garden. 'Bloody hell!' I leap off Rhodri and push my nose up against the window to get a closer look. Two lads run off. No one appears to have been left for dead inside the car. I rush to the phone and call the police. 'I'd like to report an accident . . . Sunnyside Close . . . No . . . two lads, early twenties . . . dark clothes . . . They ran off.'

'We've had a number of calls, we're on our way,' says the law-enforcing telephonist. 'Can I take your name and address?'

'I'm afraid you can't.' I don't want my house vandalized, or worse. 'I don't want police coming to the house,' I add briskly. 'Thank you. Goodbye.' Hanging up, I turn to Rhodri. 'They won't catch them,' I tell him. 'It'll be hours before they get here.'

We stand at the front door and study the angle of the car, somehow expecting something to happen – like an explosion, or a riot.

'If it weren't for the bollards it'd be in our living room,' says Rhodri. 'Look at it. The car was heading this way.'

Across the gardens, Albert emerges on his front step, his wife at his shoulder behind him. They look across to us. I shrug my shoulders: *I know, but what can you do?* They've lived here forty years, as long as Josie next door, ever since the estate was built. They were proud of the place then.

'It drives you mad, doesn't it?' says Josie, stepping out of her house, her terrier scuffling between her feet. 'You think one lot of trouble is over, then another begins.'

A few nights after the car accident, I'm woken by a man banging violently at the front door. At this time on a Sunday morning, it could only be Damien. Drunk. 'Rhodri,' I whisper. 'Rhodri, wake up.' I look across to the alarm clock – two a.m. 'Rhodri, wake up. Please wake up.' I shake him hard. 'Come on, Rhodri, wake up.'

'*Whaaat?*' he mumbles, rolling over. Then an almighty wallop startles him to life.

'Ssh,' I whisper, placing my finger on his lips. 'I don't want him to hear us. He's been out there for about twenty minutes.'

'What should we do?'

'I don't know.'

More thumps land on the door, making me jump with fright.

'Should I go out there?'

'No . . . No,' I stammer. Rhodri is strong, but Damien is wild. On second thoughts . . . 'Yes. You're stronger than Damien. See what he wants.'

Rhodri scrambles about in the dark for his trousers and a T-shirt. The bangs on the door land so fiercely that I worry he may force his way in.

'No, Rhodri, stay here.' I pull him back onto the bed.

'For heaven's sake, Maria. What do you want me to do?'

Should I call the police? No. He's not actually done anything yet. But what if he hurls a brick through the window? What if he's back to finish off what he started years ago?

'Should I call the police?' whispers Rhodri.

'No, he'll hear us.'

'But he's outside the door in the gardens. How could he hear?'

'Ssh – you're too loud. He just will.'

So we both sit in awkward silence in the dark. I take short gasping breaths, bring my knees up to my chest and nibble my nails. Another heavy bang.

'This is ridiculous, Maria.'

'*I know. I know.* We'll just have to wait until he goes away.'

Another bang.

'Come on, you bastards,' yells a voice. 'Open the fucking door!'

Rhodri wraps me in his arms. I'm quivering. I want to scream. Or cry. But nothing comes out. 'Is this how scared you used to be?'

'Yes. No. Worse. I was on my own then. At least now I've got you.'

'Open the fucking door!'

'Look out the window – see if it's him,' urges Rhodri.

But I can't move because I'm frozen with fear. 'I can't.' I whisper. 'He might see I'm here.'

Bang.

'Open the fucking door!' he yells again.

Then I relax a little. 'I don't think it's him.'

Bang.

'Open the *fucking door*!'

Bang.

'No. It's not him. It doesn't sound like him.'

'Are you sure?'

'Yes. I reckon if it was Damien he would have smashed the windows in by now.'

Rhodri gets up and walks across the room in the dark, knocking into things noisily. He pulls aside the curtains and opens the window. 'Can I help you, mate?' he says gruffly, in a bizarre attempt to sound like a northerner.

'I've come for the party.'

'Great.' I groan. 'Does it look like we're having a party?'

'Someone said there was a party here.'

'Sorry, mate, no party.'

When does Rhodri *ever* call anyone 'mate'?

'You sure?'

'We're in bed. Wrong house, mate.'

He said 'mate' again . . . hilarious.

The man shouts our address. 'That's this address,' replies Rhodri, 'but there's no party here, sorry.'

'For fuck's sake,' yells the man. Then he walks off. I hear him kick his feet down the path. 'And I bought all these beers,' he grumbles.

'He had a crate in his hand.' Rhodri climbs back into bed. 'He looked really disappointed.' He pulls me towards him and holds me tight against his chest, accidentally shoving my head under his armpit.

'You need a shower,' I tease.

'You're really shaking,' he murmurs, into my hair.

My legs and arms have taken on vibrations of their own. 'I'll stop in a minute,' I say, suddenly feeling very exposed.

'Come here,' soothes Rhodri, teasing his fingers through my hair. 'We're pathetic, aren't we? That's no good, being scared to death. I'll have to take up kick-boxing or something.'

Two incidents in one week have left me shaken. I need some respite or I'll be at the doctor's begging for Valium. Not good. When Jack and I come home from school the next day, I decide to talk to Rhodri. I can see he's in the garden.

'Can I have Ellie come over and play?' Jack asks shyly, as he tries to open the gate.

'Have you unlocked it, love?'

'Just doing it,' he says. 'Can Ellie come over one day?'

'I'll ask her mum.' I wheel my bicycle through to the garden. The front wheel collides with Rhodri's bottom, which is sticking out of the shed because he's bent over, rummaging for something.

'Ouch.' He tuts, burrowing deeper. 'I'm looking for something to make placards out of.'

'We need a holiday,' I shout to him. 'We need to get away from here – it'll do us good.'

'I'm not flying,' he says adamantly, coming out of the shed with some spray cans in his hand.

'A holiday park, then?'

Rhodri scowls. 'You know what I think about holiday parks.'

There was a feature on a green website about a family who, a few years ago, had been displaced from their houseboat by a well-known holiday-park provider that wanted to build chalets on the land. Rhodri showed me the article online. I want a week's holiday, but a child lost his home because people like me fancy a semi-posh vacation in a forest. So we can't ever visit a luxury forest oasis, or any other camp where children have fun. When I tell Rhodri I want to book a cheap flight to Nice, he shows me *National Geographic* pictures of motherless babies in India being paddled out of flooded homes. But if I don't get away from this estate I'll have a breakdown.

'Jack needs to be around other children,' I reason. 'Imagine how awful it must be as an only child.' Suddenly it dawns on me that Jack may have developed a crush on this Ellie at school. He needs some boys to play football with. A holiday should distract him.

Rhodri doesn't look like he's imagining how awful it must be. He looks like he's plotting something.

'You had your brother to play with,' I push. 'Jack can't hang out with his mum all the time.'

'I have an idea,' says Rhodri, heading into the house to use the telephone.

An hour and a phone call later our holiday is booked. 'It's arranged,' says Rhodri, flopping next to me. 'Easter week at Cobble Cottage.'

'All to ourselves?'

'Yes,' he says.

Squeezing his arm, I plant kiss after kiss on his cheek. I love Cobble Cottage. Rhodri grew up in it in a pretty hamlet in the Snowdonia National Park. There are fields to scramble over and the Cambrian Mountains to climb. We can take long bike rides along Llyn Tegid pausing for lazy picnics and peering into sailing boats, or cheering on Jack with his remote-control speedboat as it races across the lake. Or drive to the beach. Or to the old-fashioned cinema where kids queue for tubs of ice cream during the interval, and as the end credits roll the audience bursts into applause. We can bake potatoes on a campfire by the river . . .

'There should be children to play with. My mum said a boy Jack's age lives opposite and we can visit my friend Maddog – he has a baby.'

Jack will be so excited. Cobble Cottage! It's been far too long since we holidayed together. It will be wonderful. If it's cold and wet we can play cards by the wood-burner. If it's warm, we can sunbathe in the garden or sit beneath the pergola. I can pick fresh lemon thyme and basil in the garden for gorgeous slow-cooked dinners. In the evenings Rhodri and I can drink heavy red wine beneath the parasol. Or we can play games in the large sitting room, listen to old songs on vinyl and read. Jack can drape sheets over the chairs and eat lunch beneath a makeshift Bedouin tent. Or we can dance. Or make dens in the woods from broken branches and wild grass.

'Can we borrow a kayak to row on the lake?'

'We should be able to.'

'It will be just the *three* of us?'

Rhodri's parents own Cobble Cottage but live in Liverpool.

'I asked my mum if anyone else is going and she said we'll have the cottage to ourselves.'

Over the years we've holidayed with Rhodri's family. It's not that I don't like them. It's just that Rhodri and I need time together. It's been weeks since we were thoroughly intimate – discounting exhausted fumbles in the dark.

Some new lingerie, no work, good food and fresh air will bring the romance back into our lives. We used to be so *frisky*. Better to massage our relationship before it needs rocket-powered resuscitation.

'This will be so great,' I say to Rhodri. 'Thank you. Thank you.'

Rhodri bundles me tightly into his arms. Having heard the excitement, Jack dashes in and bounds on top of us.

Holi-day. Holi-day. We all need a holi-daaay. I sing like Madonna. Well, not actually like Madonna at all.

'Yes!' whoops Jack, bouncing up and down on the sofa, punching his little fist in the air. 'YES!'

15

It's Rhodri's birthday. I can't afford to take him to the Bombay Balti like I'd hoped. I may be insane, and Tina round the corner will be justified in calling me a 'weirdo' again, but as it's a pleasant evening I decide to move our dining-table and chairs outside. At weekends Rhodri and I have scoured skips looking for a garden set, but no one seems to throw them out in March. We might have more luck over the May bank holiday, or at the end of summer.

I'd no idea what to buy him for his birthday. Any extravagant gesture would be frowned upon. Last year I almost passed out in TK Maxx under the pressure. Eventually I wound up in Neal's Yard and bought an organic shaving kit – the brush was made from sustainable wood and the flannel was organic cotton. It was pricy but an absolute gem.

Or not.

Rhodri decided to grow a beard.

But I can't go wrong with adzuki bean stew, quinoa and salad. He'll love that. I step outdoors to check the temperature. It's a wee bit chilly, so we may have to wear our coats, hats and gloves at dinner. I set out wine glasses and cutlery on the table and light some candles. Now the garden looks very romantic. Rhodri should be home from the allotment soon.

*

'This is a nice surprise,' he says, stepping into the garden.

'Happy birthday! This is your birthday dinner,' I explain. 'Jack, are you cold? Do you need more layers?'

'No,' he says, his legs swinging on the chair. He's shivering, and his lips are tinged light blue but he thinks outdoor dining in the cold is a fantastic idea. He can't wait to tuck into his bean wraps. Fortunately, we're protected from Tina's view by Josie's clematis. If she spots us from her bedroom window she'll start yelling and hissing insults at us. Ever since I won the Wheelie-bin War, she walks straight past me in the gardens, smirking.

Rhodri takes a seat and loads his plate with hot food. As he eats he scans the garden, our house, and the line of terraces opposite and adjacent to us. 'I can't believe I ended up here.' He laughs in the candlelight. 'My gran would be so disappointed. She'd think all that money spent on my education wasted because I ended up here.'

Does he mean here, with me, a single mother on a council estate?

He does. That's what he means. It hurts.

'My parents worked hard so they could bring me up in a nice hamlet in a national park, and I ended up here.'

I'm terrified of what he'll say next to bring my little world crumbling down. 'I didn't always live here,' I say. 'We ended up here. You don't know how hard it's been for me to have only this.'

'Okay, okay,' he says, trying to calm me down.

Rhodri and his middle-class nonchalance. It drives me mad. Our struggles are just a game to him – if he wanted to, he could head off back to Wales and leave us. If he wanted to, he could earn heaps of money in web design or television – but he doesn't want to. He wants to paint banners while I work myself stupid. He wants to forgo a reasonable income because it goes against his principles.

'If we both worked full time we could sell this house and leave here.'

Sensing an argument, Jack makes a run for it. 'Going to play in my bedroom,' he calls, as he charges through the kitchen.

Rhodri's face turns stormy. He knows I'll land the blame on him.

'Relationships are like a seesaw,' I lecture. 'We both have to do equal amounts to balance it out. When one person does less, the other person has to do more. That's why I'm tired all the time, and that's why I get grumpy – because I have to do more. And you sit there and turn your nose up at what I've had to work for.'

I clear away the plates unhappily. 'While you loafed about at university, I was doing three jobs, studying and bringing up a baby. I was cleaning a bank at eight in the morning and working night shifts in a care home, writing up notes at four in the morning. And this is all I have for it. Do you think I want to live here? Do you think I want Jack to live here?'

Not that it's Rhodri's fault: he didn't get me pregnant; he didn't even know me then. But all I want right now is for him to feel as worthless as I do.

Two days have passed and even though Rhodri has tried to make up with me, I still feel wounded. A bitter battle rages in the kitchen. This evening a fight broke out over the potatoes.

"Don't boil them so hard,' Rhodri berated me, turning the gas down.

'You boil spuds hard, *then* simmer,' I said, turning it up again.

'I don't want my potatoes boiled to death.'

Take them out of the pan and boil your own, I think. Not that I say it. 'It's eight o'clock in the evening, Jack's starving, I'm starving, and I haven't got all night to simmer potatoes. Let's just get it done and eat dinner.'

'They'll have no nutritional value.'

So what? If they fill a hunger-hole, job done. I've cycled for two hours today, worked for nine, cleaned for one, and will spend another hour cooking. I need to bath Jack and read with him, check his homework, then start the laundry. I just want to eat. Rhodri glowers at me, and turns the potatoes down again. When he leaves the kitchen, I sigh hard and move the potatoes to the largest hob, and boil them to within an inch of their lives. Thank goodness I'm going to London next week, I think. Then I realize I haven't told Rhodri about the trip yet, and I've just discovered that I'm going to be in Edinburgh in August because the play I've been writing has been taken on by a young director.

When I go into the living room, I find Jack doing his homework and Rhodri reading up on moon cycles for our organic, reclaimed-materials allotment. 'It says here that if I plant the seeds under a full moon we'll get a better yield.'

'Oh, when will you do that?'

'I'll go out at midnight under the next full moon.'

'Okay.' It all sounds a bit mad to me. How on earth will he see what he's doing in the dark?

'I'll wear my head torch,' he says, reading my mind.

'I'm going to London next week,' I say.

'For what?'

'There's a play I want to see. I'll take the coach and stay in a hostel. Jack can stay with my mum.' I take a deep breath. 'A theatre company has found a venue for that play I've been writing. It's going to be performed at the Edinburgh Fringe the first two weeks in August. So I want to see some good fringe theatre in advance.'

Rhodri harrumphs at me, without looking up from his book.

'So I'll be away over the summer for a few weeks. I'll arrange for Jack to stay with my mum and Margaret.'

'That's good.'

'So the next few months may be chaotic.'

'They always are.'

'But then we'll have more time for one another.'

'You always say that.'

'I don't see what else I can do. I have to work to pay the bills.'

'I know.'

'I think that's great about your play, Mum,' interrupts Jack. 'Isn't it, Rhodri?' he looks directly at Rhodri as though to say, 'Appease her for once. Please.'

'It's wonderful,' says Rhodri.

'Can I watch it, Mum?'

'It's not for young people, Jack. It has swearing in it.'

'Why have you put swearing in it when you don't swear in real life?'

'Because it's a grown-up story. Not a story for children. It's what the characters do, not me.'

Jack considers this. Then he reaches for my hand. 'Well done, Mum.' He coughs at Rhodri to distract him from his compelling book on moon cycles. '*Well done, Mum.*'

'Well done,' echoes Rhodri, smiling.

16

It's Monday morning. I'm sitting in Athens's office pondering about Jack and his new romance. Yesterday Ellie came over to play. And when she left Jack said, 'When we were in my bedroom Ellie looked at me and I knew she wanted to say something. So I said, "What is it?" And she said, "I love you."'

Now we're in trouble.

'M,' says Athens, sternly.

'Yes?'

'M. I need you to send these emails, update the website and get some speakers booked in.'

'Right.'

I begin to chatter on about something to Athens, who is looking more furious with me by the second. He slams his hand on the desk, hard. 'No. M. I need you to do this.'

'Okay. Okay.' I sulk. I hate being told off. Maybe I should have stopped working for Athens, instead of giving up the listings job.

A colleague looks across the desk at me, and then at Athens. At the coffee machine later, he says 'You two argue like an old married couple.'

It's true. Athens and I have known one another for years and bicker incessantly, which must be bad for any employer-employee relationship.

Back at my desk I ask Athens, 'Do you fancy a drink after work?'

'Where?'

'I don't know. Let's see.'

I call Rhodri: 'I'm only going for one drink with Athens, and shouldn't be too late. Can you pick Jack up from school, check his homework, then put him to bed for me?'

'Have a good time,' says Rhodri. 'Don't worry, we'll be fine.'

He's being nice. Maybe the fact that I'm going away has softened his heart a little.

Athens sets down a pint for him and a glass of wine for me. I drink my wine far too quickly, so within the half-hour I'm on my feet. 'Another drink?'

'One more,' says Athens.

We relax then, and chat easily, making plans about what we're going to do over the forthcoming year. Projects we could take on and so forth. 'Another drink?'

'White wine. Then I should go.' Outside it's already dark. Jack will be in bed now. I call Rhodri. 'Sorry,' I say, 'I'll be home soon.'

'Don't worry,' he says. 'Stay out as long as you want.'

When Athens and I have finished our drinks, we move to a different bar where Athens orders another round. 'How are things with Rhodri?' he asks.

'I'm not sure,' I say truthfully. 'I don't know what I think any more or how I feel.'

A waitress shimmies over to us. 'Would you like to order more drinks?'

'Yes,' I say quickly. 'Another wine.'

'I have news to cheer you up,' offers Athens. 'You might be going to New York.'

'What?' I scream.

'An all-expenses-paid trip to New York for the organization.'

'*No.* What makes you think that?'

'There's a trip planned. Your name's been mentioned. You should apply. You stand a good chance of getting a place.'

'What about you?'

'I'll be busy here so you should go for it, on behalf of us both.'

'New York? New York!' Oh, my God. Wait till I tell Rhodri this. We could never afford to go to New York. I can't believe I might see New York. Jack will be jealous. I'd better play it down. *New York,* though. Me! In New York!

'Hangover?'

'Yes.' I groan.

'Want me to take Jack to school?'

'Yes.' I groan again.

'There's a glass of water by the bed for you. I knew you wouldn't stay out for just one drink.'

'Sorry.'

'You needed a blow-out. It's Okay.' Rhodri pulls the covers over my head and kisses my cheek fondly. 'When I come back from dropping Jack I'll make you some breakfast. Then I'm going to the allotment to dig some new seed-beds.'

'Where's Mum?' I hear Jack ask in the garden, as the bikes clatter out of the shed.

'In bed. I'm taking you today.'

Jack whines for me, then bursts into laughter at something Rhodri does. Feebly I head into the bathroom for a wash. Back in the bedroom, I pull on yesterday's clothes, then head downstairs. I am elbow high in soapsuds when Rhodri bundles merrily through the door. 'Kettle on?'

'Will be.'

Stooping down, he picks up mail from the floor. 'For you, for you, for you.'

Bills. Bills. Bills.

Because it's Mother's Day next Sunday, and we can't afford to go out for a 'Mother's Day Meal', we're heading out the Sunday before because it's cheaper. It was my idea. The plan is to find a nice country pub for lunch. But before we go we stop off at a barber's because Jack is in desperate need of a haircut. He sits on a raised chair, while I flick through a copy of the *Sunday Sport*, surrounded by framed pictures of footballers.

'How do you want it?' asks the barber.

Jack looks at me. 'I want a Mohican.'

'No Mohican,' I instruct the barber. 'Short back and sides.'

'Why can't I have a Mohican?' Jack asks, for the hundredth time.

'Because you're only eight.'

'But I want a Mohican and a motorbike.'

'Stop this or I'll shout.'

'Why?'

'Because you're getting on my nerves.' I put my nose back in the newspaper, only to realize that I'm gazing idly

149

at a model with breasts the size of watermelons. I hastily fold the paper and set it down on the empty chair next to me.

The barber places a plastic bib around Jack's neck. It's blue with red giraffes. Jack looks as if he might cry. 'So, what are you having, mate?' he asks again.

'Not a Mohican,' I remind the barber. 'Just a normal haircut.' I stand up, purse my lips, put my hands on my hips and clear my throat like a headmistress.

'Shaved at the back and sides and a bit spiky on top,' says Jack, unhappily.

'Is that Okay with you, Mum?' asks the barber.

'That's Okay with me.' Then I catch Jack giving me the look Damien used to give me. The look that means, 'You're in trouble now,' so I move to sit behind him and blow kisses to his reflection in the mirror. He ignores me.

'It looks great,' I say, brushing shorn hair from his shoulders.

Jack reaches for the tub of gel and spikes the front of his hair.

As I pay the man, Jack hovers by the counter expectantly. '*No sweets*?' he hisses, when we're out on the street. The only reason that the barber is worth a visit is for the penny chews he hands out at the end.

'*I'll* buy you some sweets. Then we're going for lunch.'

After a trip to the sweet shop we collect Rhodri and set out in search of the perfect Sunday lunch.

'What's up with him?' asks Rhodri, twiddling with the knob on the car radio, until he finds Radio 2.

'Can we have a different station on?' demands Jack.

'No. I want to listen to this,' says Rhodri.

'Some pop music?' I ask hopefully. But no, we're stuck with the golden oldies. We drive for hours in search of an idyllic country pub. Every fifteen minutes I pull over, hop out and ask, 'Is the food freshly made?' only to be honoured with the reply, 'No, it comes precooked and we reheat it on the premises.'

'Can we just stop somewhere? *Now.* I'm starving,' moans Jack.

'Just drive to the next one,' instructs Rhodri.

We repeat this little scene over and over again, until we've driven all the way from Manchester to Bakewell in the Peak District. 'The next one is the last one,' I tell Rhodri. 'We stop there and we eat.'

We drive for another half-hour until eventually we find what appears to be a gastro-pub. I ask the barman if the food is home-cooked.

'It's prepacked.'

'Do you do vegan meals?'

'No.'

'Never mind, eh?' I smile at Rhodri. I'm using my it's-a-Sunday-trip-out voice. There's tension in the air but, no matter how annoyed everyone is, I'll smile and laugh and chatter in this irritating singy-songy voice. 'Oh, look, Jack,' I sing. 'We can have lamb roast and Yorkshire puddings.'

We usually have mung-bean casserole on a Sunday, so bless the Lord for this roasted young animal.

'Not hungry.'

'Go on. You can have anything.'

'Not hungry. Don't want vegetables.'

'Have some of mine, then.'

'Don't want anything.'

Other families, nice ones with polite children, are staring at me.

'We could have gone to a pub in Manchester,' says Jack. 'You didn't have to drive two hours for lunch.'

'But it's a pre-Mothers' Day meal, a special occasion.'

Actually mothers are supposed to be treated to meals on Mothers' Day but I have to buy my own.

'But it's not Mothers' Day *yet*,' snaps Jack.

I shoot him a fierce look. He shuts up for all of one minute, but then jabbers on until I bark: 'If you can't behave nicely, you'll have to sit elsewhere.'

He moves happily to an empty table nearby. Meanwhile, Rhodri advises me to be stricter with Jack so I gradually fade him out until his voice merges with the sound of rain splashing against the window. The Sunday trip out is ruined. There will be no walk in the countryside after lunch because now we've sat down, it's absolutely pouring.

'What are you going to eat, Rhodri?'

'A plate of vegetables.'

'Very nice.' I turn to Jack. 'Isn't this lovely, Jack?' I smile through gritted teeth. 'Isn't this lovely, everyone?'

17

As the train to London pulls away from Manchester, I rest my head against the window, watching greys and browns and reds stream by until there is nothing but green fields around us. I open my magazine and lust over pictures of Helena Bonham Carter. How does she manage to look scruffy *and* sexy? A posh name must help. If I were called Mariella, I'm sure I'd be far sexier.

I rub anti-ageing cream over my hands. A Spanish girl I met at university told me you can tell everything about a woman by her hands: mine look like farm hands. If only I had graceful long fingers like . . . Who has graceful long fingers? Like Gwyneth Paltrow.

Before I left I emailed Toga to see if he fancies watching the play with me.

He emailed back:

Not the bloomin' theatre again . . .

Which made me laugh, because I knew he'd agree to come with me and he'll pay for dinner, then we'll kiss somewhere hidden away, and for one tiny moment I'll imagine that I feel this free always. I'll forget that my life is full of arguments over wheelie-bins and eco-disasters and absent violent fathers and endless bills I can't afford to pay.

Toga texted that he'll meet me on the corner of Regent

Street and Oxford Street, outside Topshop. The train will draw into Euston soon so I call him. 'Hello, Bear.'

'Hello, you.'

'How will I know where Topshop is?'

Toga sighs impatiently. 'You'll see it. You can't miss it. Catch the Tube to Oxford Circus. Six thirty?'

'Six thirty.'

It is just after six twenty-five when I emerge at Oxford Street. I check my reflection in a shop window. As I make my way from the edge of the pavement to the crossing, commuters hurtle past, knocking into me from all sides. 'Excuse me. Excuse me. Excuse me,' I mumble apologetically.

Obscured by a man holding a large placard with an arrow pointing left for 'designer handbags', I lean against a balustrade and watch Toga wait for me outside Topshop. He removes his glasses and carefully uses the tail of his scarf to wipe the lenses. He fiddles with his coat cuffs. He runs a hand through his thick hair, pulling up the front and smoothing down the back. He searches in his coat pocket for something, pulls out his mobile. Who's he calling? Another girl, maybe? My phone buzzes in my bag.

'Are you nearly here?'

'Yes.' I hang up and join the swarm crossing Oxford Street. The closer I walk towards Toga, the more I smile. He's facing away from me and trying to pick me out in the wrong crowd. I tap his shoulder, reach my fingers upwards, and draw him down to kiss me.

'Mmm.' He obliges. 'You took your time.'

I kiss him again before he can complain any more. 'Nice coat. New?'

'Not that new. We should hurry. We need to be in Islington for seven. Have a drink first? Let me take your bag.'

'Sounds good.' I hook my arm in his, and attempt to keep pace with his stride as we plough back underground.

It's when we've surfaced at Angel station that Toga drops my hand and falls a few steps behind me.

'Hello, mate,' booms a voice. 'What are you doing here?'

I turn to see a man Toga's age.

'Hi,' he says over-enthusiastically. 'This is my . . .'

What does Toga say: friend, cousin, friend-of-a-friend? Regardless of the label, I'm dismissed quickly enough.

'We're catching a show – it starts soon,' he apologizes.

''Bye,' I say, 'nice to meet you.' Not that I met the man at all. Whoever he was.

'*Shit.*'

'Why "shit"?'

'No,' he reassures himself. 'It'll be . . . We weren't doing anything. Just walking together on the street.'

A platonic distance apart, we hurry through Islington, down Upper Street towards the King's Head. My little legs run two steps to his one as I snatch glimpses inside restaurants, bars and smart boutiques. Once inside the pub we find a cramped corner, I dump my heavy bags and collapse into him.

'What would you like to drink?' he asks.

'Wine.'

'Which?'

Which is most sophisticated, red or white? I'll go for white. Red wine always leaves me with stained lips.

'Type?'

Does ordering wine have to be so complicated? I'll have the alcoholic type. The cheap type, actually – no, second thoughts: if he's buying, I'll have the expensive type.

'Lambrini,' I tease. Toga cocks his head like a disappointed spaniel.

'A good dry white wine.' I smile, pinching his bottom as he heads off to the bar. 'Do you mind if I sit here?' I ask a girl.

'Go ahead,' she says. 'That's an amazing dress you're wearing.'

'Thank you.'

'We were just admiring it,' she says, gesturing to her friend. 'It suits you.'

I'm in a black dress with a white trim: quasi-demure French maid. I'd hoped Toga would like it, but so far he hasn't said anything. 'That's very kind of you,' I say, adding, 'It's silk,' for effect.

Whatever people say about London folk being rude and arrogant is just plain wrong. These ladies are lovely. I should think of something equally complimentary. 'I love your top,' I say.

'Where are you from?' she asks.

'Manchester.'

'I went there once, years ago.' She shrieks with delight.

That's quite an achievement, I think, for someone inside the M25 to travel north, especially someone with such a plummy accent. 'It's changed a lot now,' I say, imagining that when she last visited the fronts were hanging off buildings blasted by the IRA bomb. Manchester is nothing like it seems in an Elizabeth Gaskell novel, I want to tell her. Now we generally have a toilet to each house, and send our children to school rather than the mills.

Before I can cause too much trouble, Toga returns. I take a thirsty gulp of my wine and kiss him again. I begin to brush my feet over his legs. Then I lean over for an almighty snog. Oh, he's delicious. I could unwrap him right here and lick him all over. The two women beam at me approvingly. They're thinking, She has a great dress, a gritty accent and a handsome boyfriend. I look back at them with a glint in my eye that translates as: 'Forget the dress, this man is a jolly good ride.'

At the interval we skip the bar and head outdoors for a cigarette, then skip the cigarette and instead cross the road to St Mary's Church, interrupting our steps with urgent kisses down a dark alleyway. It's drizzling, and each time Toga's cold lips touch me I shiver.

'Here will do,' says Toga, pushing me up against the church wall and wrapping his arm around my waist. With one hand, he pushes my face upwards until my neck is stretched taut, then his teeth scrape across my skin as his other hand rummages beneath my coat. 'You want it, don't you?' he whispers into my ear.

No, I want to talk about the state of the economy. Of course I want 'it'. Toga and I haven't done 'it' for ages.

If it weren't for the bracing wind whipping at my knees, I'd have passed out seconds ago.

Roughly I yank Toga's head close to mine so I can kiss him hard, then push on the railings, heaving myself up, squeezing my legs around him. 'Quickly then.'

Toga looks around – should we, shouldn't we?

Just as I think *Hallelujah! Hallelujah! Hallelujah!* we don't.

A group of men jostle down the alleyway, then another crowd, then a couple, then a man walking his dog, then five million people who have just climbed out of a bus – I dismount Toga, we wrap up and head back to the pub.

What a disappointment. Surely, the point of a lover is for the kind of impulsive sex unavailable at home. Rhodri and I used to have that but lately we've been very polite with one another. If he calls me a bitch in bed, I furrow my eyebrows and feign horror.

After the play we dine at Carluccio's. Toga pays the bill, then sees me onto a bus and waves me off as it shuttles towards Piccadilly Circus. Maybe I should have asked if I could stay at his. He's never invited me to his flat, even though he's stayed over at my house.

At the door to the backpackers' hostel where I'm staying, Spanish tourists smoke and stamp their feet to keep warm. My room is on the fifth floor. Ignoring the queue for the lift, I take the stairs, striding up moodily. In the room I haul myself onto the top bunk, then tug the thin white sheet and coarse grey blanket over me. Outside in the corridors laughter peals out as European travellers run in and out of their rooms. The air is electric with naïvety and passion. Just as I'm dropping off to sleep, the light flicks on, three Italian teenagers spill into the bedroom, and fight for the mirror to reapply their lipstick.

'*Buona sera.*' They titter. They chatter in Italian about the boys on the floor below – who should pair up with whom. Should they go with them to a bar?

I listen quietly, then say in English, 'Be careful, girls.'

To which they mock, 'Goodnight, Mother.'

They gather up their money and cigarettes. The light flicks off as they slam the door.

'No,' says Rhodri. It's the next afternoon, I'm back home and full of remorse. Nothing much happened with Toga, but even so I feel sick with guilt. Rhodri and I sit at opposite ends of the sofa. I can hear Jack singing in his bedroom as he plays with his toys. He must be happy. 'That's not what I want. I can't be in a relationship if it's monogamous,' Rhodri is saying.

Why can't he? I don't see what the problem is: the only person in our relationship larking around is me. The only remarkable change for Rhodri would be that I'd be his alone. How can he not want that? 'Are you seeing someone?' I probe uncertainly. 'Do you fancy someone? Have you been with someone?'

Even though I ask the questions, I don't want to know the answers. If Rhodri says yes, I'll be hurt. Already my eyes are filling with tears.

'That isn't the point. You know I haven't.'

'I'm not going to do this ever again.'

'You know you will.'

'I won't. If you tell me not to, I won't.'

'You can make that decision yourself. You don't need me to tell you.'

'I *can't*. I need boundaries.'

'If you want a monogamous relationship, you'll have to have it with someone else.'

'But I feel that my attention is taken away from you.'

'I don't want all of your attention. That would be too much.' Rhodri pulls me to his side of the sofa and kisses my hair. 'I'm not going to stop you doing what you want to do.'

'Rhodri, you *need* to stop me.'

'Do you want to see other men?'

'No, not any more.'

'Then don't.'

This morning I resolved to change. I'll try hard to be good. I won't text Toga. Or think of him again. While Rhodri is sowing carrot seeds at the allotment with Jack, I've cooked a special vegetable crumble, pulled out an old sheet that can double up as a picnic blanket, prepared a fruit salad and filled a large flask with rooibos tea. It will be impossible for me to transport all this on my bicycle so I'll have to drive. Rhodri won't like that: petrol consumption in exchange for food consumption.

He is weeding the onion bed furiously when I arrive. A new couple have taken over the ramshackle plot near ours and are hard at work: their allotment looks fabulous. 'Hello,' I call to them. 'Aren't you doing well!' I hope the envy in my voice is disguised. I'm trying to sound pleased for them, with their brand new shed, raised beds and pretty walkways. We look like vagabonds in comparison. I flap the sheet out, spreading it over a dense patch of weeds, adorn it with condiments and the centrepiece: a Crock-Pot of bubbling vegan wheat-free crumble.

The man digging on the allotment next to ours eyes our food hungrily, and looks at his wife. I notice she's pregnant. She looks happy. I wish I were her, with her perfect allotment, husband and imminent baby. The man nods approvingly at Rhodri. 'Lucky bloke,' he seems to be saying, 'to have a lady bring you a hot Sunday lunch on a cold March afternoon. I wish my missus would do that.'

Back home I check my emails as the washing spins out yet another load of wet clothes to be hastily dried, then packed for our forthcoming holiday to Cobble Cottage.

Drat. Just when I was doing so well, Morton has emailed me:

In Manchester tomorrow to attend an event. Will be staying overnight at a hotel. What you doing?

Jack is staying with my mum and Rufus tomorrow night. He can't stand to go a weekend without seeing his grandparents and we're off on holiday to Cobble Cottage next week. Rhodri is busy with work and activism stuff, so, I may as well meet up with Morton. If I pack for our holiday today, I can go out tomorrow and head off on Monday with Jack and Rhodri. I email back:

What a coincidence. I'm free. Meet you tomorrow?

I'm too weak. I'm sure that when I was born I was lacking a backbone.

This room is too large for a networking drinks reception, even though a third of it is filled with a stage where a band is setting up. I scan the bar for Morton. He isn't here, but I see a few familiar faces so I take a deep breath and prepare to strike up a stilted conversation. Networking parties are so difficult. Most of the time I'd rather be anywhere else.

I glance downwards. Excellent. My breasts look quite

voluptuous in this empire-line dress. I inspect the buffet. No sweet and sour pork ribs, no barbecued chicken wings, no cheesy puffs and cold pizza, just sushi, canapés and lots of classy picks. I order another glass of wine, then head back to the buffet. I lift a small parcel of rice and pop it onto my tongue: fishy, but tasty.

'Have you had a good day?' Morton leans in close to me, excluding all others.

'Yes,' I say, with my mouth full.

'Why don't we –' Morton is interrupted by a man who has come over to speak to him. I retreat, knocking the table with my bottom. I pick up a few canapés to sit pretty on my plate.

'Excuse me a moment,' Morton says to the man, and touches my arm. 'Let me get you a drink.' Gingerly I walk off with him, aware that I have stolen someone else's moment. 'We'll share a bottle,' he says kindly. 'A bottle of white and two glasses,' he tells the barman. I take the glasses. He follows with the wine. At the side of the room we stand by a window looking out onto the bustle of Portland Street. He fills my glass, stopping every now and then to look directly at me.

It's impossible to hold Morton's attention for long. Other people are keen to talk to him, including an eager, glittery woman in her fifties. A tall bald man looms over me, looking gravely down my cleavage while talking about politics and his old friend Gordon Brown. I mutter on about the disadvantaged children on our estate, that something needs to change, starting with the parents and not the kids. I tell him it's mothers of my age who are doing all the damage. He looks vaguely charmed to meet a bona fide plebeian; a real-life breadliner. I top up my glass and wander off to watch the band.

The party is almost over and so far my only contact with Morton has been glances exchanged from afar. An intelligent, pretty girl has his attention. I'm going to put my coat on and go home.

At the cloakroom, I retrieve my velvet jacket from a stubborn hanger and am slipping one arm into a sleeve when Morton appears. 'Goodbye,' I say. 'Nice to see you again.'

'Where are you going?'

'Home.'

'Perhaps we could go somewhere from here?'

'I don't know where is open.'

'I'm sure there'll be somewhere.'

'Kro, probably.'

'Well, let's go there.'

Silly me to think it would be just Morton and me going for a drink. We're seated at opposite ends of a long table. I'm perched next to a handsome academic. He's only a few years older than me and wears the rough-diamond look expertly, complete with leather biker jacket. Already he has passed me his card and insisted I must make my way to Newcastle one day. Or call him. He'll send me some books. I know I won't contact him. He's young, he's attractive, but he's not Morton – who is chatting effervescently to yet another pretty young academic. I don't like her much. She was very brisk earlier.

'Shall we go somewhere else?' asks Morton, which is tragically translated as an invitation to the whole group.

As the only local, I've directed the crowd to a gay bar on

Canal Street. We teeter drunkenly down the steps to a basement room, an anachronistic blur of fluorescent lights and burlesque wallpaper, where cute men in tight tops and young lads with funky hair chase looks across the dance floor.

'Too loud,' booms Morton, into my ear. 'What are you drinking?'

'Ocean Breeze.'

'Right.'

I hang loosely with the group, swaying rather than dancing, watching Morton watch me. It's unfair for him to be here, I think. He's so much older than anyone else. I don't even want to be here. 'I think I'll go,' I say to the rough-diamond academic.

'Don't,' he says, his fingers suspended over mine. 'Stay a bit longer.'

'I have to.

'I'm leaving,' I shout into Morton's ear.

'What?'

'I'm leaving. Do you know how to get back to your hotel?'

'I think so.' He swigs his pint quickly. 'Hang on. I'm coming with you.'

'Don't worry about him,' says the academic. 'He can make his own way back. He can look after himself.' He touches my wrist. 'Stay,' he says. 'We were just dancing.'

'I'm sorry, I can't.'

'Email me?' he adds, but I'm already walking away.

Out on the street, I wait at the door watching Morton tread uncertainly up the stairs. A lad who knows Rhodri and me is queuing to get in. 'Hiya.'

'Hiya.' He catches sight of Morton, then eyes me

quizzically. I stare back at him. Usual rules don't apply. I'm not going to make apologies.

Morton slips his fingers through mine and pulls me close to him. 'I only went into that bar because of you,' he says. 'I hated it in there.'

We set off down Canal Street, heading towards Piccadilly Gardens.

'Will you come into the hotel and have a drink with me?' asks Morton.

'Yes.' I hesitate. 'But nothing else.'

We walk up the hotel steps. Morton allows me to go ahead of him. We are abruptly stopped by the doorman. 'Is the lady a guest here?'

'No, she is not. She's a friend. We were going to have a drink in the bar.'

'I'm afraid not, sir. If you wish the lady . . .' Did the doorman really just sneer at me? '. . . to accompany you, you will have to pay at the desk. *Sir*.'

'But she's only coming in for a drink.'

'Yes, sir.' He looks at Morton, then back to me, and clearly thinks a friendly drink is improbable. 'Take it up with the desk, *sir*.'

The woman at the desk is equally uncompromising. She speaks to Morton as though he's a dirty old man and I'm a hired tart. 'If you want the lady to accompany you to your room then you will have to pay.'

'But I don't. She is simply joining me for a drink in the bar.'

'Yes, sir. As I said, if you wish the lady to accompany you to your room you will have to pay for her. You are booked in as a single.'

'How much?'

'An extra thirty pounds.'

'She thinks I'm a prostitute,' I mutter, appalled. 'I can't believe she thinks I'm a prostitute.'

'She's a friend,' Morton insists.

'Yes, sir. Of course, sir, and if you wish her to spend the night with you, you must pay.'

'She isn't going to . . . We are simply –'

'*Sir*,' she barks aggressively, 'shall I have the . . .' she stares hard at me '. . . *young* lady removed from the hotel?'

'Forget it,' I whisper. 'This is embarrassing.'

'No, don't,' says Morton, handing over his credit card. 'You're here now. What a disgrace,' he says to the receptionist.

'*Sir*. . .' she replies harshly, her frown suggesting that he is the disgrace.

I look out of the hotel window across Piccadilly Gardens. It's seven o'clock on Sunday morning and the city centre is slowly grinding to life again. I shouldn't still be here. 'I lost my purse,' I tell Rhodri over the phone.

Which is true. When I went to pay for drinks at the hotel bar, I discovered that I'd left it in the club on Canal Street.

'So I couldn't get home.'

Which is also true. No money, no cards, so no taxi home.

'Where are you?'

Morton is dozing in the bed next to me. I could tell Rhodri the truth: I'm on a bed in a hotel in Manchester with a man old enough to be my father who looks old

166

enough to be my grandfather. He would say something magnanimous like: 'Lucky you. Was it good? I hope you used protection. You didn't use Mates condoms, did you? You know how allergic you are to them. I'll make a nice dinner this evening.'

But I didn't do anything. And I don't want his understanding.

'At Emmeline's.' The lie feels horrible, like swallowing a spoonful of cod-liver oil. 'I'll be back soon.'

I tread lightly over to the kettle to make Morton a cup of tea. I leave it on the bedside table, anxious not to wake him, but then he stretches an arm out from under the duvet and searches for his glasses. 'What's going on?'

I move to the foot of the bed, and stand in front of the dressing-table, I peer into the mirror and try to scrape dried mascara from under my eyelids with my fingernail. 'I don't suppose you have a comb, do you?' I ask.

'Bathroom.'

I return with one, and begin to yank the knots from my hair.

'Are you okay?' he asks.

'Yes.'

Morton shuffles down the bed until he's sitting behind me, then reaches up and pulls me down to sit on his lap. He clasps his hands beneath my ribcage, presses his warmth into my stomach. 'Here,' he breathes through my hair onto my neck, 'let me take it all away from you. Give all that worry to me.' He holds me for a moment and we look at one another's reflection in the glass. I fall for Morton then because those are the kindest words anyone has ever said to me. I wish he could take it away, this black hole that has everything to do with Damien, Jack and me. But he has just five minutes, and to get rid of all that would take years.

18

We should be leaving for our holiday in Wales but it took me all day to pack our suitcases. Now I'm working on a last-minute feature for a magazine as Rhodri loads the car. When I have filed it I head outdoors to see how things are progressing.

'Are you sure you want to drive?' asks Rhodri. He is attaching the bicycles tightly to their rack. We parked the car beneath a lamppost for extra light. It's almost midnight, and a drunken man from the bungalows sits on the grass chatting to us.

'What you doing?' he slurs. 'Very late at night to be messing about doing that. Loved cycling, me. Years ago.' He takes another noisy slurp from a can of Tennants Super Strength, stands up, hitches his trousers, sways to his door, veers off track, spins back and loiters at Rhodri's side, repeating the same question over and over again. 'Where do you live?'

'There.' I wave in the direction of a collective mass of at least thirty houses.

'Where?'

'Shush,' I say to Rhodri, before he has time to answer. 'We don't want the house getting robbed.'

'Right,' he says. 'Just over there.' He waves in the same direction I did.

'Where?' asks the man.

'There.' Rhodri waves. 'You ready?'

'Yes.'

'Finally.'

'Did you ask Josie to look after the house and rabbits?'

'Yes.'

'And she's going to water the tomatoes and cucumbers in the garden?'

'*Yes.*'

'And the strawberries?'

'Yes. Come on. Get in. Let's go.'

I open the car door to find Jack snuggled up to his floppy bear, with his special blanket on his knee. 'Excited?' I ask him.

'Yes. But why are we setting off at midnight?'

'Because your mum was working all day,' says Rhodri, accusingly.

'Had to finish my assignment,' I remind Rhodri, 'or work would be coming on holiday with us.'

'Suppose so.'

'Are you driving, Mum?'

'Yes,' I say proudly. 'Off we go.'

I rev the car, flick on the radio and head for the motorway.

The holiday starts now.

If there's one thing Jack, Rhodri and I do well it's cramping ourselves into a small car together for a long time. We're barely out of Jackson when Rhodri belts out the Welsh national anthem, followed by Welsh folk songs, one of which is about a saucepan. That always makes me laugh – a song about a saucepan in Welsh! How funny. Jack follows the words.

'What language are you singing in?' I ask him.

'Zog.'

'Where's that from?'

'The planet Zog where I am king.'

Yes, of course it is. I begin singing 'Happy Birthday' in Spanish. It's the only Spanish song I can remember although I have a degree in Spanish and studied the language for more than a decade. Soon we're making a right racket.

'Are you certain you're going the right way?' asks Rhodri.

'*Sí*. That means "yes",' I tell him, 'in Spanish.'

He rolls his eyes at me. 'I *know* that. Are you going the right way? It doesn't look familiar.'

'*Sí, guapo,* that means "yes, fit-bit".' He rolls his eyes at me again.

'Di zwacky blod?' asks Jack, in some crazy garble that could be Albanian, Cypriot or Polish. 'That means,' he elucidates, '"Are we going the right way?" in Zog.'

I look at the surroundings as we zoom past a small town, then peer hard at a big blue motorway sign. 'Ish blob slon blop.'

'What does that mean?' squeals Jack, leaning forward so his head touches the driver's seat.

'"We are definitely not going the right way" in Zog.'

'That's not Zog language,' he says seriously, slumping back into his seat. 'You just made that up.'

Eh? Isn't that what he was doing?

'We're heading north,' I tell Rhodri. 'Have been for just over an hour.'

'Which way are we supposed to be going?' He laughs. 'South?'

'Yes, Maria.' Rhodri grins. 'Wales is south of Manchester. *South.*'

Ah, so it is. So it is.

We pull in at the next service station so Rhodri can hop into the driving seat.

I unstick my legs from the dashboard, stretch out my arms and yawn loudly. 'Crikey, where are we?'

'Almost there.'

'What time is it?'

'Three thirty.'

There is a bright smudge in the sky where the sun is rising. I turn to look at Jack. He is fast asleep, his head resting on his seatbelt.

'Sorry,' I say. 'I was supposed to be navigating, wasn't I?'

'I know the way.'

'How long have I been asleep?'

'About two hours.'

'Beautiful, isn't it?' I say woozily, looking out at the horizon.

Rhodri smiles. He's happiest here among the unspoiled landscape of the Snowdonia National Park, beneath the looming shadows of the mountains. Instantly he's easier with me. I pat his knee gently. I kiss the tips of my fingers and place them on his lips – he bites the kiss off. 'Lovely,' says Rhodri. One hand on the steering-wheel, he absently strokes my cheek.

I gaze out of the window, immersing myself in the moment. After this week together, I'll love Rhodri more. I know it.

*

It's night, and dark, by the time we have finally unpacked and are sitting down for dinner. Rhodri's father spoons onion soup into his mouth. He loads more salt into his bowl, then sneaks a peculiar glance at Rhodri. 'So, how did you make this soup?' his father asks me.

'I boiled some onions in water.'

'Anything else?' asks Rhodri's father.

'No. Just onions in water.'

'So it's onion water,' remarks Rhodri.

'Yes, I suppose it is.' I laugh.

'Onion water?' Jack laughs too. Then we're all laughing at my quite disgusting soup.

I hadn't expected Rhodri's father to be staying at Cobble Cottage because Rhodri had assured me we'd be alone. His dad is funny, though. He recites silly limericks to Jack across the table, talks about dead poets to me, and belts out classical music on the old piano. And when all that's done, he sings opera very loudly. Quite eccentric. Quite charming.

When Jack has darted from the table to play in the next room, Rhodri's father tells us a cautionary tale. 'You can hear every sound in this house, every squeak, it's not soundproofed at all . . . yes . . . so . . . *hm* . . . yes.'

'Oh,' I say, making a hasty exit from the dinner table. 'Don't worry we'll do the dishes.' I grab Rhodri by the arm and drag him to the sink.

He shrugs his shoulders and smirks. 'I think what he was trying to say was, "Don't have noisy sex while I'm here."'

'How long will that be for?'

'Few days . . . and . . .' Rhodri hesitates, then adds, 'Jack will be sleeping on a camp-bed in our room.'

I groan. I can't help it. It's not Jack that's the problem, it's Rhodri and me. 'We'll have to go to a field or something,' I suggest. 'Ask your dad to babysit Jack one night so we can go out for a shag.' Obviously we can't tell his dad what we plan to do – we'll say that we're going for a romantic walk under the stars.

Rhodri looks at me as if to say: 'Are you for fucking real?'

'Yes,' I say, reading his mind. 'Seriously, Rhodri, this is *important*.' I can't believe that at twenty-nine my sole quest in life is to secure the ultimate legover. 'We'll take a blanket with us,' I add. 'We can lie on that hill near the abandoned farmhouse. Or under the bridge by the canal.'

The bridge by the canal sells it. 'That could be fun,' he says, already imagining some seedy role-play where he can rub my arse up against a damp, earthy wall.

On day one we were up at eight for breakfast and to make a picnic for our long hike up Bera Bach, followed by a drop-in at the local pool for a swim. It was in a small country town, so we had it to ourselves and thrashed about silly. After dinner the three of us stole off into a farmer's field to play baseball.

Yesterday afternoon we cycled down the country lanes to the shops at Bala. On the way Rhodri showed us the most enormous bull, which huffed and puffed at Jack as we poked our heads over the wall. Jack laughed when the bull turned around displaying its dirty bottom. 'The bull is having a poo!' he shrieked, holding his nose. 'Eeeew.'

Today we have decamped to a mossy glade, the most

enchanted spot: harsh bracken scratches up against soft green ferns. Jack and I would never have experienced the great outdoors if we hadn't met Rhodri. I used to take Jack to places like museums and libraries and bookshops. I've always been too scared to take him somewhere isolated on my own.

Streams cut through the land. We leap over them, slapping down in sodden ground. We climb over rocks, hunting for small animals. Jack finds a sheep's skull, which he urges me to stuff into my bag so that he can take it home. When rain breaks heavily we rush frantically, gathering whatever detritus we can find to make a shelter and before long we have built a den from leaves, fallen branches and ferns.

In our makeshift shelter we huddle together, pretending to keep dry. It's Jack's house. Rhodri and I are the scouts he sends out to find yet more materials to fill the holes in the roof.

I don't care that Rhodri and I aren't on holiday alone any more, or that at the weekend the house will be full to bursting with his family, because we're having fun, and when I look at Jack, he seems truly happy.

Five days into the holiday already – it's passing too quickly. I so rarely take a holiday I'd forgotten how enjoyable they can be.

'Everything okay?' I whisper to Rhodri. It's gone nine in the morning and we're lazing in bed as quietly as possible, careful that any sudden movement could wake Jack. More guests have arrived. Beneath our room, Rhodri's brother Brad, his girlfriend and Rhodri's parents are clattering about in the kitchen. 'Do you think your mother's making pancakes?' I whisper. 'I love her pancakes. Jack does too. We should wake him before we miss them.'

'Leave him to sleep. There'll be plenty of pancakes to go around. Let's have a lie-in.'

'You're very quiet. You all right?'

'Yes. But . . .'

'What?'

'Well . . . it's quite tiring, isn't it? Being on holiday with you and Jack, it's not like being on my own.'

'Aren't you having fun?'

'I am, but –'

'I'm having a good time.' I stroke Rhodri's cheek, hoping to erase whatever he might say next. 'Jack is.'

'I'm having fun,' he says, moving on top of me. 'I am. I'm having fun.'

It's dusk when we set off for Manchester. We spent our last day of the holiday with Rhodri's old schoolfriend, Maddog. Jack is sleeping contentedly in the back of the car, worn out from playing pirates all afternoon. Seven days on holiday together and our lives feel back on track. All we needed was to spend time with one another. Bolting about working is necessary, but Rhodri is right: money isn't important, love is.

I'll try not to work so much. Perhaps there are ways we could cut down. Or I could raise the male-escort idea again. Though now it's April the party season's over so demand might be lower.

'I had such a wonderful day today,' I say, as I drive.

Rhodri fidgets with the electric windows, drawing them

up and down. I'm cheery and full of hope, doubtless irritating the hell out of my darling man.

'Your friends are lovely to be around. They're so happy and the baby is adorable. I like spending time with couples, don't you? It fuels my belief in romance.'

Rhodri's friend, Maddog, married his childhood sweetheart and they've just had their first child. Maddog loves his family deeply. It's evident in everything he does, from the way he folds the laundry, to how he mows the lawn, to how he holds his son in his arms. They have a stunning family home.

'It didn't make me feel like that,' Rhodri mutters. 'I'm sad.'

'How can you be? We've just had dinner with the loveliest family in the world.'

'I know I don't want that. I'm not going to become a male escort, Maria. And I don't want to work hard for a nice family home.'

Suddenly my head hurts. I glance at Jack's reflection in the rear-view mirror. I feel queasy, unsettled and sick. If Rhodri won't try to earn more money, then I'll have to look for other freelance projects to take on to support the three of us. I don't want us to live on that council estate for the rest of our lives. I need to move from there before Jack becomes a teenager in case he gets in with the wrong crowd.

'I don't want marriage,' continues Rhodri. 'I don't want any of those things.'

'Well, what do you want?'

'I don't know,' Rhodri says. 'But not that.'

*

The next morning it's back to the grindstone. I text Athens to let him know that I'll be working from home. Rhodri enters the kitchen/diner, which triples as my office. I watch him graze through the cupboards. He seems content enough. He doesn't look as if he's going to pack his bags and leave me. Jack went off to school singing about saucepans. So two out of three on the jubilation scale isn't bad.

When Rhodri has settled by me with the newspaper, I ask, 'You didn't mean it, did you, that you don't want all of this?'

'What?'

'You know, what you said about Maddog and a family and a house?'

'I don't want that, no, because I couldn't be involved in tackling climate change if I worked full time. But I wasn't in a good mood that day. The night before you took me to see a public toilet in Weston-super-Mare.'

'I wanted to see where my stepbrother died.'

Since that day Lucy made psychic contact with my dead stepbrother, I've thought about him more. It was years ago when a stranger found him in the men's toilets at the Winter Gardens. He'd overdosed on heroin and died there. As we were on holiday, I wanted to leave flowers at the spot but it all got a bit peculiar because Rhodri had to keep watch while I went into a cubicle, and Jack started asking questions: 'Mum, why are you leaving flowers by the men's urinals? Mum, why are you crying?' And so on.

I'm glad I went. The public toilet was on the seafront and there was a landscaped garden behind it with flower-beds and a pond. We sat on a bench beneath the pergola watching skateboarders spin by. I had imagined the place to be far bleaker. Then we all ate piping hot chips. It wasn't the day-trip of a lifetime, but it could have been worse.

'What you said upset me,' I tell him. 'It made me think, if that's the case, what are you doing with us?' Rhodri and I dated for two years before he moved in. I thought that meant we were now a family.

'I didn't think about what I was saying.'

'Well ...' I pause, searching for the right words '... That's all right, then.'

I carry on working. Rhodri flicks through the newspaper aimlessly. The best course of action, I think, is not to ask anything else.

19

A few days later, I return home from a day at work with a little present for Rhodri. I'm certain he'll absolutely love it. 'Look what I found,' I say.

Rhodri pulls off one sock and throws it across the bedroom. It lands on the radiator. He removes the other sock and flings that too. It lands in the corner on the fax machine. Then he climbs into bed next to me. 'Go on. What have you found?'

'Viagra.' This is such good luck. I was working at an office in Manchester and a solitary Viagra tablet practically threw itself at me. I have no idea who it once belonged to. I found it in the toilets at some offices where I had attended a meeting. It was longing to be discovered by me, and definitely planted there by my guardian angel. To clear up the safety issues, it's in an unopened official-looking packet that has 'Viagra' written all over it. And I Googled the side-effects just to check that we're not going to die.

'I'm not taking *that*,' barks Rhodri. 'I'm not putting chemicals in my body when I don't need to.' Not that I'm surprised. Rhodri won't consume anything that isn't grown in organic soil.

It would be a terrible waste for this Viagra to go unused. Should I take it, the possibilities will be endless. So I pop it into a pretty box I keep by the bed until I think of a plan.

*

The following Tuesday I have to travel to London for work, and because I'm in town, Toga has invited me to dinner at his house, which he has never done in all the years we've fooled around with one another. I couldn't say no. Maybe he's starting to consider the relationship between us more seriously.

I must be back at Piccadilly Circus by around eleven o'clock this evening to meet Athens and company at the hotel to plan our work schedule for tomorrow. I call Toga to make sure we're still on. 'Hello, Bear.'

'I'm busy,' he says, 'just going into a meeting. I'll see you at six.' Then the phone cuts off because the train shoots under a bridge.

Later, standing in Toga's kitchen, I feel awkward. His flat is large for someone without any children. Prints hang casually and DVD box sets are stacked against exposed brick walls: definitely no kids here. In the corners I see tokens of a Toga I'd never known about. Like the tennis rackets: I never knew he played tennis. And the Neil Diamond CD: I never knew he liked Neil Diamond. An old postcard from his mother is propped up against the kitchen window. I never knew . . . I did know that he has a mother.

He's making a pasta dish. 'Hello, you,' he says. He hooks his arm around my waist but I pull away, awkwardly rejecting his kisses. It all seems too easy now I'm here, and because Rhodri says I can do what I want, I know I will. 'What are you making?'

'Creamy mushroom sauce.' He stirs the pan for effect. 'You like it?'

I rarely eat cream because Rhodri, Jack and I inhabit a dairy-free house, but I won't tell Toga that. 'Love it.' I perch on a breakfast stool and admire him. If Toga were a tropical fruit he'd be a ripe mango, if he were an animal he'd be a yeti, if he were . . .

'What are you doing?'

'Watching you.'

'You're scaring me.'

He's such a weirdo. I turn to the counter and flick through an arcane copy of *Time Out*. 'I thought you said you had a cleaner.'

'I do.'

'It's not very tidy, is it?'

'Cheeky.' He turns the pan down and slots himself between my legs. We kiss gently.

Maybe I could skip dinner and just have Toga. I head to his bathroom with my bags where I spy a range of skincare products to surpass even my friend Emmeline's collection, and she has enough to start her own beauty spa. Good grief, Toga's one of those London metrosexuals I've read about in the weekend supplements. With all that crap, he's single-handedly polluting the South East's waterways.

'What are you doing in there?' he calls.

'Out in a minute,' I say, rummaging through my make-up bag. I'm sure I put the Viagra in here. I'm certain of it.

7.02 p.m.

I step into the kitchen in a sheer black dressing-gown and hold-ups. 'Look what I've got,' I whisper. In an attempt to look like a burlesque dancer I rummage in my bra and eventually pull out the Viagra tablet. I wave it in the air, then place it dramatically on the counter.

Toga looks at it, then at me.

'Viagra,' I say, dropping the dressing-gown to reveal the lingerie he bought me one Valentine's Day, years before I met Rhodri. The thong and camisole set is red, lacy . . . and definitely not doing the trick. '*Toga* –'

'I'm not doing it.'

7.12 p.m.

'*Oh, Toga* . . . '

I'm draped across his bed in a rather fetching tight black lace Maria Grachvogel slip. It has sexy string straps that stop just above my breasts. I think I look hot. And it only cost me five quid in the sales a decade ago. It doesn't often make an appearance, only on special occasions like this . . .

He stamps into the bedroom. 'No. I am not taking Viagra.'

7.22 p.m.

'*Oh, Toga* . . . ' I'm kneeling on the bed wearing a black raw-silk chemise with a delicate white trim. I bought it in the sales four years ago for eight quid. It doesn't often make an appearance, only on . . .

'I've told you, I'm not taking Viagra. Don't look at me like that.'

7.32 p.m.

'*Oh, Toga* . . . ' A new approach is needed so I'm sitting on the sofa reading the newspaper and wearing the ivory satin this-is-what-I-might-look-like-on-my-wedding-night-should-you-ever-wish-to-marry-me slip.

'I'm not going to take that Viagra tablet and I never will. So you can stop pestering me. I'm not going to do it.'

What a spoilsport. Yes, taking another person's prescription drug is wrong. I admit there are risks. But I didn't buy it. I didn't steal it (exactly). It was waiting for me to pick it up. Some people win on the Premium Bonds, other people find a Viagra.

'Okay. Okay.' I stalk back into his bedroom to get dressed.

Back in the kitchen Toga is guarding the pan with his life. 'Can you get the salad from the fridge?' he asks. I'm wearing my what-kind-of-lover-are-you-if-you-won't-even-take-Viagra-frown.

I crouch beside the fridge. My head knocks against his knees. He has rollmops in here. I've always wondered what sort of person eats rollmops and now I know: the Toga sort. I drop the salad on the counter, then climb onto a breakfast stool. I place the Viagra on the counter next to the cucumber.

Toga looks at it, then at me.

'Let's split it,' I say.

He runs the tap, fills a glass with water and hands it to me. He takes a knife and slices the tablet into two, then two again.

I knew Toga would. He's game for anything.

'What?'
'What?'

'You're staring at me again.'

'I can't help it.' I giggle.

Toga removes the pan from the heat.

'Are you feeling different?'

'Yes.' My face is all tingly and I feel a little flushed.

He kisses me roughly on my lips and swiftly unzips my dress. I slip off the stool so that the dress falls to my feet, then stand before him in nothing but my demure silk underwear.

Toga pushes me against the kitchen sink. I think: Lucky me! That happened quickly. Viagra's good, I'll take some more.

While Toga is nuzzling my breasts, I stretch out an arm, pinch the rest of the tablet between my fingers and swallow it dry.

This is the life, really it is: dinner simmering in a pan, a pile of magazines to skim through, no cleaning or washing-up to do, no bills to worry about, and a handsome, intelligent man lapping and purring between my thighs. If only every Tuesday night could be like this. I pick up my glass of Beaujolais, swish the lovely redness around my mouth and gaze out of the window contentedly. Toga has a shed. I think that's what I can see in the garden, although it's dark so I can't be sure. And lots of plants. How lovely. And a little patio. Delightful. I wonder if his knees are aching yet. Toga was blessed with a wonderful tongue. I was blessed with a wonderful life. And isn't the sky dark? And the kitchen light is on. And look at those flats there. I can see people washing their dishes. How sweet . . .

Ooooh . . .

Oh, no.

'Toga.'

'Yes, my little milkmaid?'

When he calls me that, I'm sure he's thinking of Tess of the d'Urbervilles.

'Toga.'

'You like that, hm?'

'Toga.'

'Mmm . . . yeah?' Spurred on by my calling his name, he licks furiously.

'*Stop, stop, stop it.*'

Toga stands up, pushes his hands down on my shoulders, forces me to my knees and unzips his trousers. Well, that wasn't what I had in mind. 'The blinds,' I try to say.

I think we may soon have an audience. He places his hand over my eyes. If I can't see the people out there, does it mean they can't see me? No, it does not. What is it with this Viagra? It's made my brain stop. All I have is *desire . . . desire . . . desire . . .* and no sense at all.

I crawl away from him to grab a shirt from the washing basket. 'Stop it now,' I say, slipping my arm into a sleeve. One can't be too careful: we could end up on the Internet.

He grabs me by the wrist and tugs me out of the kitchen and into the bathroom. He runs the shower. The room fills with steam. I stand there thinking, Where's the window? No window. Bloody windowless London flats. It's so hot I might pass out. Toga peels off the shirt, unclips my bra and I begin to sing a song I learned many years ago, because when it comes to foreplay men need lots of encouragement.

First verse

Yes

Yes

Yes

Second verse

Oh

Oh

Oh

Third verse

Just *there*

Just *there*

Just *there*

Fourth verse

Name of the person you are with repeated three times.

It's important to get the name right.

Just as I'm reaching the last verse, Toga pushes me against the sink, until my back is so arched it hurts. With his hand he presses my mouth against his ear so that he can hear every groan and – oh, my – I think I might implode or wee in the sink or accidentally defecate if he doesn't – soon.

What is he doing to me *now*?

I'm in the shower blinking away warm water raining over my face. I try to check my reflection in the taps. Panda eyes . . . I hope not. Once he has thoroughly soaped me down, he wraps me in a soft fluffy towel, like a warm present, and leads me to his bedroom. Then he gets on all fours on the bed, his rear beaming at me, and instructs me to slap his arse. Which, quite frankly, is not a request I've ever had before. 'Not like that,' he says.

I wasn't aware there was a technique to this arse-slapping business. Surely one should just wallop the other person and hope for the best.

'Use a different part of your hand.' He takes my hand in his. 'That part,' he says.

So I try again but this time hit him *really, really* hard. Which he likes. I think. Or maybe not –

'No. Not like that, like this,' he says, then demonstrates what he wants me to do on his own backside. So I swing my arm back and belt him so hard that the palm of my hand stings.

'No. Not like that, like this,' he remonstrates.

So I smack him *again*.

'No. Not like that, use the flat of your hand.'

And again. *Thwack.*

'Bit harder.'

And again. *Thwack.*

'Just a bit harder.'

And again. *Thwack.*

'Just a little bit harder.'

Bloody hell, Toga, I wasn't aware I'd signed up for spanking lessons. I slap his arse with all my might and, finally, he lets out a satisfied moan.

I am snuggled up against Toga who is flicking through some photographs he has taken of us (I think my eyebrows look good so I'll go back to that beauty salon again) when my mobile rings. It's Athens. 'M, what are you doing?'

Tricky question: it's late and Toga is talking dirty into my ear.

'Having dinner with a friend.'

'You were supposed to meet us at the hotel.'

I check the time. Drat, I've missed the last Tube. 'I'll be there first thing in the morning,' I say. 'Promise. Ready to go. Can't wait. Going to be great. Don't worry, you can rely on me.'

Athens huffs to let me know that he thinks I'm a complete pest.

'Good train journey?' I ask.

'Yes, but I expected you to be here when we booked in. We're going out to a pub, then turning in for the night.'

'I can't make it. Sorry.'

'You'd better be here first thing, M.'

'I will.'

I arrive early. I barely slept and have enough make-up caked on my face to join a dance troupe. Toga accompanied me to the hotel where Athens and the group are staying. After our performance last night, I'm surprised I can walk in a straight line.

'I'll see you soon,' I say, knowing that it will be months before I set eyes on him again. He turns on his heels and walks away from me. I take a deep breath and watch him gradually disappear into the crowds hurrying to work. If I concentrate hard on just one person, if I study that man's swagger and shiny shoes, it might just take the memories away.

Just then, I see Athens stride towards me. 'Great, M, you're here.'

'I said I would be and I am.'

He taps me lightly on the arm so I walk along with him. Then we go underground to Earls Court.

'Good evening?'

'Very good evening, thanks.'

And it was. That Viagra was really something. No wonder the older generation can't wait until they retire.

Early the next morning I sprint as fast as I can across Euston station. My overnight case bangs against my ankles, and the large bag slung over my shoulder keeps jabbing into my hips. I halt at the departures board. Manchester Piccadilly. Platform 17. Due to depart any minute. I'm about to sprint for it when Rhodri calls. I can't see how I can reach the train in time and chat. 'Hello,' I answer, running towards the platform.

'What time are you back?'

'A couple of hours. Jack okay? You okay? . . . Oh, fuck, fuck, fuck.'

'What?'

'I missed the fucking train – it's just come in.'

Rhodri falls silent for a moment. I didn't mean to curse – it just slipped out.

The sound of the train pulling out is deafening.

'Are you still there?' I shout down the phone, as the loudspeaker announces the imminent departure of a train to Birmingham New Street. 'Rhodri?'

'You've slept with someone, haven't you?'

I look around me anxiously, searching for a member of staff to direct me to the next train home. 'Pardon?'

'You've had sex with someone, haven't you?'

How long until the next train? I just want to get home now. I want to be at home this very second.

'How did you know?'

'You never swear like that. And you said the train had come in rather than that it had gone out.'

'Oh –' Rhodri is astute. I'm transparent. I'd make a dreadful perjurer. 'I'm sorry, Rhodri.'

'You don't have to be sorry. I *keep* telling you that. You don't have to be sorry.'

But I am sorry – how could I feel no remorse?

20

A few weeks have passed since I met up with Toga, and now I have dropped off his radar. No emails. No calls. Nothing. One bright afternoon Jack and I walk the long road home from school to Sunnyside. I tell Jack to look at the sky, see how blue it is. Listen to the birds, Jack, I tell him. Look at the blossom. All the while cars hum past us, mothers hastening to the shops or driving their children to swimming lessons or football club or dancing. Life feels full. I want to be at ease because years ago, after all that trouble with Damien, I didn't even notice the seasons change. I must have been walking with my eyes cast to the ground.

'We can go to the park on the way home, Jack,' I say cheerfully.

'What for?'

'To play football.'

I packed a football in the hope we may find some other children to play a game with. Otherwise it will just be Jack and me. I take his hand in mine, scruff his hair up a little with the other and kiss his forehead. He smells as good as the day he was born.

Jack screws up his nose as if to say, 'I don't want to play football with my mum.' He asks, 'Can I play on the skate-board bit instead?' He likes to hurl himself up and down the half-pipe; he has yet to try it with a skateboard and uses the aluminium curves as a slide instead.

'If you like,' I reply.

'Will you play with me?'

'I'd love to.'

Jack leans into me, pressing his head against my arm. As we walk, we trip over each other's feet.

'Everything all right, love?'

'Yes.'

'We'll have a nice evening, you and me. I'll run a warm bubble bath after the park. Then I'll read you a story at bedtime, if you're very good. And I'm sure you will be *very* good.'

'Okay,' he grumbles.

He isn't even mimicking my mummy voice and mummy words. 'Is something wrong?'

'No.'

'Are you sure?'

'*Yes.*'

'I thought going to the park would make you happy.'

'I will never ever be happy.'

He is kicking a discarded Coke can as we walk. The clink irritates me: clink, scuffle, clink, scuffle. I can't stand it when he kicks litter. But, then, maybe Ronaldo kicked litter when he was a child. I don't want to scupper Jack's chances of being a Premiership footballer.

'Of course you can be happy. I love you. You know that. You're very much loved by all of your family.'

'I can never be happy. I can't ever be happy because I don't see my dad. Because every day I only see him in my heart and every day it hurts in my heart.' He drops my hand and makes a little cross over his chest, one set of fingers fenced over the other.

'I didn't know you felt like that.'

'Well. I do. All the time. Every day. Every night.'

'I thought you were happy. Rhodri isn't your dad, but he cares a great deal for you. And for me.' I wrap Jack in my arms, swaddling him in a warm, motherly hug.

He murmurs into my dress, half in agreement, half in disagreement. 'But he's not my dad,' he grumbles. 'I'm not calling him "Dad".'

'You don't have to call him "Dad".'

Rhodri is at a meeting this evening; some public debate about the planned expansion of Manchester Airport. He won't be home until late, when he'll be all fired up about action against climate change.

'But I don't *know* my dad. I don't know who I'll grow up to be because I don't know what he does. I don't know who I am because I don't know who he is. You don't understand how it feels.' He stamps on the Coke can so hard it sticks to his shoe.

I bend down to unpeel it from the sole and drop it into a bin. 'Well, you look very much like your dad,' I tell Jack.

'Do I?'

'Yes, you have his eyes.'

'I have his mouth too, don't I?' says Jack, perking up. 'Nana says I have my dad's mouth and his is like Granddad Eddie's. It's a straight mouth. Even when I'm smiling it's in a straight line.'

'You have his mouth. And your dad loved sports. He's good at football and you are too.' There are other moments when Jack reminds me of Damien, like when he grins and tilts his head, charming me into one thing or another. Moments when I think he's delicious.

As we draw closer to the park, Jack holds my hand in silence. He is my own little boy. I don't want him to be unhappy. I don't want him to think he can never be happy for the rest of his days. 'I have some photographs of you and your dad when you were a baby,' I tell him.

'Really?'

'And a card he sent to you when you were five.' There's a shoebox in a cupboard in my room containing the little band that had been attached to his wrist, reading 'Baby of Maria Roberts, 6lb 12oz', his clamped umbilical cord, which, nearly nine years later, is withered and dried, and some cards, photographs and odd little things belonging to Damien.

'After we've been to the park, while you're in the bath, I'll pull some out for you.'

Later that evening we sit on my bed. It is our own raft in a sea of mess where Jack picks up photograph after photograph and laughs. Jack when he was a baby, wearing his dad's sunglasses, sitting on a racing car: he was dressed as a Manchester City fan then, like Damien. He supports Liverpool now, like his uncle Luke. Jack wearing underpants on his head and bouncing on the sofa with Damien, who is also wearing underpants on his head: Jack used to say that the underpants protected us from an alien invasion. I remember when I took that picture. I was standing behind the camera, underpants on my head with pigtails hanging out of the sides, laughing at Damien and Jack. In the photograph, father and son are tanned. These pictures sing with happiness and magic. No one would suspect anything else.

'Can I have this one in my room?' asks Jack. It's of him and his father on a pine bed in an apartment we rented in Spain. 'And this one.' It's of all three of us beneath a blossoming cherry tree at my father's wedding to Eleanor.

'You can take those,' I say, patting his shoulder. 'I'll keep the others safe.'

'Have we got some Blu-Tack, Mum?'

I shuffle off the bed leaving Jack with the photographs. 'You put the rest back into the box and I'll find the Blu-Tack.'

At bedtime I lie on Jack's bed and he snuggles into me as I read him another episode of Dav Pilkey's *Captain Underpants and the Attack of the Talking Toilets*.

'Sometimes,' Jack begins, as I close the book and set it down by his bed, 'when I'm playing outside, I think my dad will walk around the corner – and I feel very scared.'

'I feel that too,' I say, cuddling him tight. '*All the time*. But I promise you this, Jack, you don't need to be scared because he'd never hurt you.'

'I love you, Mum.' He plants a long kiss on my cheek.

'And I love you. Bigger than the moon.'

As I'm walking out of the room, he calls, 'I love you higher than the sky.'

I flick the light off and call back, 'I love you bigger than the entire universe.'

'I love you more than that,' he calls back.

'I'm a lucky mummy, then, aren't I?'

As I close the bedroom door, Jack blows me a kiss through the gap. I catch it and throw it straight back.

*

The next day, I collect Jack from after-school club and we go shopping. 'Scarlet can come over tonight,' I say. She's been spending more time with her mum, which is good. That's why we haven't seen her.

Struggling to carry grocery bags, I pass Tina easing herself into her car. Jack shouts hello to her son. I pretend to be very busy juggling bags and searching for my keys so that I don't need to look at her sly smile. If she weren't bigger than me, I'd – I'd – Stupid woman.

Rhodri is at home. He has been cooking and a savoury aroma fills the house. I peer into the oven and see the Crock-Pot. Turning to Jack, I say, 'If you do your homework quickly, the longer you'll have to play with Scarlet.'

'What's for dinner?' he asks.

'A surprise.'

Jack groans and runs upstairs. Experience has taught him that 'a surprise' is synonymous with 'I've no idea what's in that Crock-Pot.'

While he's in his room changing, I have the opportunity to string up the badminton net I bought from Argos as a treat. I hope he'll like it. I can't drive the poles into the hard ground so I tie one end to the drainpipe, and the other to the tree across our stretch of the communal gardens.

'Surprise,' I shout up the stairs.

Not a peep. Can't say I blame him. He probably thinks the surprise is roasted parsnips in Marmite.

'*Jack*, surprise!'

He appears at the top of the stairs, hands on his hips. 'What?'

'Come out and see.'

'I'm not eating that stuff, whatever it is.'

'Come and see what's outside, Moody Bum.'

Fortunately Scarlet has arrived. 'Can I play?' she hollers through the door.

'Course you can.'

Now Jack's thinking, Can I play what? He runs down the stairs and out through the door. He runs back in and hugs me. 'Thanks, Mum.' Then he darts back out again to adjust the ties on the drainpipe and the tree. 'You haven't tied this very well,' he calls. Then he chooses a metallic blue bat, picks up the shuttlecock and gets ready to play.

'Girls against boys?' I suggest to Scarlet.

'Yeah!' they both shout. Jack runs indoors to grab Rhodri and drag him outside.

Us girls won. Those boys cheated. A few children walking down the estate stopped to play so Rhodri and I left them to it. Now I'm sitting on Rhodri's knee, watching the news and overhearing children bicker in front of the window. Moments later everyone has fallen out with one another, the game is over and children are storming off in different directions. You can't buy children happiness, not even from Argos.

The next morning I watch mothers gather in clusters outside the school. Jack is off playing. If I made an effort to befriend some mummies, Jack might feel more involved. I sit on the bench by the tree stump, wishing someone would talk to me. I may have missed the boat on this one because they've formed mystical inner-circle groups. I'd need to be Robocop to bust into one: I'd have one of those synthesized voices and bellow, 'Make room, single mother on the verge of a nervous breakdown coming through.' Even though Rhodri lives with us, I still feel very much a single mother when it comes to raising Jack. If I were married, maybe I wouldn't feel as if my life is temporary.

I divide the mums into groups so that I can try to figure out where I fit in.

Grade-A mummies.
Mostly housewives. Their husbands have good jobs and they live in dream houses. They spend a lot of time in front of the mirror, have good clothes, good hair, sports cars, attractive children, and are permatanned (not the nasty streaky stuff, but the result of fancy holidays with fancy sun lotions). The kind of mum I'd love to be.

Grade-B mummies.
The sporty mothers who jog five miles at least twice a week, followed by an hour at the gym. And the career mothers who work in law, broadcasting and the medical profession, but not as domestic assistants, more like consultant cardiologists and so on.

Grade-C mummies.
The struggling mothers. I think I fit in with them. We always look harried and as if we should be whipped off for an instant makeover. I'm sure I must look jobless. That's probably why no one talks to me. My shoes are knackered. My clothes are too. And I hang around with the aura that I'm going off to the DSS to get a social loan to fund my addiction to the Shopping Channel.

'Would you like to come to my exhibition?' says a mummy.

I turn my head in disbelief.

It's not voices in my head. A mother *is* actually talking to me. She hands me a postcard. 'I'm a photographer,' she says. 'My exhibition is on at the gallery across the road.'

'I'd love to go,' I say, hoping to hold her for conversation. Then the bell rings for the start of school. I kiss Jack goodbye and scan the playground in search of the friendly mum, but I'm too late: she's already left.

21

I sit on the dirty steps to the office block where I work for Athens. The enormous steel doors are locked. My keys are at home so I read a newspaper and pick at a bacon sandwich I bought from the Koffee Pot nearby.

'Morning,' says one of the music girls, rattling her keys in the lock. 'You're early.' She lets me in, then slinks off in a cool fashion towards her end of the office.

I switch on my computer, clear away dirty mugs, leaf through papers on my desk, then check my emails. Last night Rhodri said he'd take on some gardening work, which is a relief. Holy goat. There's an email from Cici, the girl who was handling the applications for –

I'm going to *New York* on an all-expenses-paid work trip! *I* am one of the chosen few! I call Rhodri. 'Guess what?' I screech.

'What?' He sounds as if he's still in bed.

'Are you still in bed?'

'Yes, it's my first lie-in for weeks.'

'I'm going to New York!' I holler.

'When?'

'In about *ten* days.' Do I have a current passport? Yes, yes, yes, I'm sure I have. 'Athens!' I yell, spying him walking down the corridor. 'I'm going to New York!'

'I'll talk to you when you get home. Are you going to work late?' shouts Rhodri, over my excitement.

'No. I'll be back around seven.'

'We've a lot to do today, M,' chides Athens. He's in a foul mood, I can tell.

Oh, yes – New York, New York, New York!

Somebody likes me.

When I arrive home I find a young bearded lad in the kitchen. This reminds me very much of when an Iranian friend came to stay for a fortnight and, four months later, was still sleeping in my office-kitchen-diner, and Buddhists used my lounge for their weekly chants. Then, like now, life was one big hullabaloo.

Rhodri collected Jack from after-school club and they are now making posters at the kitchen table. I look to see what Jack has drawn – the world exploding under the effects of climate change. How lovely. He leaps off the chair and flings his arms around me.

'Hello, honey.' I lift him onto my hip, as if he were a toddler, and rub noses with him. 'Have you had a good day?' I turn to the bearded lad and offer to shake his hand. 'Hello,' I say to him.

'Joel,' he says, returning the handshake awkwardly.

I must remember to stop doing that handshake. It's so working class. People embrace nowadays. With this in mind, I go to kiss his cheek. He veers away. 'Nice to meet you, Joel. I'm Maria.'

'I know,' he says. 'We met before Christmas.'

Ah, *that* Joel. The subvertising one. The vegan-glue one. Now I remember.

'Rhodri,' I call, as I struggle through the kitchen, Jack still clinging to my hip, in search of my darling man. Rhodri is making stencils in the living room. He glances up, catches sight of us and shakes his head affectionately. I slide Jack down my body, headlock Rhodri and give him a delightful kiss. 'I'm so excited,' I begin.

But Rhodri harrumphs at me. 'About what?'

'New York!'

'How are you going to be getting to New York?'

He isn't going to be happy for me, is he? I knew it. 'On an aeroplane,' I say. 'How else would I get there?'

'I thought so.'

'Well, I can't jolly well catch the boat to the United bloody States of America one week in advance, meet the convoy there and return two weeks later. A five-day trip to New York would take a month.'

'You could say no. You don't have to go.'

I could say no, but I'm not going to. 'It is a training trip,' I argue. 'I need to go for my *career*.' I'm not altogether sure what that career is, but I'm quite sure I have one.

Jack scowls at me. 'You're going to New York and I'm not. I don't believe it.' He folds his arms across his chest furiously and slumps on to the big leather armchair.

'It'll be all work, sweetheart, not much fun.' Is it really necessary for everybody to hate me today? 'Tell you what, if I think you'll like it, we'll go one day. Hey?'

'All right. Can I have one of those T-shirts with "I 'heart' New York" on it?'

'If I can find one, yes.'

'And a present?'

'Yes.'

*

That night everywhere I look in the house reminds me of the imminent disaster that is climate change, and the fire-breathing dragon that is capitalism. I switch on the television to find a documentary on wind farms and how that's no good. I watch the news and discover that across the world people are starving or drowning or being exploited in the drive for globalization. Children in India are holed up in factories sewing beads onto ethnic-style clothing for export to the UK, their eyes and bodies blistered from years of being locked in a room. Elsewhere women and young girls are trapped in the sex industry. I sit on the sofa and cry at everything I watch, starting with *Coronation Street* at seven thirty and ending after *News at Ten*. What a disaster, I think. But would any of this be solved by my not getting on that aeroplane?

New York was incredible. Our fabulous hotel was situated at the foot of the Empire State Building. I took a special lift to the penthouse to get to my room, which was an *executive suite* with a remote-control queen-sized bed that had an adjustable mattress. I pressed the button to make it firm, then again to make it squashy, firm, squashy, firm, squashy, on and on for five glorious nights. Each morning a paper was delivered to the door, then a maid cleaned the bathroom, folded the towels and made the bed while I was out at executive-type meetings. We took trips to Brooklyn and Greenwich Village, and went to the National Arts Center on Gramercy Square. I trawled Fifth Avenue, like Holly Golightly in *Breakfast at Tiffany's*. When I tired of that, I napped on the grass in Central Park to the sound of children screaming and laughing on the fairground, a jazz band played, and I heard the clip-clop of horses taking tourists here and there. We rode the Staten Island ferry to catch a glimpse of the Statue of Liberty at midnight. Cocktails were served in the executive lounge each day from five until seven.

One evening I looked out across the skyline of New York City, martini in hand, fellow travellers lounging on the sofas engaged in intellectual conversations about poets, and it dawned on me that what I crave is opportunity. I don't want to downsize my life until I live in a commune wearing recycled potato sacks. I want to help people and make a difference. I want to travel with Jack and experience other ways of being. I don't want to be a single mother on the verge of a nervous breakdown for the rest of my life.

Tonight as I lie in my own bed, giddy with jetlag, I plan to remedy our dire financial situation. Rhodri won't allow me to pimp him out to cover the mortgage but during my stay in New York I worked on a top-secret plan to start my own business. It's a terrific idea – despite a looming recession. I've spent the last few days putting together a business proposal and my projections demonstrate that I'll be a mega-multi-millionaire in five years' time. A former banker can downsize to my house, and I'll upsize to a flash city pad. All I need to do is to find a business angel with heaps of money and convince her to give me some cash, so that I can make heaps in return. I told Rhodri about my plan and he stormed away from me in disappointment. I said: 'Think of it as a redistribution of wealth. Rich people give me money, I'll make money, and in turn I'll help out charitable causes. Think of me as

Robin Hood. I'll be robbing the rich to give to the poor.'

To which Rhodri replied, 'But it could involve people flying from one country to another and I cannot give you my support for that.'

So I'm going to travel to London for a business seminar on how to attract a venture capitalist. It's a *Dragon's Den* environment, but in the real world not the television one. Since my trip to New York, I've been designing my new entrepreneurial lifestyle by signing up for business start-up meetings and networking breakfasts. It's very likely that we'll be off this estate and living next door to Tamara Mellon in a jiffy. I've booked to stay at a cheap hotel in Paddington because I cannot bear to stay at that backpackers' hostel again, even if it does only cost twelve pounds per night. As I'm soon going to be a multi-millionaire, I'm counting on being able to recoup the fifty pounds.

'Your room is located in the building across the street,' says the receptionist. I take the key, then drag my case across the foyer and towards the exit. 'It's on the top floor. Do you need help with your bags?'

'I can manage, thanks.'

The receptionist reaches for the telephone. 'I can call someone – it isn't a problem.'

'Thank you, but I'll be fine.' If I'm going to be a world-class entrepreneur, I first need to handle the challenge of a few stairs. I struggle out of Reception and over Gloucester Terrace to the annexe facing the hotel. With some difficulty I unlock the heavy door, then push against it until it gives way to a rather depressing and dusty hallway. I stand at the bottom of the stairs, looking at the banister that curls up and up and into itself. How am I going to get to the top floor? I can barely even see it.

I scan the hallway for a lift. This hotel reminds me of the place my father moved into after his divorce from my mother. It was a grand old house divided into bedsits, with a shared bathroom on each floor. It was the kind of place you'd end up in should things go wrong, or if they never went right in the first place.

I pull my case up the stairs backwards, one step at a time. The seminar I'm due to attend is near Trafalgar Square. That gives me two hours to shower and polish myself. Afterwards I've arranged to meet Morton for a quick drink.

By the time I've climbed countless flights of stairs to my room I'm breathless and sweaty. I shuffle my case through the door, then throw myself onto the double bed and take in my surroundings. It's shabby without the chic: the carpet is dirty, ragged, and poorly fitted at the edges, and the slatted blinds obscure the view onto the street. The room is filled with the noisy throttle of buses and traffic outside. I lie back and close my eyes. The sheets feel clean, but the air smells musky and thick with other people's encounters.

Later I stand under the hot jets of water in the tiny shower cubicle and try to shave my legs. When I drop the soap there's barely room to bend down so I squat to pick up the slippery bar. Eventually I open the shower door and stick one leg out then the other, dripping water over the floor as I glide the razor over my skin.

I spend much of my evening with entrepreneurs and stressed venture capitalists. I sit next to a young multi-millionaire looking to invest in cutting-edge businesses to prop up his doomed ones. I follow him out on to the street, lean against the wall and smoke with him. He's quite a dish. We talk about his business ventures (vast but steadily losing money), the weather (hot), the Tube (unreliable). Then he walks one way and I another until I find myself sitting on a bench in Trafalgar Square, looking up at Nelson's Column.

I dig in my bag for my mobile to ring home.

'Maria Roberts's phone. She's not here right now, how can I help you?'

'Jack, it's Mummy.'

'Hello, Mum. Where are you?'

'Trafalgar Square in London.'

'I want to be in London.'

'Did you have a good day?'

'Yes.'

'Did you go swimming?'

'Yes.'

'Did you swim well?'

'Yes.'

'What's Rhodri doing?'

'Cooking dinner.'

'You haven't eaten yet?' Oh, no, it'll be a vegan dish. Jack will howl, Rhodri will moan. I'll feel bad. Jack talks briefly, but seems bored already. 'Please could you put Rhodri on? Love you.'

'Love you, 'bye,' says Jack, dropping the phone and yelling, '*Rhodri.*'

There is the clatter of pans, some grumbles and the rising sound of *The Simpsons* in the background.

'What do you want?'

'Nice to speak to you too.'

'I'm busy cooking dinner and trying to get Jack to do his homework.'

'I just called to say hello and goodnight.'

'Right.'

'It would be nice if you sounded like you want to hear from me. I am your girlfriend.'

'I'm tired, that's all.'

'What are you doing for dinner?'

'Fish fingers and oven chips.'

'But you don't believe in convenience food.' I get it. Home-cooked meals when I'm around, oven food when I'm not. I'll store that one up for ammunition.

'How was the seminar?'

'Very dull. No good at all. Not what it said in the description and an utter waste of time.'

'What are you doing this evening?'

'Meeting up with a friend.'

'Well, have a good time. Love you.'

'You too,' I say. 'See you tomorrow.'

The sky is a grey blue fading into dusk. Buses rattle past me, followed by motorcycles. All I can hear is the sound of irritated honks and the scream of an ambulance siren. There always seems to be an emergency in London. I call Morton and he picks up quickly.

'Hello? Morton, it's me.'

'I'm still at dinner across the city.'

'When can you meet?'

'I'll have another drink and be with you in forty minutes What are you going to do in the meantime?'

There's a networking event connected to the meeting

but I don't want to join in. All this talk of money has left me feeling hollow. 'Go for dinner.'

'Meet me in the Garrick Arms.'

'Where is it?'

'Behind the National Portrait Gallery.'

'Where's that?'

'It's huge, you can't miss it . . .' Morton is momentarily distracted by someone talking to him. 'I'll see you in there,' he says, and then he is gone.

I spot an American place, Garfunkels, across the square, so I make my way there.

'Table for?'

'One.' I sound like such a loser.

The waiter seats me at a small table by other lonely diners: a woman of my age, and a man who is probably just over thirty. I smile at the woman – she ignores me. I smile at the man – he looks down to his newspaper. I take a book out of my bag and pretend to read. If this is women's liberation, you can stuff it.

Morton calls to tell me he's already in the Garrick Arms. This is followed by an almighty calamity. I think he and his phone have just crashed to the floor. 'Are you okay?' I hear a woman say. 'Are you okay?'

'Help him,' someone else calls. 'Is he injured?'

'Morton,' I shout. 'Morton?' I hastily pay the bill and leave the restaurant in search of the pub. Standing in Trafalgar Square I try to figure out where I am. There is an enormous building ahead of me. That could be Buckingham Palace or something so I won't walk that way. I'll walk up and down Charing Cross Road instead.

I hate London. I do. This road goes on for eternity.

After haranguing passer-by after passer-by I'm still lost. No one in this Godforsaken city knows where they are or where they're going, and if they do then it's some mystery they don't want to share.

'Morton.' My phone is tucked between my shoulder and ear, my fingers searching through the *A–Z*. I turn the map upside-down. 'I'm lost.'

'Where are you?'

'Back at Trafalgar Square.'

'You're practically here . . .' Morton begins to direct me over the phone until I realize the big building ahead of me is actually the National Portrait Gallery, not Buckingham Palace, after all.

'What's with the hole on the knees?' I ask pointing to his torn trousers.

'I fell over,' he says. 'An attractive woman helped me up.'

'Good dinner?'

'Yes . . .' Morton doesn't finish his sentence, but nods sagely and closes his eyes.

'Are you falling asleep?'

'No.'

'I'm going to get a drink.' Probably not wise to offer Morton one. Some night this is going to be. When I return from the bar with a large white wine, I balance on a small stool next to him. Morton barely registers my arrival.

'What do you want from me?' he asks, eyes closed as if he's dozing or wishing me away. 'What are you doing here?'

'I've been to a seminar about setting up my own business.' Once I've convinced Morton that my intention is not to seduce him and whip him off for a night of passion, he relaxes a little. I tell him about my top-secret plan to become stinking rich. He tells me it's a fantastic idea and I should go ahead and do it. I'm quite wonderful, he tells me, and different from anyone he's ever met. Maybe he can help me in some way. Then he begins to crack daft jokes – between which he pauses to gaze into my eyes until the warmth tickles my insides, then at my cleavage. I move the stool closer to him. 'I like you,' I tell him. 'You make me laugh.'

Soon we are kissing. Then we move out onto the road where I hang my arms around his neck as he searches in his pocket for his wallet. He hails a black cab. 'Are you after my money?' he murmurs. 'Is that what you want?

The only thing I want from Morton right now is the same thing he wants from me.

In the hotel room Morton slumps on an armchair in the corner, he removes his glasses to rub his eyes.

'Can you see me?' I ask, from the bed.

'Yes,' he says, gesturing that I should walk towards him.

It's just after midnight. Morton's asleep. I tease the slats of the blinds open with my fingers and peer out onto the dark London street. Buses cut across the road, black cabs stop and start, and a young woman clatters down the pavement in high heels. I gaze at Morton, smiling. Every girl should sleep with a silver fox once. I feel as if I've been dipped in a vat of warm runny honey while humming angels untangle my hair.

I try to sneak back into bed without waking Morton, but as I creep under the sheets he pulls me to him. 'Where have you been?' he murmurs.

'I was restless, I couldn't sleep,' I whisper, as he kisses the nape of my neck. I turn and wrap myself around him. By the time morning rages through the window, I'm exhausted.

On the train home, commuters shunt by with bags, searching for seats. 'Is this one free?' a man asks.

'I think so.' I'm not in the mood for conversation. Remorse is settling in. And I'm so tired I just want to sleep. So I curl my coat into a ball, wedge it against the window and draw my knees up for a nap. As the train rocks out of Euston, I fall asleep.

When I wake the man is looking at me. 'You slept a long time. I'm Michael.' He shakes my hand steadily.

'Why are you heading to Manchester?' I yawn. 'Do you live there?'

'Business,' he says. 'I am looking to invest in a bed company. Do you live in Manchester?'

'Not in the centre no, but I work in an office there sometimes.'

'Are you working there tomorrow?'

'Yes.'

'Then let's meet for a coffee,' he suggests. 'I'm in Manchester for a few days, then return to London and back to Nigeria.' Michael tells me that he's a management consultant in London, that he uses his income to fund business ventures in Nigeria. There, he's a wealthy publisher. I ask if he helps the poor in his country; he says he has no time

213

for them. If they didn't want to be poor, they should work harder. He says I should move there. I'd have a better life there, with him.

'You're married?' I observe, gesturing to the ring on his finger.

'Yes. Four children. They're looked after by their mother.' He waves his hand as though to sweep them aside. 'You are an intelligent, beautiful girl. I never met a woman like you.' He writes down his email address on the cover of my notebook. 'I wish I had a woman like you as my wife.'

'Yes, but you have a wife.' The man can't just go proposing on a train when he already has a wife in another continent. It seems . . . let me think . . . a little *hasty*.

'But I would be so happy with you as my wife.' He tells me he has three cars in Nigeria, one of which is a Rolls-Royce, that I should move there because I would have a glamorous life and a big house, even a pool and staff. There are many opportunities for a girl like me, clever, white – being white will work in my favour. I tell him I have a child. He says, 'Bring the boy too. Email me and visit. You will love Nigeria. It is beautiful. More beautiful than here. I will look after you.'

When we pull into Piccadilly, he stands up reluctantly. 'You will email me? You will come to Nigeria?'

'No.' I laugh. 'I have a boyfriend here, my home. I have a family.'

'I will never get over meeting you,' he insists. 'You beautiful girl that could have been my wife.'

22

I pull the car in at the edge of the communal gardens and look over at my house. It's almost midnight but the living-room light is on, which means Rhodri is awake. It's a fortnight since I saw Morton in London, and during that time I've given up my job with Athens, and moved to work on a freelance project for a local magazine where I earn ten pounds more per day. I dropped by a contact's workplace one morning and was offered the job. The hours are long, and much of the work needs to be completed in the office rather than from home. I love my new job, but it's making our household unhappy. I see less of Jack, and Rhodri says he's been asking regularly about Damien. I have no choice but to spend long days out of the house: my business venture seems increasingly impossible now the national economy is wobbly, and the bills are piling up. Rhodri has taken on some gardening, but the money goes nowhere. A woman once told me: 'When poverty comes in at the door, love flies out of the window.' I thought she was clueless, but now I see that she was speaking the truth.

To make matters worse, Margaret No. 2 has been having troubles of her own. For years she has lavished all her love and attention on Jack and me, but now Eddie is protesting that it isn't fair on their other grandchild: Damien has a three-year-old son with his present girlfriend. She has agreed that when Damien is released from prison in a few weeks' time, he will move into her house. Which means Jack won't be able to stay. And I'll have to keep my distance. More so now than ever, it feels as if Damien's world is going to collide with mine.

I climb the stairs to find Rhodri in the bath. We used to bathe together: we'd sit in candlelight telling stories to one another. He would wash my hair, soap my limbs, and twiddle his fingers between my toes. It was a tight squeeze because it was a very small bath, and Rhodri is so tall and spindly he had to bend his knees to fit into it.

'Evening,' I say, leaning over to kiss Rhodri's cheek. Tonight I will be loving and adoring, even if I feel like shooting myself. He doesn't reply. I look at him more closely. 'Is something the matter?'

'No.'

'Rhodri,' I ask again, more gently, 'talk to me.' There's something about the look on his face that makes my stomach sink. 'What's wrong?'

'I was thinking of my life without you.'

'Don't worry, I'm fine,' I soothe. 'I'm not going to die or anything.'

'I don't mean that.' Rhodri looks at me. 'I was imagining my life without you and Jack. I was imagining what it would be like if I didn't live with you and have to do all this.'

He means family stuff, the ceaseless shunting from one thing to the next and feeling like nothing ever improves. 'So you were thinking of leaving us?'

'No . . . yes . . . well, no . . . no . . . I'm not –'

Shaking, I sit on the edge of the bath. 'Rhodri, are you going to leave me?'

I don't want him to leave me. Maybe I thought I did, but I don't. I know that now. 'Don't leave me, please.'

'I'm not going to leave you.' Rhodri's hot wet hand grabs mine. 'It was a silly thing to think. It's just . . . you, Jack, working, bills – it's a lot for me.'

I know it's hard for him: before he moved in with us he lived in a squat, worked when he wanted, spent very little and enjoyed a completely different lifestyle. Maybe he should never have fallen in love with me. 'It's a lot for me too. I'm only just getting used to it and I've done it for nine years.'

'I'm not going anywhere,' he insists, drying his face on the towel.

'Promise?'

'Promise.'

Well, that's a relief.

The next day I'm running to a tight deadline again. This is the third night I've worked until almost midnight. The later I return home, the less I seem to want to walk through the door. I drive the car past our house and park by the garages. I throw my arms over the steering-wheel, my forehead touching my fingertips. 'I don't want to go home,' I say, out loud, to myself. Are these the thoughts that bother men and women who one day set off for work never to return? Do they approach the front door one fateful evening thinking, I can't live like this any more, before fleeing for ever?

'You're unhappy,' I say to myself. 'But what are you unhappy about?'

I drive back towards the house, park the car and walk along the garden path, willing this feeling to change.

'Evening,' calls Rhodri. 'You're late.'

'I'm tired. I'm going straight to bed.' I change into my do-not-undress-me pyjamas: fluffy, white, emblazoned with pink rabbits, and when Rhodri climbs in next to me I pretend to be dead with sleep.

It feels as if I've only just dropped off when I wake with a start. Jack is moaning loudly in his bedroom. I hear him getting up and stumbling across the landing, shouting, '*No no no.*' I jump out of bed and take him in my arms, then back to his bed. 'Sssh, sweetheart, sssh,' I coo.

'*No . . . no . . . no . . .*' He looks at me, terrified, his hands moving up and down my face. 'No . . . don't . . . Mum . . .'

'What is it?'

'They're all around you,' he shrieks, between sobs.

'What?'

'Lots of little balls.' He screams, backing away from me. I hold him tightly in my arms, breathing into his hair, rocking him like a baby. He cries and cries. 'They're going to get you.'

'What's going to get me, Jack?'

'The balls,' he cries. 'The little white balls that are heading for earth.'

When eventually I manage to calm him, I lie by his side, stroking his hair and shushing him softly. He drifts in and out of his nightmare. Each time I try to move from his bed, he stirs and cries. So I lie, wakeful, by his side, waiting for him to slip into a deep sleep. It's almost morning when

I return to my bed and the birds are squawking up a riot outside on the telegraph pole.

A few hours later Jack sings his way to the bathroom, sits on the toilet, pyjama bottoms around his ankles, and calls, 'Good morning, Mum,' in his usual way. He runs the tap, washes his hands, then climbs into bed with Rhodri and me.

'You had a nightmare last night, Jack. Do you remember?'

'No.'

'You were shouting and screaming. You got up out of bed and walked across the landing.'

'Did I?'

'Yes.'

'Don't you remember anything?' asks Rhodri.

Jack grips my face in his hands. 'No,' he says. 'Can we not talk about it, please? Can I watch television before school?'

Rhodri shrugs. It's all quite peculiar but I shan't push it.

'Night terrors?' suggests Rhodri.

For a change of scenery, and to give Rhodri some space, Jack and I stayed at my mother's last night. I'm longing for a break and the opportunity to relax before I go stir crazy.

'Morning,' calls my mother, as I walk across the landing. 'Getting up now?'

Not yet, I think. I *need* a lie-in. I slope back to my bedroom, hoping to huddle in bed for a little longer. When I lift up the duvet to climb in, I discover that Jack is hiding beneath it and promptly springs to life. 'Morning, Mum,' he says, pulling me to him for a kiss. 'Shall we watch television?' With that he pulls out the remote control and Saturday-morning TV blasts into the room.

Someone help me, please. I'm so exhausted I can barely peel my eyes open.

'Jack, get dressed we're going out to the shops,' calls my mother.

Thank goodness. That means I can sleep for a few more hours. I check the time on my mobile, 8.36 a.m. – far too early to do anything. Only real mums go food shopping at this time on a Saturday.

Lying there in bed, I think about my relationship with Rhodri, and how it's not looking good. I take the opportunity to compile my Love Curriculum Vitae. Should I find myself truly single again, I can post it on an Internet dating site. From the look of it, the offers will be rolling in.

Love Curriculum Vitae

Full name: Maria Lynn Claire Roberts

Age: 29

Appearance: just under 5ft 3, brown hair, stubby nose, thunder thighs.

Education: lots, but none of it proving useful.

Relationship status: cohabitant with environmental activist (open relationship, but not yet swinging).

Former relationship history: father of child, absent.

Location: a council estate, Manchester.

Estimated assets: minus £90,000 (if you include the mortgage).

Likes: champagne, good hotels, posh restaurant meals.

Dislikes: rarely being able to enjoy any of the above.

Strengths: falls in love quicker than it takes to scratch a lotto card.

Weaknesses: falls out of love in the same time it took for the Triassic period to turn into the Jurassic period. (That is, many millions of years.)

Bonus features: ample breasts, tiny waist, extra-large arse.

Additional extras: might make ideal partner for a hobbit fetishist who appreciates the shorter, dumpier, less trendy version of Cindy Crawford.

And then I fall asleep.

It's almost lunchtime when my mother and Jack return, complete with her disapproving look and a bag of pasties from the bakery down the road. I've showered and slapped on some make-up, blow-dried my hair, and slipped on the dress I wore last night. I've sprayed it with her Chanel No. 5 to make it smell nice. We sit down to eat.

'When do you go to Edinburgh?' she asks.

'In about three weeks.'

'Are you going to eat your lunch?'

I look at the pasty. 'Give me a minute,' I say. 'I haven't had breakfast yet.'

I'll be at the Edinburgh Festival for almost the entire month of August. Last week I caught a glimpse of my play at rehearsals, and it doesn't look like I imagined it. The lead female dropped out on Christian principles, the next choice turned up, then ran a mile, and the director is heavily pregnant. Now the venue managers where the play is to be staged have gone bankrupt. Everything is going wrong. If I believed in Fate, she's wagging a finger and saying, 'Do not go to Edinburgh. Stay at home.'

'Margaret [she means Margaret No. 2] is going to take Jack on holiday and then we're going to take him away with his cousins. The following week we'll come to the festival to visit you. We'll book into a hotel.'

I turn to Jack. 'That sounds exciting, doesn't it, darling?'

'Yes,' says Jack, his mouth crammed with pasty.

'Rhodri could travel in the car with us,' adds my mother.

'He's protesting at the camp for climate action at Heathrow.'

'All summer?'

'Not all summer, but he can't take time off for holidays after that.'

I'm going to be on a low income during August. Our bank accounts are overdrawn and it looks likely that the magazine project I've been working on will end in October. Maybe I shouldn't have left my job with Athens. If our financial situation doesn't improve, come November I'll have to sell my lady eggs to Americans, then a kidney, and the dodgy little toe on my right foot.

23

'Do you know how to read that?' I point to the map on Zelda's knee, laughing. I haven't seen my best friend for ages, because we've both been too wrapped up with men. 'Do you know any good jokes like "How many academics does it take to read an *A–Z*?"'

It's impressively early – well, ten o'clock, which feels early for a Saturday. It's a glorious August morning and I am outside Zelda's flat. Our suitcases are packed into the boot of the car and strewn over the back seat. Zelda is wearing a bright silk scarf, which prevents her curly hair falling into her face. Her oversized sunglasses make her look like a glamorous Hollywood starlet in search of romance, coffee and *panettone*. She climbs into the car and crosses her long slim legs so that one hangs spidery over the other.

'I have a picnic!' she says.

'Have you got your seatbelt on?'

'Just doing it.' As she reaches back for it, her bracelets jingle. She rummages in one of the bags wedged between her feet. 'We have fruit, coriander hummus, water, and lots of healthy snacks for the journey.'

'Let's go, then,' I say. 'This is going to be so great. We'll go mad in Edinburgh. It'll be like an 18–30s holiday in Ibiza, only in Scotland and nowhere near a beach, packed with the literati rather than clubbers with glo-sticks.' How thrilling! 'We'll have passionate affairs with famous writers or actors, or both at once, every day. I'm so glad you'll be with me,' I add, as we turn out of her road and head towards the motorway.

I'd expected to be alone for the summer in Edinburgh but then Zelda chucked her boyfriend, and decided last night that she'd come too. 'Forget that bastard,' I say, pausing to check that 'bastard' doesn't tip her into tears . . . No – brilliant: this is a break-up that requires lashings of feminine vitriol for the wounds to heal.

'What a bastard!' she agrees.

'Oh, he's *such* a bastard. A real twat.' Am I pushing it with that last expletive? No, we're still on safe territory: she must be well and truly mad with him.

'Fucker,' she adds.

'What an utter, utter, utter fucker,' I agree. 'You're so much better off single. You're hot and you're going to have so much fun in Edinburgh. Where are you going to stay, you crazy girl?'

'With my cousin. He's a banker and has a flat in the city overlooking the castle.'

Now, why didn't she tell me sooner that she had a cousin who's a banker with a flat opposite the castle? Tsh. Girls really should pass this kind of information on to one another.

Once in Edinburgh, we're lost.

'Maybe we should turn the map upside-down.'

Zelda turns the *A–Z* upside-down. 'We need to pass the castle,' she says. We shoot up and down the road in search of it. 'Where's your flat?'

'Murrayfield,' I say.

'If we just go down this road, we should get to it soon.' Zelda calls the landlord to say we'll be arriving in five minutes. We've just picked up the keys for the flats where the actors are staying: soft carpets, plump cushions and loads of books. Very lush. I'm hoping mine will be too.

This is far worse than I imagined. There must be a mistake. I call the theatre-company manager. No mistake.

This flat is a fleapit. It's worse than that hotel in Paddington. It's is even grottier than my house – and I thought I was slumming it there. 'I don't want to stay here,' I whisper to Zelda.

'Everything okay?' asks the landlord.

'Tremendous.'

Everything is so not okay. I open the door to my bedroom to see that the carpet is made from that nasty cord stuff, the bed is a metal monstrosity and the curtains wouldn't make it into a charity shop. Frankenstein might be happy sleeping there, but not me.

'You can come and stay with me any time,' says Zelda. 'My cousin's flat is supposed to be luxurious.'

Later when I've dropped Zelda off at her swanky retreat – which is virtually *in* the castle grounds and so swanky even the entrance hall has plush cappuccino carpet, walnut antiques and an impressive Georgian door – I unpack my case into the crappy wardrobe. Thank goodness I brought some bedding. I'd be sleeping on a bare mattress otherwise. There's nothing about the place that feels homely. And through the walls I can hear a couple having sex. I slope to the kitchen in search of food and a cup of tea. No such luck, so I slip on my shoes, and head down to the Spar beneath the flat.

When I'm back in the kitchen ten minutes later, the sex session is still banging on at full force. I try to take a nap, but find it impossible because of the constant groaning.

Exhausted, I call Rhodri. 'Hiya, it's me.'

'I know it's you.'

'How are things? When are you leaving for the protest? Have you arranged for someone to look after the rabbits?'

'I forgot about that.'

'Ask Scarlet and Philomena – they'll do it, no problem. Tell Scarlet we'll pay her five pounds a week.'

'Okay.'

'And Josie will look after the post and the plants if you give her a key.'

'You all right?'

'I think the couple next door are loved-up because they've been shagging all afternoon. And I mean *all* afternoon. You missing me?'

'You missing me?'

'Yes.'

Then Rhodri speaks softly and warmly to me, which makes me think that he does love me, after all, and instantly I miss him. When I say goodbye to him, I call Jack, who is holidaying in a caravan with Margaret No. 2, and then I'm even more homesick.

A week has gone by. My play is on in the Arctic, far, *far* away from all the fun in town. Only teetotal depressives make it to this end of the city because there ain't no action, and there ain't no pubs either. The set doesn't fit the stage, and neither does the cast. Thankfully, Zelda has been nursing me with red wine in the Traverse Theatre bar, where I've developed a crush on the security woman, who gazes upon me with pity. Meanwhile actors have been hitting on Zelda.

I've also discovered that it's not a loved-up couple on the other side of my bedroom wall but a sauna-and-massage parlour so 'saunas and massages' noisily take place at all hours of the day. Last night, tortured by lack of sleep, I shared Zelda's bed at her cousin's luxury flat. Sleeping with a girl is so much nicer than it is with a sweaty hairy man. Zelda is so scented and floral – everything she has is dainty and pretty and sparkly.

Tonight Zelda is going out with some academics she met at a conference, but luckily I have plans, too, because Morton called to say that he's at the Edinburgh International Film Festival for a few days. This evening we're going to meet for a quick drink. He's flying here from London. I wonder if he'll have to charge past Rhodri and other protesters at the airport. I put some bacon under the grill for a sandwich, then strip off and plunge into the bath. By the time I'm ready for my evening out dinner will be ready.

Stepping out of the bath, I pull the plug, grab a towel and make my way to my bedroom. The humping from the sauna-and-massage parlour is drawing to a climax so I play some music on my laptop to drown the grunts and moans, then kick my feet up onto the bed and take deep breaths. Apparently a bath followed by a serene rest is equivalent to an expensive hydrotherapy treatment at a spa.

I'm just beginning to relax when a smoke alarm shrieks.

I leap up and run into the hall in my towel, remember the bacon and pull it out from under the grill. Then I try to spot where the smoke alarm is: the ceiling is the obvious place – but even if I stood on a chair I couldn't reach it. I hunt for a ladder and find one in a cupboard the size of a morgue. I haul it out into the kitchen, wobble up and switch the alarm off – only to be startled by the scream of another from the hall. I drag the ladder there and switch that one off too – only to hear the scream of a third, this time from the bedroom.

Silence, thank God for that. I breathe a sigh of relief – only for all three to strike up again. I run through the flat on a mission to open as many windows as possible but someone bangs aggressively on the door. 'The alarms are going off,' a woman yells.

No shit, Sherlock. 'I'm dealing with it,' I call back. 'Sorry.'

She bangs the door harder. 'They've been going off for twenty minutes.'

'I know, I'm sorry, I'm trying to turn them off. They'll stop soon, I promise.'

The only way to do this quickly is to shed the towel. It's holding me back. Naked, I run from room to room, climbing the ladder, pressing the button, climbing down, running to the next, but the bloody things will not stop. I use the towel to waft smoke out of the window.

The woman returns and bangs on the door harder. 'The alarms are still going off!'

I look through the spy-hole on the door. I can't see her. 'I really am very sorry.'

'Do you need any help?'

'No, I think I'm Okay,' I call, flapping the towel beneath the smoke alarm in the hall. It stops, as do the others.

'Are you sure you don't need any help?'

'It's under control.'

I hold my breath, waiting for one or another to start up again. But they don't. Eventually the woman walks off. She must think me a lost cause – what kind of lunatic refuses to open the door? My heart is pounding so hard that I feel sick.

Some half-hour later I'm dressed to meet Morton, but after all that dashing around I am a nervous ruddy mess, not clean and glowing as I'd hoped to be. I begin to pack my bag for the evening: lipgloss, a map of Edinburgh, purse, hairbrush . . .

Now someone else is knocking on the door.

'Excuse me,' a man shouts through the letterbox. 'Excuse me.' He bangs again. 'Excuse me.'

I peer through the spy-hole. He leans against the wall: nice hair, good clothes, smart, but nevertheless a potential rapist. I creep away from the door, suddenly cold with fear. I cup my hand over my mouth and nose so that he can't hear me breathe.

'Can you open the door? I'd like to speak with you.' He raps the letterbox so hard I jump and shake with terror. 'I know you're in there.'

I creep down the hallway and slump onto the floor, listening to his relentless shouts. If I hold my breath and close my eyes, he might just go away.

'We live in the flat beneath you,' he calls through the letterbox. 'There's water pouring into our kitchen. When you're able, please come down and speak with us.'

When he's gone I flop my head between my knees and cry: this is ridiculous, *I am ridiculous*. What kind of woman would hide, rather than answer the door?

It's past seven when I meet Morton. He's waiting for me in the Traverse Bar, two glasses of white wine on the table. He looks professional, like an old and clever doctor. I climb up onto the stool, and as we talk I swing my legs, causing the stool to pivot from side to side. His voice seems to boom loud and deep amid the general chatter. I'd like to catch him between my legs, pull him to me and kiss him. But just as I reach out with them he introduces me to a spectacled and jolly colleague, and they dive head first into some discussion about politics.

We drink up quickly, then head outdoors. Morton has a meeting at eight, so I walk with him through throngs of people handing out flyers. We stride past the tents at the book festival, and past bars spilled out onto the pavements, their tables filled with animated ladies sharing bottles of wine and talking about literature.

'I stop here,' he says, gesturing to a grand building.

'Five more minutes?' I ask.

'Tomorrow,' he says, 'we'll catch a play. Meet me at six.'

He grins hopefully, so I pull his shirt collar until his face is close to mine. Teasingly I bite his ear. 'I'll see you tomorrow, then.'

As I walk the long road to Murrayfield I place my daily call to Jack. 'Hello, darling. What are you doing?'

'I'm still on holiday,' he shrills. 'No, Granddad, *stop it – stop it . . .*' He laughs. 'And we've been shopping and I bought some new games and I made some friends and Nana's making dinner and . . .'

'Sounds like you're having lots of fun.'

'I *am*. You wanna speak to Nana?' He hands the phone to my mother.

'You eating okay?'

'Yes.'

'We'll be with you at the weekend. Jack says he isn't missing you but I think he is because he falls quiet from time to time.'

'I just want to come home now,' I say. 'This is too long to be away from him.' The hours are so torture and the pressure of promoting my own play, which no one wants to watch and is located in Festival Arctic, is surely on a par with being locked in a cupboard with a spider if you're an arachnophobe. If it weren't for Zelda, I'd have offered myself to the Edinburgh Tattoo as a human cannonball.

Thank goodness I'm seeing her later.

I drop into the venue on my way to see how many tickets have been sold for this evening's performance. Hmph . . . not a lot.

'I have something here for you,' says the girl at the desk. 'At least, I think it's for you.'

I see the most enormous bunch of flowers. And an elegantly wrapped box. I hope they're for me.

The girl hands me the bouquet. 'I wish someone'd send me flowers like this.' She grins.

Who loves me so much that they'd go to all the trouble of sending me such an expensive display of my favourite lilies?

It's a struggle carrying the bouquet more than a mile to

my dismal flat, then heaving it up the endless flights of cold stone stairs. I set it down so the weight of the water in their wrapping makes them stand upright. I open the box of chocolates and pop one into my mouth. I don't recognize the writing. It's a small card. To prolong the surprise, I hold the envelope up to the sunlight at the window and try to deduce who it might be from.

Rhodri would never send me flowers. He might grow something for me from seed, or plant a tree, but he would never send me a bunch of flowers: the carbon footprint is simply too great. Not to mention the overuse of pesticides and cheap labour.

Morton. He may have been stricken with love for me last night.

Toga. Perhaps he feels bad that he visited Edinburgh the week before I arrived, and never did take me to the Hilton.

Or someone totally random who has simply taken a fancy to me.

I open the card . . .

. . . the flowers are from my mother.

I dial her number again. 'Thanks, Mum. They're great . . . Not too big . . . No . . . It was a lovely thought. I have them in my bedroom . . . Yes, I'm enjoying a chocolate right now.' I put another into my mouth and suck it appreciatively. 'Mm, delicious. I'll eat them all and get fat.' My mother chuckles. 'It was a beautiful thought and cheered me up no end. Thank you.'

'I thought it would. Well, you take care, love. See you at the weekend.'

*

'George made dinner,' proclaims Zelda, proudly. I'm seated with Zelda, her cousin George and his economist friend John around the dining table at George's flat. Outside, fireworks at the Edinburgh Tattoo are bursting, whiz, pop, bang, above the castle. I'm weary after my night with Morton. He took me for dinner at a chic little restaurant in Grassmarket. Now, from my own experience, I wholly believe that oysters are indeed an aphrodisiac.

'This looks fab,' I say to George. 'Thanks for having me over. I was in need of some home comforts.'

'No problem,' he says. 'You're welcome.'

'And thanks for all your kindness while I've been here. It's very good of you.' George has taken me under his wing, as he has Zelda. Right now, my dresses are in his washing machine, and my bras and pants are drying on his radiator.

George talks about his work at the bank. 'But I'm leaving for Afghanistan soon,' he adds.

'Why?'

'With the Territorial Army,' explains Zelda. 'George will be leaving his job as a banker for the army.'

Then the doorbell rings: a sergeant major in full uniform has dropped by for a cup of tea.

I think of Rhodri. He'll be at Heathrow, campaigning with the other activists and attending workshops, talking about direct action, like anti-war, anti-globalization, anti-cheap-airline protests, and here I am, a traitor in his midst, drinking imported wine with a soldier, a banker and an economist.

*

By the time Jack arrives with my mother at the weekend, I'm shaking with exhaustion. I see them waiting for me at a picnic bench in their hotel garden. I take a seat next to Jack, kiss him hello, hug him tightly and listen to his tales about his holiday, then retreat to the toilets to cry. I'm washing my face with cold water when my father rings. 'Hello, petal,' he says. 'Everything okay? I just wanted to warn you – now don't get upset about this – but I went to your house yesterday to see how Rhodri is getting on. You probably wanted to return and find everything tidy and nice . . .'

'Is it that bad?'

'I think so, yes.'

'It might not be when I get back.'

'I'll see if Eleanor and I can get over there this weekend and sort it out, but we might not have time. I'm sorry, darling, but the house is a mess.'

I've just put my phone away and am brushing my hair, preparing to head back outdoors to Jack, when Toga calls.

'I can't talk right now,' I say.

'Are you still with Rhodri?' he asks.

'Yes. Why?'

'I need to see you,' he says. 'Soon.'

Why does he need to see me? He won't tell me over the telephone. Then it dawns on me that maybe Toga is in love with me and, in that brief moment, it feels as if my life is about to change.

24

Three weeks have passed, the September school term has started, and already my jaunt to the Edinburgh Festival seems a lifetime ago. My father was right. I returned to find the house upside-down. Rhodri is so fired up with activism from spending summer at the camp, that I have secured my position as Environmental Enemy No. 1. Toga has called a number of times, suggesting weekends when he might visit, but the timing just doesn't seem right: pulling my family back together needs to be my top priority.

It's Jack's birthday today. He is nine. I'm skint. Last month the mortgage wasn't paid, and some of the cheques for the bills bounced. This month I need to pay out twice the amount of money. Some of my freelance projects have come to an abrupt end. I have to find more work, which means toiling for longer hours, which means Jack and Rhodri will be even more despairing with me. Today as I scrub and clean the house with some sort of vegetable derivative in preparation for Jack's party, I'm once again plotting how to put my top-secret business idea into action. I'm also wondering if I should file for bankruptcy and live in the car. If I did, all this would end. I want to drop into a coma. If I were in a coma, someone else would handle my worries. Then I could wake up and start my life over again.

Is it so wrong for me to want nice things for Jack? I

didn't drag myself through university to exist like this. Someone somewhere in government promised me a graduate lifestyle with a professional income. Toga may be a metrosexual and spend more time in front of the mirror than I do, but he has a career, he is solvent, and therefore not an altogether appalling father figure for Jack.

By evening thoughts of Toga have been cast aside and Rhodri and I are putting on an Oscar-winning show of togetherness. Despite our squabbles, splintered lives and fractious relationship, he and I are gallant and loving when in company. We snuggle close to one another on the sofa and watch Jack regale the party with endless impressions of me dancing and talking.

'Would you like a cup of *tea*?' Rhodri mimics me to my mother, which starts him laughing and snorting. Then Jack mimics how Rhodri runs, and I mimic Jack. It's a funny old hootenanny. A couple of glasses of wine later, I threaten a rendition of the Welsh saucepan song and Rhodri threatens to sing the Welsh national anthem.

Last year we had a free party for Jack and his friends at a family funday arranged by a theatre in Manchester. This year we're having a simple get-together at our house. Right now our family is packed into our tiny living room, lined up on chairs like passengers at the back of a bus. I've bought Jack a digital camera. It wasn't an expensive one, but I'm sure he'll love it.

Well, that is until he opens his present from Margaret No. 2, a computer, and then his present from my mother and Rufus, a Motorola Razr mobile phone. Rhodri, who has been thoroughly helpful all evening, handing out food, drink, tea, coffee, biscuits, and joking along in his lovable way, gives me a look, which I translate as 'We'll talk about this later.'

Now there are more mobile phones and computers in our house than there are people. I could start an empire to rival eBay and sell off all the cast-offs we've accumulated from strangers' skips.

Margaret is the last to leave. She stalls in the doorway to rifle through her bag, then pulls out a card. 'For Jack, from Damien. I didn't want to hand it to him earlier in case it upset him. I don't know what you want to do with it.' She tells me that Damien is just out of prison and is staying with her for a few weeks until he gets a job, so we mustn't call round to her house. She says that he has asked if I will meet him to talk about his having contact with Jack. She has seen him playing with his other son, and she really thinks he's trying to be a good dad. But the answer is no: it doesn't seem to me that Damien has changed. Maybe I'll regret this decision in the future, but right now it seems the best thing to do.

'I'll have to give the card to Jack,' I say. 'I can't not.'

When all the guests have left, with party cake wrapped in tissue, and we've cleared the room, I go upstairs to see if Jack has fallen asleep. 'Jack,' I whisper. 'Jack?'

'Hello, Mummy. Get into bed with me. Give me a hug.'

'Have you had a good day?'

'Oh, yes.' He hooks his arms around me, pulling me down until I'm lying next to him.

'I have something for you,' I say, taking the bright yellow envelope from my pocket. 'I think it's from your dad.'

Jack sits up, takes it from me and tears it open quickly. Three ten-pound notes fall onto his lap. He doesn't pick them up. He reads the message:

Happy Birthday, Son
Here is my telephone number, call me when you want.
Love Daddy
xxx

'Can I call him?' asks Jack. 'Can I call him? He's given me his number . . . Mum, can I call him now?' He's already leaping out from beneath his duvet.

'Calm down, Jack. Not now. Let me take the card and put it up for you on the bookshelf with the others.'

Reluctantly he hands it to me. 'Can I call him tomorrow?'

'I'll have to think about that. Can we talk about it in the morning?'

'Okay,' says Jack, turning away from me and kneading his head into the pillow.

'Good night, darling.'

'Night,' he says darkly.

'So what are you going to do?' asks Rhodri, one arm slung heavily over my shoulders as I lean into him on the sofa.

'Damien shouldn't have written his telephone number in there. He's put me in a very difficult position.'

'Are you going to let Jack call him?'

I stand up and slot the card between some books on the shelves. 'I just can't,' I say to Rhodri. 'I'll explain to Jack.'

'I think you're doing the right thing.'

'He was in prison. How do I know that won't happen again? Jack will meet him only to lose him.'

The following morning Jack chatters all the way to school about the card.

I say, 'We'll discuss it tonight.'

'And you know where it is?'

'Yes.'

I return home to enter into a debate with Rhodri about the Motorola mobile phone. 'Jack should not use a mobile phone. He's too young and it will damage his ears.'

'Well, what am I supposed to do? Take that away from him too?'

'Yes. For his health. You specifically said, "No mobile phone," and they bought him a mobile phone. It's not just dangerous for his health, he might get mugged. He's got a better mobile phone than you. Tell your mother to take it back.'

'Rhodri, I can't argue with the whole world.' Some battles you just have to lose. That's my opinion. Sometimes it's better to accept defeat before you even begin.

'I cannot agree to Jack having a mobile phone.'

When Rhodri makes a point, there's no shifting him.

'Okay,' I relent. Because I think he's right. We specifically said, 'No mobile phone for Jack.' So Rhodri places the mobile phone still in its unopened box at the top of the bookshelves out of sight.

When Jack is doing his homework he asks, 'Where's the card? Where's the mobile phone?'

I explain that, because I love him, I've had to make some tough decisions.

He says, 'Yesterday I had the best birthday ever. Today it's the worst birthday ever,' then stomps up the stairs, slamming his bedroom door behind him.

He sulks for hours. I enter his room, he ignores me and continues to watch television. I switch the television off. He scowls at me. 'Jack,' I begin. 'Don't be angry with me for protecting you, please. Nothing's changed, has it? I said no to a mobile phone, I said no to your dad. I'm afraid they're both still a no. I'm not going to change my mind. I'm sorry.'

'*I know, I know,*' he says. 'Okay.'

'All right?'

'Yes,' he relents, 'all right.'

And, thankfully, that seems to be the end of it.

September passes and October arrives. It's like harvest festival in our house. I should invest in a smock and a harmonica. Pumpkins, knobbly green squashes and bunches of garlic clutter the kitchen worktops and windowsill. I have scoured recipe books for soup and stew ideas, and catalogues for storage solutions. Despite his insistence that he'll visit soon, Toga is yet to arrive in Manchester to 'talk'. I really don't see why we can't 'talk' on the telephone. He must want to talk to me about serious stuff . . . like a marriage proposal.

Unusually, my father has temporarily been hit with the generosity stick: he has invited us out for a Sunday meal with Eleanor and her son Luke. It's Eleanor's birthday so the extravagance starts now. One year my father bought her a toolkit, and the next, an anorak. Perhaps this year he'll really push the boat out and buy her a cordless drill.

I'm surprised my father has offered to pay because on a weekly basis he sets himself a challenge. 'Look,' he'll say on a Sunday evening, opening his wallet and showing me the contents, 'I have one ten-pound note in my wallet and I'm going to keep it there until next Sunday. Just you see.'

To which my exasperated stepmother, Eleanor, says, 'Yes, but you'll just spend my money instead, won't you, Trevor? Won't you?'

Rhodri has gone off to a squat party in Liverpool. He said he'd be home for the meal, but it's gone two o'clock and he still isn't back yet.

'I'm sorry,' I say to Eleanor, 'I don't know where he is and I can't call him to find out. We should order.'

She tilts her head sympathetically and smiles. 'It doesn't matter. Just the five of us, then. What are you having, Jack?'

We leave the restaurant at around four. Jack seems tired so I send him to bed for a quick nap – he hasn't had an afternoon snooze since he was a toddler. Rhodri called half an hour ago to say that he's waiting for someone to give him a lift to Manchester from Liverpool. I'm furious with him for letting me down so spectacularly.

It's just after Rhodri gets home that Jack begins sobbing. Over the past few weeks his night terrors have escalated. I barely drop off to sleep before he's shouting for me. He dreams about something attacking me, or the world ending. Right now he's sitting upright in bed shrieking with terror and staring at me as if I'm covered with wasps. I sit next to him holding his hand, which is cold and clammy. I try to make him laugh. He stares at my face, screaming and shouting. When he looks out of the window he says he can see white balls falling from the sky destroying the earth. I ask him to draw me a picture, which he does, but then he drops the pencil and again begins to cry. I give him a spoon of Calpol and hope it will work, but it doesn't. Almost an hour later Jack's breathing has become panicked.

I call NHS Direct, and on their advice we rush Jack to the out-of-hours doctor, then to the hospital. By the time we arrive at A and E, Jack is hallucinating and verging on delirium. We stay the night. Blood tests are carried out. The next morning a young doctor declares Jack a healthy boy and we are discharged, but he is to have a brain scan. A letter will follow, with the appointment.

I'm worried that all this talk of the planet ending, not to mention the memories of Damien, are causing Jack's nightmares. If they are, then something is going to have to change – and fast.

25

Despite our rapprochement since Jack's birthday, Rhodri and I still aren't on loving terms. We have moments when we're tender with each other, but they're becoming rare. Maybe I am paranoid, but Rhodri is grumpy. And he's been acting suspiciously this past month. He's always checking his email account, has started taking unexpected walks in the evening, and is generally very distracted. I have a strong feeling that he's keeping something from me. Maybe he had a summer romance at the camp. If he did, then I'm surprised he hasn't mentioned it because Rhodri is a completely honest person. He wouldn't see the value of keeping quiet about something like a fleeting infidelity.

A few months ago he returned from work and said casually, while spreading peanut butter on a Ryvita, 'There's a really nice girl at work. She's in her early twenties, I think I might ask her on a date.'

And I said: 'You're kidding me, right?' I couldn't deal with him dating someone younger than me: that would be like a slap in the face.

And Rhodri said, 'No, I'm not kidding you. I think she likes me. I might just ask her out. What's wrong with that?'

'Because I don't want you to start *dating* someone. What am I supposed to say if you tell me that you're going off on a *date* one night? "You look nice, darling. Have a good time?"'

'Well, yes. I suppose so.'

'No-no-no-no-NO!'

'Who are you to talk?'

'She'll fall in love with you. And she'll be heartbroken because you're in a relationship with me. She'll feel all lonely.' I'm speaking from experience here.

'I might or might not ask her out.'

'If you do, don't expect me to be sorted about it. I always said, "Just because you can handle the thought of me being with someone else, don't expect me to be so magnanimous."'

'Maria, it'll happen one day. That's what we discussed. That's what we agreed. When it happens, you'll have to deal with it.'

'I'm warning you in advance,' I explained. 'I'll probably get jealous about it. That's the way I am. You're obviously a far better person than me.'

That's why I think it's unlikely he'd keep the news to himself that something's going on, but I'll ask him when he returns this evening.

It's after six when Rhodri returns from a gardening job. He heads straight for the computer to check his email.

'Would you like a cup of tea?'

'Hmm?'

'Tea?'

'Yeah, yeah.'

'Hungry?'

'Hmm?'

'Rhodri, did you have a romance at the Camp for Climate Action?'

'No, Darren did, though. [Darren is his Welsh friend.] There were these girls who came into the tent, and we were drinking cider, and I thought I might, but then I didn't.'

The morning I left for Edinburgh, Rhodri kissed me fondly and said, 'Have a safe journey, have a good time, and don't come back pregnant because I'm not going to look after any more of your illegitimate children.' It was supposed to be a joke, but I didn't find it very funny.

I wonder how many couples across the UK have ridiculous casual conversations like ours over rooibos tea: 'Have you had a good day, husband? Think about shagging any of your colleagues today? No? Why not? That is a shame. Better luck tomorrow.' It's absolutely insane – I live this life, and even I can see the lunacy in it.

'I didn't really fancy the one I was talking to. If I'm not interested in the girl, and if I don't really like her, I don't see the point.'

Well, that's okay, then.

Rhodri's mysterious behaviour has continued all week. Which makes me wonder whether he's telling the truth, after all. Last night he shouted out another woman's name, Fiona, in his sleep. I'm going to try to be the most wonderful girlfriend possible again because I don't want Rhodri to leave me for this Fiona woman. I now see the error of my ways. I'm sorry. I'll even turn vegan, if that's what it takes to keep my man.

To prove how sincere I am about saving this relationship,

I've even promised Rhodri that this weekend I'll join him in his activities. Tonight we're going on a date of Rhodri's choice. We'll be attending the launch of works by 'an underground collective of artists' exhibiting in an abandoned warehouse. An evening with the future Emins and Hirsts of the art world, a couple of glasses of wine and merriment. It all sounds good to me.

Come the end of the afternoon, I feel very tired. This morning I dragged Jack around a market, trying to figure out how to feed the three of us for a week on just twenty pounds. I think we'll have to do without tea and coffee. They're too much of a luxury. We'll have to drink water. I'm not sure we can even afford to drink concentrated juice. Now my head hurts from the worry of balancing a food budget with complex vegan recipes.

'I don't want to go out, I'm too tired,' I tell Rhodri, as I flop onto the sofa.

'There's a surprise,' he says.

'What do you mean by that?'

'You never want to go where I want to go.'

One last shot, I tell myself. That's all our relationship needs. I lumber off the sofa and change into my best art-loving clothes. Quick glance in the mirror: yes, I look French peasant, *circa* 1930s, good hat, good dress, good shoes, now just a lick of red lipstick . . . there, all done.

'Will it be full of hippies?' I ask, as we walk to the tram station.

Jack interrupts: 'Mum don't be racist against hippies.'

'No,' says Rhodri, bursting with pride that Jack is on his side. 'It will be full of different people.'

'Will I stick out?'

'No.'

'Will they all be wearing funny clothes?'

'No. It will be full of normal people.'

At the station I spot an old schoolfriend. Next to my French peasant get-up, she looks like an *über*-groovy Ibiza chick. 'Hiya,' she beams, 'where are you off to?'

'A warehouse.'

'You going to the Warehouse Project?' She's giddy with the idea that I'm going to a famous club night. *As if* I'm as cool as she is. *As if.*

'No, we're going to a warehouse to look at some art.'

'Very cultural.' She disappears back to her friends, her long blonde hair flapping behind her.

In the warehouse I look around me with horror. I stare hard at Rhodri. 'What is this?' I croak.

'A squat party! Great, isn't it?'

This is so not great. Oh, this is so not great.

'Come on. I've got some pens, let's draw on the walls,' says Rhodri, collecting a bunch of markers and indicating to me where people have created their own graffiti art. 'Or you can help yourself to that.' He points to a pile of junk, comprising broken mirrors, pictures, ornaments and a big sign declaring, 'Take Me.'

I feel like that: TAKE ME AWAY. NOW.

Rhodri and Jack are scribbling happily on the walls. What I am supposed to do? Join in. That's what I promised Rhodri I would do. I look around for something sane to keep me occupied. In the corner people are juggling for the pleasure of it. Over in the café area trees have been planted in old toilets, and . . . oh, my Lord, what's that? What have the other 'art exhibition' attendees drawn on the walls?

There's an enormous cartoon sketch featuring a meat-eater and a cow, and a story about how meat-eaters are *bad, bad* murderers. I hide my red-leather gloves in my red-leather bag, and hope that no one will notice my red-leather shoes. I'm wearing a cardigan from the high street. I would have felt less exposed if I'd turned up naked.

Rhodri and Jack have disappeared. I scan the warehouse for them and locate Rhodri on a chair, scribbling high up on a stone pillar. What's that I hear? It can't be. *It is.* Someone in the far corner is beating a tambourine. Please don't let this be true. Then the chanting begins. Chanting and yoga on a Saturday night in Hulme.

I will not give up. I'm going to participate if it kills me. I can't say I don't like this world if I've never tried to enter it. I wander to another corner to spy on a group of women chatting on a couple of battered sofas. Please don't be knitting, I think. But they are *finger-knitting* woolly hats. They're wearing purple, have messy hair, facial piercings and are *finger-knitting* woolly hats.

A couple of adults race past me on a Little Tykes coupé car. Get off the toddler truck, I want to yell. You're grown-ups!

I take a deep breath and sit down with the ladies. I pick up a wire hanger, and some orange wool. 'Have you any feathers for a dreamcatcher?' I ask the group.

'Well, we don't,' one woman answers kindly, 'because these are *vegan* dreamcatchers. But I can show you how to make a tassel out of wool?'

But wool comes from an animal. Are these women crazy? WOOL comes from an ANIMAL.

The chanting in the corner is getting on my nerves and that tambourine needs whacking over someone's head. I catch sight of a thin man standing on a mat spinning glass balls in one hand. The walls are hung with enormous photographic prints of protests: it would fair to say that these people are not the greatest fans of the British police force.

I make my excuses and dash to the toilet. A man follows me in to have a conversation about how they plumbed in the water supply. 'I'm sorry,' I say, 'but can we finish this later? I really need to wee.' I close the door on him. The toilet floor is *disgusting*. My patent ballet pumps are soaked in urine.

When I eventually find Rhodri, he and Jack are having great fun dipping their hands into paint and leaving prints on a long strip of rolled-out wallpaper. 'I need to leave now,' I say

'Not yet,' replies Rhodri. 'In a while.'

'I need to leave now.'

'You're so racist against hippies.' Jack grunts, after we leave the warehouse. 'I was having a good time.'

We wait for the tram at G-Mex. The Hilton Hotel towers above us. That's where I want to be, I think, in the bar up there, sipping cocktails and looking out across the city, loving life and looking forward to the future.

It's Sunday afternoon and Rhodri is sitting on the big leather armchair, sewing a sock for his scythe. He uses it on the allotment because fuel-powered strimmers pollute the environment.

I say, 'I'm going to get new curtains for winter. Thick ones for the bedroom. We didn't replace the window last year. It's draughty now.'

Rhodri looks up. 'I'll find you a sewing machine and you can run some up. You could get the material from a charity shop.'

'Rhodri, love, I don't have any free time to make curtains.'

'I don't agree with you buying new things for the house.'

I love this man, he's a good man, but I'm starting to think that we're never going to work. I feel like I can't do 'us' any more. I'm so weary with the pressure to be eco-perfect that I constantly feel a failure. It's my house, I think. It's my house. And I don't even have the liberty to decide to buy curtains or choose which washing powder I want to use.

Then, just when things seem like they can't get any worse, Toga calls again. And Morton texts to say that he'll be passing through Manchester tomorrow. I make arrangements to meet Morton for an hour in a bar on Canal Street, then wave him off at the station when he gets on his train to London.

26

During the week, Rhodri took up a one-man crusade at a shopping mall handing out homemade leaflets on climate change. If only he'd use his free time to look for more gardening work, I wouldn't feel like my innards are about to fall out. Today I received an email from the magazine project explaining that at the end of the month there will be no freelance opportunities, so I'll lose my main source of income. By the time the bills come in during November, we'll be on red alert. Oh, shit. What if Jack and I end up homeless again?

I'm watching *Coronation Street* but not really concentrating because I'm panic-stricken. Jack is running around the garden trying to catch the rabbits. We need a new hutch. They're eating their way out of that one.

'Come into the hallway,' says Rhodri. As I'm functioning on autopilot, I oblige.

'Sit down.' He points to a step.

'Why are we whispering on the stairs?'

'The telephone might be tapped.'

'What would it be tapped for? How can they hear when we're not even on the phone?'

'They just might. Look, I'm staying over at Fiona's tonight.'

'Fiona? That's the name you called in your sleep. You

can't just tell me you're going to stay the night at this woman's house and then leave.'

'It's not like that. Other people will be there.'

What is it, a free-love house? 'What's going on?'

'I can't tell you.'

'I'm your girlfriend, of course you can tell me.'

'You'll find out tomorrow. We're going to be involved in some direct action.'

'Rhodri, please think about this. Don't get arrested. How will we cope if you go to prison?'

'It's a risk I'm prepared to take. Climate change is a very real threat.'

'I *know* that. But what about our world?' If Rhodri goes to prison, I may just fall apart. On the other hand, I'll have plenty in common with my neighbours, whose boyfriends are in and out of clink. 'What is it you're going to do?'

'I can't tell you.' Rhodri lifts up his bag and swings it on to his shoulders, then zips up his waterproof, kisses my cheek and heads off.

He thinks I'm one of them, doesn't he? The people opposing his beliefs. The wrongdoers. The enemy.

The next morning I think, Sod it. It's absolutely freezing and Rhodri isn't around so we'll drive to school rather than cycle. We come to an abrupt stop in a traffic jam. Half an hour later we've moved three centimetres. If only we'd cycled, we'd have been there by now. Jack fiddles with the knob on the radio. At nine o'clock the news begins with a report that 'A group of protesters are blockading domestic flights at Manchester Airport and have locked themselves together at the check-in desks.'

'I bet that's Rhodri!' says Jack.

'I bet it is.' I laugh.

At work I search the Internet for more information.

Rhodri has been locked to Fiona and the other protesters for hours. Already I'm jealous – it's been months since he used handcuffs on me.

On my coffee break, I call Zelda. 'That Fiona may not be as hot as you,' she says, 'but they have common ground, and before you know it, ethics will win the day.'

By lunchtime Rhodri's face is on newsreels and websites. It's just after six o'clock when my father calls. 'We've just seen Rhodri on ITV,' he says. 'I'd recognize that bearded face anywhere.'

Thankfully, Rhodri wasn't arrested. Instead, due to all the media coverage, he's something of a regional celebrity. The next evening we sit in Cornerhouse drinking wine with Zelda – she saw Rhodri on the news too and lavishes praise on him.

'I'm very proud of you,' I say to Rhodri, 'and what you do. But I don't agree with it. By targeting the budget airlines you're creating problems for the poor. Pick on the rich. Protest against them. Don't alienate people who can't afford to travel any other way.'

By the time we head out onto Oxford Road I'm drunk, and Rhodri and I are arguing. I think I'm right; he thinks he's right. I say, 'I'm sick of you sneering at me because I'm a single mother.'

He says, 'I've never sneered at you. How can you say that?'

I say: 'You and your middle-class ways. Living poor like this is a choice for you. You can choose not to live like this. But for me and Jack it isn't a choice. I didn't struggle through university when I was homeless in that refuge to spend my life on a council estate. I want more, Rhodri.'

'How can you say I sneered at you for being a single mother?' he says again. 'When I moved to Manchester to *be with* you and Jack?'

'I think you have. Nothing I do is ever good enough. You talk to me as though I'm stupid. Everything I do is wrong. And I'm sick of it.'

Rhodri says, 'You can make your own way home.' He leaves me opposite the Palace Theatre and heads off in the opposite direction to catch a bus.

I arrive back at the house before Rhodri and lock the door behind me. I grab all his clothes from the wardrobe and throw them on to the living-room floor. Then I go upstairs to lie on the bed and wait for him to return so that we can finish the argument.

By the time I realize I've been asleep it's too late. It's dawn. I left the key in the door all night and Rhodri couldn't get into the house. There's no sign of him. I take the key out of the door and head back to bed. He has a pager for work so I call it. I have to send him my apologies through a stranger.

Approximately five a.m.
Man: Can I take your message?
Me: Where are you? Can you come back now?
Man: So that's 'Where are you? Can you come back now?'
Me: That's correct.

Approximately five forty-five a.m.

Man: Can I take your message, please?

Me: I really am very sorry. Call me.

Man: So that's 'I really am very sorry. Call me'?

Me: That's correct.

Approximately six thirty a.m.

Man: Can I take your message?

Me: I am very, very sorry. Call me, please.

Man: So that's 'I am very, very sorry. Call me, please'?

Me: That's correct.

Approximately ten thirty a.m.

Woman: Can I take your message?

Me: I am very, very sorry. It was a petulant prank that went too far. Please call me. Please.

Woman: So that's 'I am very, very sorry. It was a petulant prank that went too far. Please call me. Please'?

Me: That's correct.

Rhodri returns just after lunchtime. 'Hello,' he says gruffly. I know he's annoyed with me for locking him out of the house, which was wrong, but then I fell asleep and it ended up being more wrong than I intended because he had to sleep in the shed for five hours.

I leap into my apology straight away but Rhodri won't forgive me.

'I genuinely am really very sorry,' I say, over and over again, but Rhodri just shakes his head.

He gathers his things. 'I'm going to stay with my friend Aiden for a few days. I'll speak with you next week.'

*

Alone throughout the day, minus the eco-warrior, my thoughts are: I didn't see that coming. (What am I? Stupid?) Followed by: I'm slicing up steak in my kitchen. In the house I own. I don't feel guilty. My God, I feel free. This is brilliant! Then: There's nothing for it but to be like Rhodri. Love is love, and if that's what it takes to keep my man, I won't wash and I'll go hippie. I slice more steak with a shiny sharp knife. Heaven above, it looks delicious. What I need is an omnivorous man: a man who loves meat and would roast a leg of lamb for me with his strong hands and then serve it up on a rosemary-scented platter.

I plop handfuls of carrots into a saucepan. I need to keep quiet and agree with Rhodri on everything. Conflict is not a girl's best friend. I add some *petits pois*, also known as peas. I can use beauty products again – without the lecture. Anti-ageing creams, deodorant, perfume, yes, perfume. I'll buy myself a bottle of the most fake-smelling expensive concoction I can get my hands on. And bath salts. And make-up!

I slide Yorkshire puddings into the oven. Jack saunters in. 'Is there anything I can help you with?' he asks. Sweet boy. He's salivating at the thought of a meat and gravy dish.

'No, thanks, love, you watch *Top Gear*, if you like,' I say, closing the kitchen door. If Rhodri were here, Jack would have to watch *Top Gear* in another room.

I'm so alone! I cannot manage the house on my own! Who will do the composting? I can't compost!

I stand on my tiptoes to get the plates out of the cupboard: Rhodri usually does this for me. Rhodri is tall. And I, I am small.

I may be small but I can compost. I'm Superwoman and I can compost. I, Superwoman, can achieve anything. I'm going to start that business. I'm going to be a better person. I'm going to succeed.

I look out of the window. It's almost dark and I'm scared of the dark. Rhodri isn't coming back. His bike isn't going to squeak down the path. The gate isn't going to slam shut. Rhodri is not going to walk back through those patio doors until next week.

On Monday, Rhodri returns with his dirty washing. A tent hangs over the banister. He must have been camping. I head out of the door with Jack and an overnight bag. 'Where are you going?' he calls after me.

'To review a show.'

'I thought we were going to talk.'

'We were "going to talk" yesterday.'

'Where are you staying?'

'At my mother's,' I say, on the brink of tears. 'You didn't call all weekend.'

'You didn't call me.'

'You don't have a phone. I have two.'

'I have a pager.'

'I did page.'

'I didn't get it.'

'I can't talk to you through a pager.'

At home the next evening, Rhodri and I are still barely on speaking terms with one another. I want to say something significant to get our relationship back on track, but I can't muster the words or the enthusiasm. Then, before I can stop myself, I gabble, 'I can't go through another Christmas like last year, I'm dreading it.'

He tells me that he can't either, and that he still feels the same about climate change. I'd stand a better chance of winning my man over if I was competing against another woman – but as it is me versus an entire planet . . . After one final debate, I lose.

I say: 'I can't enter another New Year like this. I was unhappy in my twenties. In a month's time I'll turn thirty. I want my thirties to be happy, and about leading the life I want to live.' Then I take a deep breath and tell Rhodri that I want us to split up. He needs to move out. He can stay here until he finds somewhere else to live.'

It seems he already has: his friend Aiden has offered him the spare room.

27

I should be trying to save my relationship but it's no use: I'm absolutely fed up with this life. I've avoided speaking to Toga so that I can think clearly about Rhodri. I can't sleep, and there have been days when I've felt too dreary even to walk. If I go on like this I'll ruin everything. I can stop the meltdown now by begging Rhodri, 'Please, please can we try again?' But my heart just isn't in it. What I need is a cure, so I go in search of holistic healing.

Dr Li, a Chinese herbalist, has his fingers wrapped around my wrist examining my pulse. He looks at his assistant, Mrs Yu, and then at me. He stands up, walks behind my chair and feels for something on my neck. I stick my tongue out for him and he scratches his nose, bemused. He speaks in Chinese to Mrs Yu, who translates: 'Doctor say is very strange. He say you not ill, but heart-beat is very slow and faint.'

'Goodness,' I say, but I'm not at all surprised. My heart feels as if it's about to stop.

'He ask: "Have you been ill? Going to toilet okay? Not constipated?"'

'Not constipated,' I reply. Mrs Yu translates this to Dr Li, who studies me more intently. He bends down, bangs my knees and examines my ankles. He attempts to speak English to me: 'I can help,' he breathes, 'but you mast tell me whot problem h'is.' He speaks again in Chinese to Mrs Yu.

'Is very important you tell Doctor what is wrong. He cannot help if you do not tell what is wrong.'

'I think I'm heartbroken,' I say quietly.

Mrs Yu translates this to Dr Li. He closes his eyes and nods. Again he speaks in Chinese to Mrs Yu. 'Your partner?' she asks. Mrs Yu and Dr Li have met Jack and Rhodri many times; they greet us like old friends when we see them. At one point last year we stopped using NHS doctors altogether.

'Yes, but not just him.'

'The father of your son?'

'No.'

Dr Li stares me intently as Mrs Yu translates my monosyllabic answers.

'Then who?'

'A man. He doesn't live near here. I don't see him often, but . . . we meet up from time to time and now everything's in tatters and I feel so sad.' I wipe tears from my cheek.

'Does he know?' asks Mrs Yu. She stretches her hand across the desk and places it over mine.

'No.'

Dr Li speaks again in Chinese, this time directing his words at me. I try to understand him, but it's impossible, so I purse my lips gratefully and nod.

'Doctor say there is no Chinese medicine for broken heart. Doctor say you must tell this man.'

'I can't.'

'You mast tell him,' says Dr Li, wagging a finger at me. 'Pulse is very weak. Not good. Not good.'

'Can't you give me some of those little balls?' In the

past I've been sent home with bags of herby little balls, which work wonders for migraines, skin problems and period pains.

Shielding me like a baby bird, Mrs Yu leads me under her elegant arm to the door. Dr Li stands solemnly behind her, as though I am being sent out to do battle with the enemy. 'Is no little balls for heartache,' says Mrs Yu. 'You tell him you love him, then you feel better.'

I meet Zelda for a drink at Cord in Manchester. She's travelling to London in a few days to watch our friend Prince read at the Southbank Centre. He'll stay at a luxury boutique hotel. Zelda has already bagged a space in his bed, but she reckons there'll be plenty of room beneath the duvet for me too. Like a bunch of seven-year-olds, Prince, Zelda and I have been known to cram into a bed together in a completely non-sexual manner, though the hotel staff may not see it quite like that.

I arrange for Jack to stay the night with Margaret No. 2. I shall drop him at school, go to the event and dart back the next day. I look for accommodation as a back-up. Not at *those* prices. I email freebedandbreakfastandsex.com instead.

Dear Bear,

Have been invited to an event in London. Sorry for the short notice would you like to come (ha ha)?

Naughty Bear xxxx

Once I ended an email 'Love X'. I didn't hear from Toga for weeks. Another time I randomly slotted in 'Yup, that's why I love you. x' And didn't hear from him for almost a month. The lesson learned: when emailing Toga, never use the word 'love', but if I need an immediate answer do allude to sex. If it's very urgent, kinky sex.

Now all I need to do is wait . . .

Why hasn't he emailed back?

Ping!

Someone offering me a test pack of Viagra.

Ping!

An email from . . . Toga:

Busy at work. On deadline. Call later.X

I reread the email over and over again. What a love: a big 'X' not a little one. He must really like me.

And with a few details in place such as breakfast club, after-school club and swimming lessons, it's all organized. Except for the train tickets: which I can purchase on the day. Or I could drive? Train tickets are very expensive. No. Not drive. Perhaps drive. I email Toga:

Do you have a driveway? And are you in the congestion zone?x

He responds instantly: very peculiar, unless he thinks that 'congestion zone' is a euphemism for an orgy:

Have a driveway (of sorts) and not in the congestion zone. X

Last night I shaved off every bit of body hair I could see and even hair I couldn't: a dangerous pursuit that required the agility of a contortionist, combined with the thrill of a Gillette razorblade. It looks like Toga can't make it to Prince's event because he's off to some fancy-pants do at

a hotel in Mayfair. I asked him if he could forfeit sch-
moozing for a bite of literature but he put on his firm
I'm-a-man-and-I-mean-it voice: 'I don't know where I'll
be and I don't want to leave the party early. It'll be a good
night: we're going for a meal, and then to a hotel for champagne. I'm looking forward to it. I can't make plans to
meet you, sorry.'

'I might book a hotel then.' What would I pay with?
Dried chickpeas? I have kilos of them.

'There's no need to book a hotel,' he said, 'when you
can stay at my flat.'

About forty minutes from Euston I carry my bags to
the train toilet to get changed and start the cosmetic over-
haul. Then I see it: A Very Big Queue for a Very Small
Toilet.

By the time the train pulls in at Euston, I'm standing in
the cubicle, naked, frantically trying to change into a dress.
If I don't hurry up, I'll be on my way back to Manchester.

Eventually I rush back to my seat where I find a man
standing guard over my bags. 'I thought you were never
coming back,' he says.

I'm to collect the keys to Toga's flat from the offices
where he works. I lean against the railings on the square,
gazing enviously at the cars lined up to take sleek, success-
ful people to the party – limousines with tinted windows,
four-by-fours and shiny black Mercedes. Preened girls
wearing little dresses and high heels merrily clamber into
the back seats. I'm certain Toga would prefer to be with
one of them and not me.

I cross the road and squeeze between a giant black

Range Rover and a black Mercedes. A security man listens to instructions in his earpiece, and as girls teem out of the shiny revolving doors he checks their names on his official-looking clipboard.

Rhodri would be horrified to see this. He'd have a group of protesters flinging their naked hairy bodies over the bonnets of the cars. They'd have placards in their hands with 'Balls to Climate Change' scrawled in vegetable-ink marker pen, with an arrow pointing to their bollocks. He'd say they should choose a venue close by, rather than transporting such avid consumerists in oil-guzzling cars across a congested city.

In the foyer, girls, girls, girls tumble out of the lift, kissing the head of the bald concierge. 'You coming to the party?' asks one.

'Maybe.' He shrugs. 'Maybe.

'Yes?' he asks me. 'Can I help you?'

'I've come to pick up some keys. Toga left them here for me.'

'I have an envelope.' He hands me a large padded one. Perhaps Toga's left me a present: it's so large that there *must* be a present in it . . . No present. Just a very small set of keys. I hand back the empty envelope. 'You can reuse it,' I explain. 'Shame to waste it.'

I head outdoors with the partygoers.

'That car, please,' says the security guard with the head-gear on. He points me in the direction of a limousine. Tempting.

In the early hours of the morning I catch a cab to Toga's flat. Unfortunately the driver is not in possession of the

Knowledge, I am very drunk and we are lost. What if Toga's pulled a girl at the party and brought her back to his? Will I end up on the sofa? My mobile's ringing. I burrow in my bag, trying to retrieve it.

'Hello, Bear, where are you?'

'Standing outside my flat waiting for you. Where are you?'

'In a taxi. *Lost!*' Toga obviously doesn't find this as entertaining as I do.

'For God's sake.'

I get the feeling Toga isn't a happy bear this evening.

'I'm standing in the freezing cold waiting for you. You have my keys. Where are you?'

'On a busy road.' That's not a good answer, is it? All roads in London are busy. 'By a park?'

'Which park?'

'A big one.

'I'd better get back quickly,' I say to the cab driver, who has pulled over to look through his *A–Z*. 'He's not very happy with me. Out in the cold, poor love. You want a big road with a Nando's on it,' I tell him for the tenth time. 'There!' I yell. 'There!' Suddenly everything looks familiar. Lucky Toga – he'll be with me in no time. The cab pulls up at the end of the road. I walk down the icy street and see him. Lovely Toga. With his cute bobble hat on and glasses. He wraps his arm over me and pulls me towards him for a kiss as we head indoors to bed.

Toga sleeps, but I'm restless and cold. I get up and wander to his living room where I find a pile of photographs. Next to them is a silly card I gave him many years ago. I'm surprised he kept it. I read the daft poem I wrote to him. How embarrassing. I wrap myself in his zebra dressing-gown, make a cup of tea and stand in the doorway, watching him sleep.

'There's a zebra in the bed,' he says in the morning, pulling me onto him. I make what I think is a zebra sound, but possibly sounds like a warthog. I kiss the little scar in the shape of a bear's paw on his chest, then his lips. 'Good morning.'

Toga gets out of bed to shower for work, then stands at the foot drying himself from the shower. I watch him pull his clothes from his enormous wardrobe. 'You look very handsome this morning,' I say. And he does. Looming over me, it's quite impressive. 'I fancy you rotten,' I say. 'Come here.'

Toga lurches over to me pretending to be reluctant until he gets close enough for me to pull him onto the bed. He groans. But obliges.

'That was nice. I'll have another,' I say, grabbing his collar.

'Go on, then, if you must.' He kisses me quickly. 'I'll make you some breakfast,' he says, then pads off down the hall to the kitchen before I can wrestle with him again. From the bed I hear him gather pots together, flick the kettle on and switch the radio into life. Leaves clatter over the conservatory roof like children running riot above us. I curl into the duvet and listen to a love song playing on the radio. I feel warm and content. If this is happiness, I like it.

'Toast,' says Toga, handing me a plate with *I Love Skegness* in big red letters across it. I put it on the cabinet by the bed and gaze up at him. 'No,' he says. 'I've got to get to work. I gave you a good seeing-to last night and this morning.'

'Just a *kiss*, that's all I'm asking for.'

He rolls his eyes, then kisses me. "Bye, love. Call me when you're on the train.' He grabs his keys and makes for the door.

'Toga,' I shout. 'Toga.'

He strides back into the bedroom, grinning. 'What?'

'Another. Just a little one.'

'Oh, all right, then . . . I'm really going now.'

I wait until he's walked further this time. 'Toga,' I call.

Toga plods back into the room, shoulders slumped. 'Go on, then,' he says. 'If you must. Kiss me, then.' He lunges at me until his cheek is next to my lips and I hoot with laughter. He stands up, smoothes down his jumper, ruffles his hair and is off.

I'm lying in Toga's bed, daydreaming about (in no specific order): our big house in the country (somewhere just outside London, of course, so he can keep his job) with a dog, and our lovely little children, probably girls, blonde, plaits, identical twins, very pretty little dresses, their adoring big brother Jack, and our days out to galleries in the convertible, the wedding (a small luxurious affair with me wearing a demure and simple dress that cost a fortune, a beautiful white-gold ring, gorgeous little diamond earrings, a tiny but very expensive single-diamond necklace), our holidays in Mustique with drug-addict rock stars . . . and we're happily ever after. The sex is *fantastic* – always. In fact, it only gets better. Throughout our long and happy life together (he'll die before me, leaving me wealthy but heartbroken) we experiment in all sorts of ways, even frequenting swingers' joints, which we laugh off as a 'silly phase' in our sixties at the nudist club in Brighton. And then, in our seventies, when the grandkids have gone home, I'll bring him coffee only to find him dead with a smile on his face and I'll think, We had a good life.

I'm just at the end of my saga when my phone vibrates with a text message:

Be careful love. It is very icy and slippery out there x

A few days later, I'm washing the dishes in my kitchen trying to fade out the sound of Rhodri packing his belongings into cardboard boxes. He's removing his records from the bookshelves, and his Welsh books. Each time I've stepped into the living room it looks emptier. We're caring and careful with one another, which makes me uncertain that we're doing the right thing. As I perch on the sofa it takes all my strength to hold off from saying, 'Stop! Put everything back. I've changed my mind.'

Rhodri said goodbye to Jack last night and explained that he won't be here when he returns from school, and Jack seemed all right with that.

'I'm sorry, Rhodri,' I say, perched on the sofa feeling glum. 'For everything I've ever done. And the other men. I'm sorry about that too.'

He places his hand on my knee and takes a swig of his tea. 'Maria,' he says, smiling, 'you don't need to be sorry. I keep telling you that. You didn't do anything wrong.' He thinks for a moment. 'I changed,' he adds, 'and so did you. We were never going to work, were we?'

He laughs a little and so do I. Then I slope off to the bedroom where I begin to pack away his clothes and shoes.

PART THREE

28

Forget the Sunday lie-in and festive bollocks in preparation for Christmas. I'm going to blast all the dust out of the house. I'm going to wash the towels and the bedding. I'm even going to wash clothes that don't need washing but have been soaked in vegetable-derivative detergent for the past year. I will also mop the floors and clean the windows.

New start, new attitude.

I'll be a housewife, just for me. What a liberation!

Jack wasn't too keen on the plan. 'I know I *said* we'd go on a bike ride today,' I explained, 'but Santa doesn't like messy houses and he'll be on his way here soon.'

Jack had wanted to play at Margaret's house, but he can't because Damien, who now lives with his girlfriend, is visiting her today, and he's the last person I want to bump into when I'm sloping about with a broken heart.

This morning, like a rebel, I went to the shops and purchased a truckload of products that were banned during the Rhodri years:

- Vanish

- Persil Colour

- Fairy fabric conditioner (almond milk and honey)

- L'Oréal Elvive colour protective shampoo

- Pantene colour protective conditioner (couldn't find the L'Oréal one to match)

- Stardrops multi-purpose cleaning fluid

- Toilet Duck

- Flash Power Action *with bleach*

- Those things you put in the toilet to turn the water blue when you flush it

- Flash floor cleaner

- Mr Muscle oven cleaner

- Plug-in air-fresheners ('festive aroma', get rid of those dank compost and kitchen-bin smells we've been harbouring)

- 1001 carpet cleaner

- Pledge

- Olay anti-ageing moisturizer

- Johnson & Johnson facial wipes

- 2 Radox bubblebath (one is relaxing to calm me down, and the other is invigorating to get me going again)

- Impulse Temptation (should I bump into a handsome man *by*, rather than *on*, the conveyor-belt at the supermarket)

- A frozen pizza and some cheap and nasty oven
  chips for tonight's dinner

I bought a copy of *Cosmopolitan* because it has a feature on things to do before you turn thirty. I'll have to get cracking with planning. A quick skim of the magazine, and I discover that it's far too late to do any of the things it suggests I should do before I turn thirty because it's evidently aimed at women who have only just turned twenty, not those like me who turned twenty almost a decade ago.

I throw the magazine into the recycling pile and pick up a broom instead. Cleaning is addictive. The house smells of artificial citrus and feels spick and span. After I've sprayed Mr Muscle inside the oven, I'm going to have a hot bath in my relaxing Radox bubble bath. Between mopping and dusting and generally being a multitasking phenomenon, I managed to iron Jack's school uniform and prepare his packed lunch for tomorrow – I even cut the crusts off his sandwiches. He has Vimto in his flask, not organic Fairtrade pulp, so I'll be a much-loved supermum before I know it.

The next day I'm on a toxic-product come-down when I hear the key turn in the front door and Rhodri walks in. 'Hello. Needed something from the shed.' He grabs a banana from the fruit basket, wolfs it, then heads upstairs.

'Where are you going?'

'Toilet.'

He is up there for a suspiciously long time – the time it takes to have a number two. I've only just rid the bathroom of man smells. The toilet flushes and, before I know it, he's in the kitchen, rooting through the cupboards, grazing on what he can find and snaffling oatcakes. Forgive me, but I thought he'd moved out.

'You don't live here any more.' Surely this is obvious. He packed his things himself, although I have been finding shoes and other things around the house, placed there, I'm beginning to think, so he has no choice but to come back. 'You can't just wander in and eat my food,' I say.

His mouth is stuffed with oatcakes, and he has a big jar of olives in a vice grip between his knees. 'I've come to fix your bike. You want your bike fixed, don't you?'

'Yes.'

'Well, then.'

The cost of bike repairs must be a banana, four oatcakes and a handful of olives. No, hang on, he's in the cupboards rummaging for more. What else has he found? Peanut butter.

Rhodri goes to the shed to pull out my bike. I have about an hour before I'm due to collect Jack from school. I'll make Jack something he likes for dinner: Heinz ravioli on toast? Hmm . . . If Rhodri is here, I can't let him see that we've started to eat convenience food.

'You're a very lucky girl,' he tells me, as I watch him fiddling with the brakes.

'Lucky how, exactly?'

'You slept with other men, asked me to leave, and here I am repairing your bicycle for you.'

'Yes, I am lucky,' I say. 'But the environment is even luckier. If you didn't do it, I'd have to drive.'

*

Jack and I arrive home from school to find Rhodri still in the back garden, unscrewing parts from my bike, cleaning them and putting them back.

'Cup of tea?' I yell.

'Yes, please, dear.'

Just like old times. Scary.

He heads into the kitchen, taking his dirty boots off at the door. We stand a distance apart.

'How's the bike going?'

'I need to order some bearings. It'll ride smoothly when it's done, though.' Rhodri takes a noisy slug of his tea. If he was still my boyfriend, I'd have nagged him about that. Now he lives elsewhere he can do as he pleases. He grins pleasantly at me. 'Good cup of tea, love.'

'Thanks. And thanks for doing the bike.'

'Do you want that?' he asks, nodding towards an over-sized pumpkin sitting on the kitchen counter.

'No. You can take it.'

'Actually,' he says, 'you have it. You can make pumpkin soup out of it, or pumpkin pie.'

'I don't know how to cook pumpkin and I've still got pumpkin in the freezer from last year. Take it.'

'You have it.'

'No, you.'

'No. It's all right.'

'If you stay, we can share it for dinner.'

'I'm having dinner with some friends this evening.'

'That's nice,' I say uncertainly. 'Are they vegan?'

'Yes.'

'How do you know them?'

'From meetings and protests. We like the same things.'

'That's great.'

We both fall quiet for a moment.

'I bet you're missing my cooking?' I joke, seriously.

Rhodri thinks about this. He's about to lie to please me, but then at the last minute changes his mind: 'Aiden's a very good cook. You're a good cook . . . but Aiden, well, he's older and he's had more experience. You'll get better.' Rhodri smirks.

I grunt and turn to wash the dishes. But I'm happy he's happy. No, I am. Well, perhaps not *happy* as such.

29

It's less than two weeks to Christmas. Margaret No. 2 has taken Jack to her house: they're going to watch Christmas films and eat Christmas food. She's disappointed that we can't visit her on Christmas Day because Damien will be there. I said, 'Don't worry about us. Think about what's good for Jack in the long-term. It works for everybody if Damien sorts himself out. Maybe he needs your help right now, and we'll be okay. We can see you after Christmas.'

'I'll try,' she said.

The perfect antidote to a life collapse is some girl bonding time, so my friends Sybil, Nancy and Emmeline are coming over for a pre-Christmas and pre-birthday meal. Zelda and Prince couldn't make it. I'll turn thirty soon. After that night with Damien, I'd wanted to bury my future birthdays in a field. But as I approach thirty it feels time to forget the bad stuff and celebrate again.

I'm wearing the red Christmas apron with the reindeers laughing all over it. The turkey has been stuffed, basted and roasted: it's settling on the side, ready to be carved. The vegetables are cooked. When Emmeline gets here, I'll ask her how she makes those fabulous roasted vegetables she does, and we'll quickly shove them in the oven. Nancy is vegetarian so she's having vegetarian haggis. The table is set with candles and crackers.

The front door is wide open so the girls stride in,

spreading festive cheer, bags of wine, chocolates and champagne weighing them down.

'Hello,' says Sybil, handing over a beautifully wrapped parcel of homemade mince pies as she kisses me.

'Hello, darling,' says Nancy, handing me a parcel of homemade cookies.

'Hello, hon.' Emmeline wraps me in a tight hug. 'How you doing? Smells gorgeous. Oooh, look at that turkey!'

'I'm a vegetarian, and it even smells good to me,' says Nancy.

'Where shall we put these?' Sybil asks, clinking bottles of champagne and wine together.

'In the fridge. I have a bottle of champagne chilled already. Who wants a glass?' It was given to me as a birthday present last year. No better moment to drink it than now.

It's only three o'clock and, a bottle of champagne down, we're seated around the table, sipping wine and waiting for the roasted vegetables to crisp.

'You okay, honey, since Rhodri left?' asks Emmeline.

'A bit sad,' I say. 'It was the right thing to do.'

'You changed everything about yourself for him,' she says. 'You couldn't have compromised much more.'

'I can't help thinking, If I'd just done this or that it would've worked.'

'And all this see-other-men business,' she says, 'I don't think that could work.'

I don't know if Emmeline's right. Rhodri and I separated because ultimately he would have wanted us to move to a commune and drop out of working life altogether. And I couldn't scrimp any more. I couldn't inflict that on

Jack. 'Maybe I wouldn't have stayed with Rhodri so long if I hadn't had the other men.'

'I don't think you can truly love someone if you allow them to go with someone else,' says Nancy.

'Rhodri would say that that's love. He sees it quite differently. It's hard to apply the usual argument because the usual argument doesn't apply.' Rhodri told me that he was never heartbroken or made jealous by any of this. I think for a moment. 'I'll never do it again,' I add. And I really mean it. I tried all that free-love business but I understand now that I want to be with just one man, not many.

I arrange the food on the serving dishes and take them to the table to a welcome round of applause. Emmeline sets about carving the turkey while Sybil cracks open the next bottle of champagne.

After dinner we head into Manchester, where we drink underground at the Temple, a public toilet that was converted into a bar. I'm going to change. I'm going to clear out the men in my life, like I'm sorting out my wardrobe.

30

Last night I cleaned the house until one twenty-three a.m. so this morning we're late for school. I'm beginning to suspect that all the cleaning may have something to do with wanting to bleach out my old life. Despite my good intentions, I didn't succeed in getting up at six to shower. I'd meant to wear a nice dress, perfect my hair and make-up, and arrive in the playground looking like Audrey Hepburn.

'Why are you still wearing those pants you slept in?' asks Jack.

'They're also jogging bottoms,' I reply. 'Suitable for jogging to school in when I want to keep fit.'

'But you wear them in bed.'

'No, I don't.' That's a small white lie, but never mind. 'Have you got your lunchbag?'

'Yes.'

'Reading book?'

'Yes.'

'Homework?'

'No.'

'Oh, Jack.'

'What?'

'Why no homework?'

'I forgot.'

'I can't remember everything for you,' I say, trailing off.

I can't remember anything for myself, let alone Jack. I can't even get dressed. The only space to park the car is a good ten minutes on foot to school. As I'm walking, running, walking towards the entrance I'm aware of the self-pitiful stoop I've adopted. My whole body feels as though it's urging me to give up, collapse on the pavement and be washed into the gutter with the other detritus.

At the school gates glamorous mums glide past us on their way for coffee at Café Exploit the Third World.

'Let's run a bit faster, Jack,' I say breathlessly. I nod to the mums as I race towards the doors, hoping they don't notice that I'm wearing my pyjamas and haven't washed my face or brushed my hair.

Back home I sip my decaffeinated Fairtrade organic instant coffee with Fairtrade organic rice milk and half a spoon of organic Fairtrade unrefined sugar, wishing that one day someone would invite me for mummy-type gossip over coffee. I look in the mirror, hoping to God that Helena Bonham Carter will gaze back at me, but, no, I'm still me. After some mental preparation and a few deep breaths, I take my mobile from my bag, take a seat on the stairs and call Morton. 'Hi, it's me.'

'Hello, you. Listen . . .' he says, before I have chance to ask him whether he has any honourable intentions towards me at all, and that the purpose of the call is to bring some order to my life by downsizing on the men in it. '. . . there's something I've been meaning to tell you.'

'What's that, then?' I'm hoping it might be that he wants to take on Jack and me as an investment, and fund a decade of Jack's education at a top public school.

'I've met someone. You know how it is, when you meet someone special and . . . Well, it doesn't happen every day, does it?'

'Go on.'

'So all this with you and me, it can't go on any more. I get the sense you want a country cottage, with a gate leading up the path and roses growing around the door. I'm not the one to give that to you.'

'What's wrong with wanting a cottage with roses growing around the door?'

'Nothing at all. But I don't want that sort of commitment. This woman, she's the same age as me, and I'm quite happy sitting with her and filling in the crossword.'

I'm not hurt. Not really. I'm relieved it's over. I'm very fond of Morton, but I suppose I always knew he was too old to be the One. We chat for about an hour. He's enjoying a rare day off and is in a pub filling in a crossword as we speak.

'I'm going now,' I say finally, because it feels like neither of us wants the conversation to draw to a close.

'But we'll still be friends?' he asks. 'I really want that. I've travelled the world and met some impressive people, but . . .' he pauses '. . . Maria, you're the only woman I've ever met who's dragged me in the pissing rain through a graveyard.'

This next afternoon I arrange a meeting with Jack's teacher, Miss Lamb. I'm worried about him: two men have entered, then disappeared from his life, and I wonder if he's having problems at school.

'Take a seat,' she says, pointing to a very small chair at a very small table. 'How are things at home?'

284

'Not bad,' I say cautiously. 'Why?'

'Is everything okay with Jack?'

'Well, he's been a little upset. Some boys have been teasing him. And he said you told him his maths is slipping. He's proud of being good at maths and he took it very much to heart. He's a sensitive boy.'

'He's been quite upset at school.' She reaches behind her to take one of Jack's books from a pile. She opens a page and shows me that Jack has scrawled some rather sad faces on what should have been a bar chart. 'This is all he managed to do during one whole lesson.'

Quite worrying, I agree. The lines are wobbly, as though he couldn't hold his pencil still – he's barely managed to draw a graph at all.

'Jack has broken down crying in class a number of times. When I took him outside to ask what was wrong he told me he missed his dad.' Miss Lamb looks at me expecting an explanation. But I've done that thing I do, pressed my lips together. 'You don't have to tell me anything,' she says sympathetically. 'But it might be helpful if you do.' She asks, 'Is there any chance he could see his father?'

'I don't think so.'

We're not the only single-parent family in the world. I'm not the only mother who works. There are other children whose families have broken up. I'm not the only single mother in the playground.

'My partner has recently moved out. Jack said he wasn't bothered but maybe he is more than he realizes. Maybe he thinks he's missing his dad, but he's missing Rhodri, who was like a father to him.'

'Can Jack still see Rhodri?' asks Miss Lamb.

'Yes. He'll still come over. It's amicable,' I say.

'That's good,' says Miss Lamb.

I drive with Jack over to my mother's house. She and my stepfather are at work but the heating is sure to be on, so the house will be cosy, and she always has a fine selection of tea, juice, sweets and biscuits. It's the ideal neutral place for me to have a chat with Jack. Our own house is too full of history.

When we arrive, I make us some snacks and we head up to my old room and snuggle up in bed watching television, Jack tucked under my arm. I hand him biscuits and hot Vimto, which I let him sip as I hold it.

'Jack,' I say gently, 'I had a word with Miss Lamb today. She's worried about you. She says you walked out of the classroom crying the other day.' I try to detach him from me, but he clings on, all arms and legs. If I could just see his face, I could make him smile. But, no, he won't let me.

'At school,' he says, beginning to cry, 'they keep asking me about my dad and they know not to. I told Saul that I didn't see my dad and he told everyone that my dad is a *murderer*, so I threw him against the wall.'

'No, no, you mustn't do that. You must tell a teacher.'

'I have told the teacher but she doesn't do anything, just says to them, "Don't do that." Finlay's always, always going on about his dad and it drives me mad and he's doing it on purpose, I know he is, and then he asks me where my dad is and I have to say I don't know.'

'What about deep-sea diving with sharks in New Zealand, like we said?'

'Because he *isn't*.'

Imagination, Jack, use your imagination.

All of this hurts Jack, I can feel it. It's not like when he cries at being told off, or when he's fallen off his skateboard: these sobs come from deep down in his stomach, somewhere even Vimto can't reach. Not even hot Vimto. When will we stop struggling with this? It's been years.

'It's all right for you, you have a dad,' he says. 'You don't know how this feels. And you go to see your dad and you have a sister and you have stepbrothers.'

'You have three granddads and lots of people who love you, and friends and cousins and uncles.'

'But it isn't the same.' He unhooks his arms from my neck, turns his back to me and presses his cheek against the bedroom wall. 'You don't understand. You don't know how it feels.'

'I'm trying to understand, Jack, but you're right, I don't know how it feels. But I'm trying, love.'

Jack becomes distraught. I'm not helping him at all. I'm making things worse.

'I want to see my dad and I want to see my half-brother,' he says angrily. He thinks that if he says this firmly enough I'll give in.

'Sweetheart, I don't think he's changed. If he had, then you could see him. And when you're older, able to catch a bus, that kind of thing, fifteen perhaps, you can. But right now you need your mum.'

Jack furrows his brow. Not good enough, I hear him think.

'It's better to have a mum who's healthy and happy,' I try to explain, 'and able to look after you and have fun with you, isn't it?'

'Yes.'

'And if your dad was around then maybe I wouldn't be able to do that – because he made me very unhappy, Jack, and I wasn't able to be a good mum. I was sad and crying all the time. I don't want him in our lives. I don't want him coming to the house.'

'He wouldn't have to come to the house.'

'No.'

There's silence between us. I don't know how to pull Jack back to me.

'What did he do to you?' asks Jack.

'He hurt me.'

'I know that, you told me that. I want to know what he did. Tell me.' He says it again, persuasively, softly: 'Please tell me.'

There's a moment of awkward silence between us. There's only one right answer: 'I'm going to, Jack.'

For a long time we sit on the bed. Jack curled up on my lap, holding on tight, weeping hard, trying to talk, but not able to. 'I can't say what I'm thinking,' he says.

'You must,' I urge. 'If you say it, it won't feel so bad.'

'It's too bad to say.'

'Nothing's that bad.'

'It's horrible to say.'

'Say it, then it's gone. Whisper it.'

I brush my hair to one side so he can whisper in my ear: 'I wish I never had a dad.' He says it again strongly: '*I wish I never had a dad.*'

31

I've failed my son because I'm absolutely incapable of sustaining a relationship.

What a fuck-up.

Last night Jack slept in my bed. He was fitful, coughing and kicking out, so I moved and slept in his bed. I had an awful nightmare, the one where a beast creature enters the house and tries to kill me. It has hairy legs and a nasty face. I tried to get back to sleep but the dogs next door barked and barked, the rabbits banged about in the hutch and a drunk couple picked a fight by the back gate. It's past ten o'clock, and I still can't lift my head from my pillow. Which means we're very late for school again. Which means I must have hit snooze. So I'm still in bed, but Jack is obviously awake because the television's blaring downstairs. What will the note say? 'Mummy couldn't be bothered to take me to school yesterday, so she didn't'?

As I'm stranded in bed for the foreseeable future, I decide to use my horizontal status productively. Unable to do that, I brood. What now? Do I get up, get dressed, feign a dental appointment for Jack, or just stay here in bed? I try again to get up. No, not happening today.

Who now? I consider past boyfriends, former bosses, acquaintances I bump into from time to time, any man who has ever sent me an email/smiled/delivered post to my door. Neighbours. God, no, not one of my neighbours.

Did Rhodri and I actually make the decision to split up – and *stick* to it?

I actually made a decision. I made a decision? Things are looking up.

Jack tumbles up the stairs muttering, 'Ouch, ouch.' It's his favourite word at the moment. 'What you doing, Mum?' He yawns.

I'm on his bed, wrapped in his fake *Doctor Who* duvet, a Dalek pillow under my head and his favourite teddy under my arm. 'You took up all the room in my bed, so I got into yours. Give us a hug.'

Jack throws himself on top of me, wrestling my neck into a headlock.

'Why didn't you wake me?' I ask.

'I have stomach ache.'

'Oh dear,' I say, thinking, That'll do. No school today. Jack said he was ill and I can't be cruel and force him to go to school. 'Is it a very bad stomach ache?'

'Yes,' says Jack, screwing up his face and rubbing his tummy for effect.

'Oh, you poor thing,' I say. 'No sweets and crisps for you today but lots of green veg to fill you up with vitamins to help fight that bug!'

'Okay.' He grimaces.

Even a diet of salad and vegetables seems preferable to him than a day at school. I check his forehead. No temperature. He could really be ill. But he climbs off me and hunts for PlayStation games, so perhaps not.

'No PlayStation if you're ill,' I say.

He pulls out a *Dandy* from his bookshelf and reads to

me, putting on an accent that sounds Scottish for the voice of Desperate Dan.

'That was wonderful reading, fantastic expression and intonation.' I clap enthusiastically. 'I'll get up and make some breakfast, have a bath and then we'll do something. A game of chess? Not too much television, though.' I don't know how to play chess. Rhodri was the one who could play chess.

Jack pulls me from his bed. It's an effort to put one foot after the other. I don't know why I suggested chess. I can barely muster the enthusiasm to fill the kettle with water. I shake out a bowl of Shreddies for him, sprinkle some sugar on, pour out the soya milk and place it on the coffee-table in the living room. Then I crumple up on the sofa to drink my tea. I'm pathetic – even for me, this is quite pathetic. I force myself to get up again and tread heavily up the stairs, turn on the taps, sit on the edge of the bath and watch the room fill with steam.

My thoughts are confined to one-word sentences: Bath. Hot. Cold. Water. *Why?Me?*

I plod hopelessly from the bathroom back to bed. Have coped on my own before. Will cope again – the bath sounds like it may spill over.

'JACK!' I yell. 'The bath.'

'Mum,' he yells back, 'WHAT?'

'The bath!' I groan.

'*Oooo–kaaaaaaaay!*' he yells back, then bounds up the stairs – a very healthy boy, not a poorly boy.

I hear Jack get into the bath. He starts to talk to the cars and the *Star Wars* figures he's lined up on the shelf.

'Don't pee in the water,' I shout to Jack. 'I'll get in after you.'

'Why would I pee in the bath when we have a toilet?'

Fair point.

I'm clean, sort of, if you count bathing in another person's dirty water as washing.

The telephone rings. Jack answers. I hope it will be Rhodri.

'Zelda,' Jack says. 'For you.'

'How are you, love?' asks Zelda.

I look down at Rhodri's green Y-fronts, which I'm wearing as a kind of homage to the times we wore one another's underwear.

'Are you upset?'

'No.'

'You shouldn't be. It was going to happen. It happened. You need to get over it.'

Yes, yes, yes, for God's sake. Can a girl not be weak? Not even for a day?

'Meet me for lunch. One o'clock. Kim by the Sea.'

I look to see what time it is: twelve fifteen. I'm not –
'I'm not dressed,' I say to Zelda.

'Well, get dressed. *'Bye!*'

Before I can argue, she hangs up. Jack is standing brazenly in the doorway, hands on his hips, naked little peachy pecs and full tackle on display. 'Why,' he asks solemnly, 'are you wearing Rhodri's green underpants when you're a girl? Where's your own knickers?'

'Don't have anything clean.'

Jack glares at me, totally unimpressed by what I think is a logical answer.

'And these are warm and comfortable and it's cold outside.'

'You shouldn't be wearing them. You're a lady. I'll tell him.'

'Well, I am wearing them because I have nothing else and need to keep my bottom warm.'

'You shouldn't.'

'How can I take you seriously,' I say, 'when you aren't even wearing underpants?'

He turns around, shakes his little bottom at me, then slams his bedroom door shut.

'And get dressed,' I call. 'We're going to meet Zelda.'

I go to the bathroom, still wearing Rhodri's underpants, to brush my teeth, only to discover Rhodri has taken pretty much everything, including the toothpaste, and possibly even my knickers. I haven't felt so depressed since the last time I felt depressed.

We step into Kim by the Sea – it must be a mother-and-baby afternoon because there are lots of mums cooing at their babies. I'm mesmerized by them. I wish I had a baby. The mothers look affluent and Bohemian. I just know that their cupboards are brimming with Meridian food products, tofu and falafel. One of the little girls will be called India or Summer or Sunshine, something like that.

'India, darling, give that to Mummy.'

I knew it.

I see a vacant table by the door, beneath the specials board. Jack picks up the menu and hunts for something he likes.

Zelda arrives, looking glamorous as usual, and sits opposite Jack.

Then the waiter walks over, a generic-looking boy with a beard and skinny pants. 'What can I get you to drink?'

'Coffee. Black,' says Zelda.

'Organic lemonade,' says Jack.

'And for you?' the waiter asks me. He fancies me. Course he does. *Course* he does.

'Can I have organic egg and organic homemade chips?' Jack butts in. He's becoming more middle class by the day. He'll be changing his name to Theobald before he has his first shave.

'Organic egg and chips twice,' I tell the waiter. 'And a Coke.'

Zelda looks at me with disapproval, a look that says: Coke, egg and chips, you can do better than that. 'What's wrong with him?' she says, pointing at Jack. 'Fancy a day off school, did you?'

'I had stomach ache but I'm feeling better now.'

'You'll be well enough to go to school tomorrow, though, won't you?' I add.

Zelda turns to the waiter. 'I'll have the falafel with salad,' she says. Then Jack launches into an incredibly long monologue about his magazine, *Worm Warfare*.

'Can I speak?' I ask, half an hour later.

'In a minute, Jack's talking,' says Zelda. 'Carry on.'

There's a lot of oohing and aahing, some slapping of

hands on the table, and some laughs as Zelda and Jack compete to be the loudest and most theatrical. They're one step away from standing on the table and performing a tap dance when the food comes.

In the car on the way home Jack asks, 'Was I good?'

'Yes. I don't think you're ill, though, are you?'

'I was but I'm feeling better now.'

'You were good, but I didn't get chance to talk to Zelda. You two were chatting all the time.'

'That's because she's my friend too,' says Jack. 'I've known her nearly as long as you. You can't keep all your friends to yourself.'

That evening Jack tucks into sweets, repeating lines from old films over and over again. He's rooting around on my desk, looking for heaven knows what but he's very intent on finding it. It's almost the school holidays, so it can't be his homework. 'What are you looking for?' I ask.

'I need a pen and some paper.'

'What are you going to do? Is it to make another edition of your *Worm Warfare* magazine?'

'I can't tell you.'

'You can. I'm your mum.' I hand him some paper and a pen, and he runs off to his room.

He's been up there for a suspiciously long time, a sure sign that he's up to mischief, so I knock on his door.

'Don't come in.'

'I'm just collecting things for washing,' I lie, entering his bedroom. Jack is sitting at his desk, writing furiously. 'Come and watch *The Simpsons* with me,' I say.

'I can't,' he replies.

'Why?'

'All I can think about is Ellie. That's what happens when you lose your girlfriend, you can't think of anything else.'

'You'll get another girl,' I say, expecting him to think that girls are like skateboards.

I'd thought Jack and Ellie were a fleeting playground romance. I knew he liked her, but not as much as this. The other week he mentioned his friends are in love with her too, but I brushed it off as a childish game. Now it seems that his best friend wants to be her boyfriend too.

'I'm going to write a letter to her and tell her I love her and want her back.'

I sit at the end of his bed, and try to tickle his feet, amazed that while I'm so down in the dumps he's coping fantastically. Still, I am his mother. And it's my duty to protect him, especially from girls. 'Don't do that. Ellie has the other boys after her. You might end up upset. She's been your special friend for a while now, and it's time to move on.'

'It's taken me four years,' he replies seriously, 'to tell her that I fancy her. I'm not going to give up now. That's not what you do. Can you leave me alone, please?' He stands up and pushes me out of the room.

'Would you like me to help you?' I call, as he closes the door behind me. 'I could check your spellings.'

Jack slides the letter to me through the gap beneath the door. It is written on A4 computer paper and folded in half. He has drawn a heart on the front and written in capital letters: I LOVE YOU. 'Dear Ellie,' I begin to read it aloud. Jack opens the door and gazes up at me with pride. 'You are the most beautiful girl in the world. I fancy you. You have the most beautiful eyes and the most beautiful hair. You are also the kindest girl I will ever meet. I want you to be my girlfriend. Let me know what you think and you me and Tyrone and Tai and Mark can talk about it. I hope you decide it is me. Love, Jack.'

Tyrone, Tai and Mark are the other boys vying for Ellie's love. 'What a wonderful letter,' I tell Jack. 'Are you sure you want to send it?'

'Why wouldn't I be?'

'Just . . . are you sure?'

Jack folds the letter and slips it into an envelope, with a furry koala bear key-ring. On the front he writes in big letters: 'FOR THE EYES OF ELLIE ONLY'. 'I'm putting it in my school bag,' he says. 'I want to give it to her.'

As I'm making supper, I try to imagine how it must feel to be only nine and so fearless you can write a letter to the one big love of your life, and ask that love to choose — even just to ask that love to start a conversation that ends somewhere. I'm completely in awe of my son. And I wonder if perhaps it isn't Rhodri or Damien's absence that has upset him, but that he was feeling the first pains of unrequited love.

32

It's just over a week until Christmas and I'm ashamed to admit that nothing is planned. We haven't even got a Christmas tree up yet. And, horror of horrors, I'm very soon going to turn thirty.

'We're not having that plastic one we had last year,' says Jack, throwing his school bag into my arms when we get home.

'The one Granddad very kindly gave us?' I point out.

'It was small and awful,' proclaims Jack. Interior design being his new calling, I must remember to ring *House & Garden* to find out if they're looking for a nine-year-old columnist. 'I do not want that plastic Christmas tree in the house.'

'I haven't any money for a real one,' I tell him. 'They're very expensive.' A real tree is, what, about forty pounds? My Christmas budget is what? I haven't even got a Christmas budget.

'I'll use my pocket money.'

'You're not using your pocket money to buy a Christmas tree.'

'I have loads of pocket money. In my *Doctor Who* Tardis piggy-bank.'

Playground sales of *Worm Warfare* magazine must be rocketing. But Jack isn't going to buy the Christmas tree, even if he is a Felix Dennis-style entrepreneur. I shall purchase the tree. Trouble is, it's too early to get a reduced-price one. We have bought real Christmas trees before, but only when they were going cheap. One Christmas Eve I bagged a six-footer for six pounds just hours before the shop was due to close.

Jack looks as if he might cry. Maybe what we need to make everything better is a *huge* Christmas tree.

'Okay, okay. We'll get a real tree.'

'Now?'

'Now. This very instant.'

We slide around Christmas tree vendors' yards in the mud, Jack yelling, 'What about this one?' while I try to keep up with him. I look at the price tags and gasp, 'Fifty pounds for a tree? Robbery! Next year I shall grow my own.' I haggle with the vendors. No use. All the best trees have been sold, but there are still plenty of fools around to pay over the odds for the crap that's left. I take Jack's hand and pull him out of there. 'Supermarket,' I say. 'They'll be cheaper there.' I can't let my principles get in the way of the purse strings.

'But I want –' Jack stops. 'Okay,' he says, swinging his legs into the car.

It's dark, it's raining, and Jack and I are laughing as we struggle to carry the biggest Christmas tree we could find across the supermarket car park. He has the trunk, I have the spiky end, and we're stumbling all over the place as if we might fall over at any minute. Jack is cackling, 'Mum, *don't, don't*, I'm going to pee my pants.' He pauses to breathe. 'I will pee my pants!' he says sternly, which encourages me to behave even more ridiculously. We throw open the boot of our little car, set down the rear seats, move the front seat forward, and try to ram the tree in. Jack scrambles into the back and climbs all over it like a lumberjack, hoisting and tugging. I'm pushing and shrieking, 'Pull! Pull! Heave-ho!' and Jack is yelling, 'I'm going to pee my pants, I'm going to pee my pants,' when a very classy black Audi TT pulls up in the bay next to us, and out steps a man, not much older than me, in a suit.

Thank you, Santa Claus. My three favourite things, all at once. A man. In a suit. And an Audi TT. You get a much better class of man in a Sainsbury's car park. If we were at Asda he'd be wearing a boiler-suit and driving a clapped-out Ford Escort.

'Would you like some help?' the man asks.

Oh, heaven, yes. You can help me get out of these wet clothes back home. Help with the tree? I ponder for a moment. 'No, it's all right,' I say. 'All part of the festive fun. Getting it into the car is the best bit.'

'You sure?'

'Sure.' I smile.

Audi TT shrugs his shoulders and walks off. Nice bottom. What a very nice bottom.

Tree up. It was too tall for the house so I held it between my legs while Jack sawed the top off with a steak knife. Lights. That's what we need. Out to the shed for the ladder, then up to the attic. I hate the attic. Not that I spend much time in it. Usually I just flail my arms about in the hope I'll touch the things I'm looking for. Torch in hand, I discover it's a relationship graveyard in here: the bag containing lights is next to many boxes containing Damien's belongings – old copies of *Strike*, photographs, clothes. Other boxes contain toys from when Jack was a toddler, and baby clothes from when I'd naïvely hoped I'd have another baby. I find a box of Rhodri's things and a pile of Welsh books. What do I need Welsh books for? It's like a curated exhibition of my life up here – complete with the gold Lurex boob tube I wore when I was nineteen, sexy and slim.

Downstairs, we struggle to wrap the lights around the tree.

Jack stands on the sofa at the far end of the room, flicks the light off and I switch the fairy-lights on. He claps wildly. 'It's *beeeeeoooootiful,*' he gasps. The tree has taken the place of furniture in the living room and, 'extravagance' being my new middle name, is resplendent with purple, silver and white baubles I bought on a three-for-two offer at Sainsbury's.

We sing 'Walking in a Winter Wonderland', followed by 'We Wish You a Merry Christmas', a veritable medley. We hop about the living room in what could be described as ballroom dancing, but really shouldn't. Jack stands with his legs apart so I can try to crawl under them, he twirls me in and out, then I throw him under my legs, and struggle to pick him up again.

Margaret No. 2 knocks on the door, comes in, plants herself on the sofa with her dogs and exclaims that we have the best Christmas tree she's ever seen.

The next day I'm determined that this year nothing is going to interrupt Mission Happy Christmas. I take a deep breath and insert my cash card into the ATM to withdraw cash to spend on Christmas presents and food. The machine asks: 'Would you like to check your balance?'

Yes, go on, then.

'Your current balance is: £1653.24 OD. Your available balance is: £1876.03 OD. Would you like to use another service?'

Yes.

'Choose a service.'

In the absence of 'Withdraw money from Richard Branson's account' I press: Withdraw cash. Amount £100.00 Money dispensed. Things are looking up: the bank is still happy to give me money when I have none. What a helpful, helpful, bank.

Drat. The Christmas present Jack really wanted, a punch-bag with boxing gloves, is sold out. I should have shopped earlier. I order one at Argos, which will arrive two days before Christmas. I've no idea where we'll hang it without the ceiling caving in. I go to the pet shop and order a new hutch for the rabbits.

I'm just leaving the store when Zelda calls: 'Hi, love. I'm coming over for a coffee. Be there in about half an hour.'

'I'm just out shopping.'

'Where?'

I can't say, 'The pet shop': she's a John Lewis kind of girl. 'I'll make it back. See you soon.'

Zelda is ill, bless her. From upstairs I heard her hammering on the front door and sneezing. 'Open the door!'

I make her a hot drink. 'Have a cup of coffee, keep warm.'

Zelda takes a sip and puts it back down: 'What type of coffee is this?' she asks, appalled.

She likes my Christmas tree: 'Very nice.' Hates my mess: 'Oh, my God, what happened in here?' Thinks my romantic state needs an instant remedy: 'You're lovelorn all the time.' And that my clothes, skin, general self, et cetera, need urgent attention: 'Get a facial. Join the gym. Go shopping and buy some new clothes. That's what works for me after a break-up.'

I do look drab. I bought this dress at a charity shop four years ago, my coat is torn, my tights are laddered and Oxfam would decline to resell my shoes. 'I'll sort myself out,' I say.

'I'll arrange a night out,' she says encouragingly. 'You're a wonderful girl, Maria. Anyone would be lucky to have you. I've always thought that.'

33

The day before Christmas Eve I'm woken by the shrill of the telephone. It's bound to be my mother. Only she would call me the morning after I've been out with Zelda, Nancy, Emmeline and Sybil for Christmas drinks the night before. I stumble to the windowsill to pick up the phone. Catching my reflection in the dressing-table mirror, I see my lip is cut and swollen. I look down to my knees, which are scabbed and bruised. When the black cab dropped me at home, I took one step onto the pavement, slipped on some ice and fell flat on my face. I hope no one saw me.

'Maria.'

'Yes, Mother?' I can barely speak, my throat is so hoarse from shouting over the music in the bar.

'Maria, I need you to get hold of Josephine. Are you dressed?'

'No.'

'Get dressed and drive to the hospital. Intensive care.'

'Why?' I panic. 'What's happened? Mum—'

'Last night there was a terrible accident. It's your cousin. You need to get hold of your sister.'

'I will, I will, I'll try. But, Mum, I can't drive. I was drinking last night.'

'Maria, you have got to be quick.'

My mother's voice cracks. I hear her sniffle, then regain

control of herself. Mothers have a habit of being so strong that they trick you into thinking everything's going to be easy.

'Mum, tell me he's going to recover. He's just badly injured, right?'

'Maria, he's only got a few hours to live. They've given him until one o'clock. Get hold of Josephine. Phone a taxi.'

I look at the time on my mobile. It's almost eleven o'clock.

I ring and ring Josephine. Jesus, Josephine, where are you? Come on. Not at home or on her mobile.

I call my father. 'Where's Josephine?'

'Shopping probably. It's a busy time of year for women. How are you, darling?'

'Dad, you need to come and get me now and take me to Hope Hospital. There's been an accident.' I fill in the details. 'It's urgent. Get hold of Josephine. Get her to yours and tell her there. Don't tell her when she's shopping.'

I call Margaret No. 2. 'Please can you hold on to Jack?' I cry. 'I need to go to the hospital.'

When Josephine and I enter Intensive Care we're escorted to the relatives' room. We open the door to find our entire extended family of uncles and cousins there. We weren't due to see them until Christmas morning, at my mother's, for Irish coffee and the swapping of presents.

My uncle John nods quietly. I scan the room: their faces are grave and white. My young cousin, who was in his mid-twenties, is going to die. One bad decision last night changed everything. He got into a car. The young driver had been drinking. The car skidded and flipped on ice. It landed upside-down in a garden. One other passenger is dead. Two more are in a critical condition. Outside the quiet of the relatives' room, his young sons slide up and down the hospital corridor. His sons, his sister, his mother – my aunt Sophie – his little brother.

My mother takes my hand. 'Do you want to say good-bye?'

Yes. No. I don't know.

She walks me to his bed. Aunt Sophie and his sister wait by his side.

'But he looks so alive. He looks like he's going to wake up.'

'He's not going to wake up, Maria,' my mother says. 'He's brain-dead. The machines are keeping him going because he agreed to be an organ donor.'

I take his hand. It feels warm. Josephine tells him all about her shopping trip. Poor love, I think, poor, poor love.

I collect Jack and bring him to the hospital; he leaves a card and a teddy bear at the foot of my cousin's bed. We wait some more in the relatives' room. My cousin holds on for longer than they thought he would. When, finally, it's time, and the priest arrives to read him the last rites, many of us stand around his bed, shaken with grief. At some point his spirit leaves. His youngest son reaches out with his little hand to hold on to his daddy.

'Thank you, Father,' says his mother.

Uncertainly, we each kiss him and say goodbye for the last time.

Shortly after, I leave the hospital.

Christmas Day passed unnoticed. It's Boxing Day morning when I receive the call to say the life-support machine has been switched off and my cousin's organs are due to be removed by the transplant team.

Much later, Jack walks into my room. I'm lying in bed, a towel wrapped around me, the duvet plumped between my arms. 'You have to get up,' he says softly, stroking my leg. 'Come on, Mum. We have to be at Nana's. You said we had to be there for five thirty.'

'I will.'

'It's five o'clock. You've been saying that for ages and you're still in bed. Put your pants on, and a T-shirt. Come on.'

'I will, when you leave the room. I'm naked under here.'

'I'll help you get dressed. But I'm not putting your bra and knickers on you. You'll have to do that yourself.' Jack is cajoling but insistent, using the tone I employ when he's ill and tell him, 'You must eat, you must take your medicine, you must rest.' Closing his eyes, he takes my arm and pulls me from under the duvet until I'm on my feet.

I feel light-headed. My feet are rocks at the bottom of my legs and it seems as though little pebbles are running through my veins, willing me to lie down again. 'I'm up, see? Leave me now and I'll get dressed.'

'If you go back to bed, I'll hear the bump from downstairs. I'll be listening out for it.'

What to wear? I have no clothes. I choose a hotchpotch from what's hanging up. I dry and straighten my hair.

When we arrive at my mother's, Grandma is swinging on a high stool at the breakfast bar. My mother is taking buffet food from the oven while my stepfather is on the sofa, watching cartoons. I find a packet of soluble paracetamol in my mother's medicine box. I drop a tablet into a glass of cold water. Grandma watches me. 'Not too much water,' she says. 'You're supposed to have just a bit of water with it.' I grimace and gulp it down. My head hurts. My whole body aches.

Josephine arrives with her boyfriend and the kids. Aunt Sarah arrives with her son. Great-aunt Katrina, who is here for the holidays, sits next to Grandma, at the end of the breakfast bar, scanning the kitchen for gluten-free food. 'I can't eat any gluten,' she says. 'Nothing with gluten in it for me. You have such good gluten-free food here in the UK. The food you find in Canada.' She pulls a face and sticks out her tongue. 'It's not like here anyway. It's so cold over in Canada, and you should see the snow. It's up to here,' she adds, pointing to her shoulders.

When the roast potatoes are out of the oven and on the table, my mother shouts, 'Come on now, everybody, before the potatoes go cold. Tuck in.'

'Come on, lads,' says my stepfather, to the kids. 'Get to the table, boys, and eat.'

'Wait now,' says Grandma, ever one for tradition, 'until the men and boys have got theirs.'

So we wait. When the boys are done, we load our plates with turkey, salmon, garlic bread, prawns, chicken-satay sticks and salad. We eat until we're full. Then Josephine starts the call for Grandma's sherry trifle.

Grandma knows how much we all adore her sherry trifle. When I was a little kid she and I made trifle together in her kitchen, tipping sherry in by the glassful. I love her trifle almost as much as I love her treacle bread. Grandma and I haven't made treacle bread together for years.

Josephine pipes up: 'How much sherry is in there, Nana?'

'Two big beakers,' says Aunt Katrina.

'Two big glasses full,' says Grandma. 'Well, we had to – it was to serve eleven and it was a big bowl, you see. That trifle's been here, there and everywhere, that trifle has. It's been carried to three houses over Christmas and it hasn't gone yet. Make sure you eat it.'

'We poured the sherry into these big glasses,' says Aunt Katrina, 'and then we poured it into the trifle and we didn't drink any of it, did we?'

My mother's in the kitchen, pulling off the clingfilm.

'I can smell it from here,' says Josephine. 'We'll all be drunk. Maria won't be able to drive home. Will you, Maria?' She laughs heartily, holding onto Grandma.

'When someone opens a bottle of wine two miles away, Josephine can smell it,' I chime in. I make a gesture like the child-catcher sniffing out children. 'She has a nose for alcohol, our Josephine.'

Aunt Sarah turns to Grandma and Aunt Katrina. 'I bet you drank the rest of it, didn't you?'

'We did not!' says Aunt Katrina.

'Ach, enough now,' says Grandma. 'You'll be okay eating it.'

My mother brings the bowls in, piled high with trifle. I don't know if I can manage so much food.

Grandma takes the first spoonful. We watch her and wait. 'It's good . . . Yes, it is. It's good.' She smiles, then giggles, like I've seen her do with her old schoolfriend. She giggles like a young girl, even though she's on the other side of eighty.

I take a spoonful. It *is* good. 'This is amazing,' I say.

My mother's sitting at the far corner of the table. The men have moved into the other room, captivated by *Father Ted* on the television. I don't know how she found the energy to lay out such a feast, what with my cousin having died. But we're eating, and we're smiling.

Only yesterday my mother said, 'It's been a difficult couple of years.'

'It has,' I said.

'You're looking better today, Grandma,' I say. 'You have colour in your cheeks. You were so pale yesterday, I was worried about you.' She'd been as white as her hair.

'Thank you,' she says, 'for being so observant. I'm glad I'm looking better.' She strokes her cheek with a trembling hand, then smiles her winning smile. And she looks beautiful then. In her wedding photographs she looks like a film star. 'He was only twenty-four,' she says.

We all fall quiet for a moment.

'The doctors,' my mother begins, 'say that he'll provide life for seven people.'

'They can use,' adds Aunt Sarah, 'his heart, his lungs, his eyes, his kidneys . . .'

'There are two of them,' says my mother. 'You only need one to live. He had two to give.'

'And two eyes,' says Grandma. 'You can use the corneas to help blind people.' And she tells us the story of a friend's child who was blind but was able to see because of a donated cornea.

'What else is there?' asks my mother, because it's hard to think straight, and the sherry trifle's almost gone. We're scraping for the cream and the custard at the bottom of the bowls. I can hear the spoons hitting the glass above *Father Ted* on the television. Upstairs, Jack and his cousins are laughing and playing.

'Liver?' I suggest.

'It was in the news,' says Grandma. She turns to me. 'If you find the clipping in the paper, will you give it to me?'

'I will,' I say.

'Seven families are spending this Christmas full of hope because he was an organ donor,' my mother says. Then she brings out the After Eights. The coffee machine bubbles, and my young nephew, who's asleep upstairs, wakes and shouts for Josephine. We eat more chocolates. And we talk.

34

Every day since Christmas Eve I've tried to speak to Toga. He's in Manchester for the holidays, visiting his parents, and I'd hoped to see him. He was too busy to pick up his phone or return my calls, and when we finally spoke this morning he said, 'You sound like you've caught a cold. If you have, we can't meet up tonight because I'm going scuba-diving over New Year and if I catch a cold I won't be able to equalize.'

Jack is staying with my mother so that I can enjoy a birthday night out. Tomorrow I turn thirty. I want to wake up to find that my life has been transformed overnight. My cousin's death has made me realize that I need to get my act together.

Toga's due to come over this evening so I'm on a last-minute mission to make my entire life seem perfect. I scrub the bathroom wearing a basque, a thong and stockings because I don't want to get my new dress dirty. If Toga could see me now, I'm sure he'd want me for ever, for keeps. A girl who cleans the house in stockings: how could he turn her down?

Original plan to celebrate my birthday with Toga: a romantic walk in the country followed by dinner and a night of passion in a four-poster bed at a rural retreat. This was changed to: a romantic afternoon walk across the river to Boho for something to eat. This became: after Toga's shopping trip for his imminent scuba-diving holiday I'll meet him in town. He'll be grumpy and laden with bags. We'll go for a quick bite to eat and afterwards to a bar. Then I'll bring him home. 'I don't want a big night,' he said.

'Okay,' I said, thinking, I want a grand night with bells on it.

I sit at the dressing-table and prepare to undergo some drastic renovations. I dry and straighten my hair, then tease in a few tempting curls. I slap on some foundation and create dark, brooding eyes, framed by incredibly long, sweeping lashes. I'm rubbing some Orgasm over my cheeks (what a ridiculous name for a shade of blusher) when my phone vibrates with a text message. Toga. What does he want now – to cancel?

Didn't go shopping. Will meet at 6.30 p.m. Where?

I text back:

Outside Cornerhouse. X

This means we can pop into Odder on Oxford Road and have a quick drink with Zelda, Emmeline, Nancy, Sybil and some others who are enjoying a night out. The girls can meet Toga and give me the 'pursue' or 'don't pursue' look.

My phone vibrates again. Toga:

Somewhere more central? X

This is Manchester, not London. Once you're in the centre, everywhere is central. Is it absolutely impossible for Toga to say:

> I'll be there at 6.30 p.m. prompt. You may not be able to see my face because of the enormous bouquet of white lilies and red roses I'll be carrying, especially for you, but you'll be able to sense my passion and love. If you're still uncertain, there'll be two sweet doves perched on my shoulders.

I text back:

> How about outside the library at St Peter's Square?

My lip is still swollen from the night I stepped out of the taxi and slipped on black ice. I try to disguise it with red lipstick. I don't look sexy, I look like I've had a stroke. My arse and hips throb and the bruises on my knees are visible even through the stockings. I also have a scabby red streak on my arm where I burned myself on the grill. All in all, I look like a chick who's heavily into S&M.

Toga texts again:

> Low key. Then back to yours for adult fun. X

Does a game of charades count as adult fun?

Toilette completed, I change the sheets. Which is no easy task in these high heels. Finally I slip on my dress.

Tonight I will drink slowly and steadily. I will not get drunk. I will gaze at Toga adoringly. I take a Beecham's flu remedy to disguise my cold and prepare to leave the house.

The pills were a *bad, bad* idea because now my body is on *fire* – and not in a horny way either. My ears and my vagina itch, and my legs, arms, neck and face sting. I examine myself in the mirror: I'm covered from head to foot in white lumps surrounded by angry red blotches. I'm allergic to it. What a time to find out. Oh, God, what if my throat swells? I might die here, alone in my bedroom. I strip off my underwear and run naked to the bathroom, rummage through the medicine box and pull out some antihistamines. Recommended dose: two small pills. I take four. I won't die on four, but I may pass out in the throes of adult fun. I run a cold shower, then squirt freezing water into my ears, down my throat, over my shoulders and up my orifices. Minutes later I wrap myself in a towel and lie on the bed with relief.

It's now six twenty and I'm late as usual. But at least the red blotches are fading. Result!

I arrive at St Peter's Square and take a seat on a bench in the metro stop and begin to scan the surrounding streets for Toga. I can't see him. My mobile rings. 'Where are you?' he asks. He's playing the I've-been-here-for-ages game.

I can play it too. 'I'm here, darling. Can't see you. Where are you?' Then I spot him over by one of the white pillars at the entrance to Central Library and begin to stroll towards him. A little bag is swinging from his hand and it looks like a present for me. An expensive one.

'Hello,' he says. I stand on tiptoe to catch his kiss on my lips as he hands me a Jo Malone gift bag. 'Happy birthday.'

'Happy Christmas,' I answer.

We walk down Peter Street in the direction of the Hilton Hotel.

We're standing in a queue, waiting for the lift to take us to the cocktail bar. 'I should have put our names on the guest list,' says Toga. 'Last time I came here we had a booth.'

'When did you come here?'

'Earlier this year.'

I hesitate for a moment. 'You told me you couldn't make it. You said someone came in your place.'

'Did I?'

Does Toga tell so many lies he doesn't even remember the truth?

'It's no matter,' he says. Then he continues to tell me about the room, and the bar, and his friends who joined him.

'But you lied to me,' I say.

'I didn't know how to tell you.' He shrugs me off as if I'm being difficult. Then it's our turn to step into the lift and be shuttled up to the bar.

Toga buys me a 'Shaker Maker', a drink the barman recommended the last time he came here.

I say: 'I can't believe you lied to me when you knew the nature of the relationship I had with Rhodri. If you were here with someone else, you should have said.'

Toga doesn't want to talk about that. He leads me over

to the windows where we look out across the city. He says, 'The architecture in London is so much better than it is in Manchester.' He loves the buildings in London and so do I. But when I look out across the skyline, I think, This is my home.

We end up at Wings, a Chinese restaurant on Lincoln Square. The service here is perfect. You don't even have to lift a napkin yourself or pour the wine. They do all that for you. The minute the level in your glass dips, they top it up. I drink much faster than Toga so I'm rewarded with more wine. I'm just beginning to relax when he says, 'I've been trying to figure out what we are to one another. I've never really known, but now I do. We're friends, aren't we? We get on well together and we've known one another for years.' He studies his glass for a few seconds, then adds, 'I can't stay this evening. I can come back to yours for a while but then I must go home.' He means to the single bed at his mother's house. 'I need to go shopping tomorrow and I don't feel well.'

I've spent the Christmas period in and out of an intensive-care unit, waiting for my younger cousin to die. He knows I've done nothing but cry for days. I need to feel loved and I need this man, in whom I've invested too much emotion for years, to care for me. Just for tonight, I don't want to feel that I'm striding through life alone. What I want more than anything, and what I need, is a man to depend on, someone to trust. I don't want *adult fun*.

'You're not coming to my house, getting what you want and then leaving. No. That is not acceptable and it's not polite.' I place my glass down on the table and pull my handbag towards me, searching for my purse. The restaurant manager must have noticed the change in mood because a waitress hastily brings the bill. I take a look at it and throw some notes on the table.

'Don't be like that. I never said I'd stay,' says Toga.

'You did. You texted it.'

'I didn't say specifically I would stay.'

'I said, "Stay over," and you said, "Yes, that should be fine."'

He's going to play with words here: 'should be' being his get-out clause.

'I'm going home tonight.'

'Fine,' I say. 'Your choice.'

'Don't be like this. Don't behave like this. I knew if I mentioned it early on you'd be like this.'

'I'll behave as I see fit. You disrespect me by ignoring my calls, then suggest coming to my house for a bit of fun and leaving. You take me for a fool.' I grab my things and storm off towards the exit. I'm slowed down because I have to wait for the maître d' to bring my coat. 'Is everything okay?' he asks.

'Yes,' I say. 'The meal was fantastic. Thank you.'

I step out of the restaurant and into Lincoln Square. Toga follows me. 'Have you any cigarettes?' he calls gently. Which stalls me because I'm about to cut and run.

'Yes.' I rummage in my bag for a packet, then pull out one for him and another for me. I spend too long hunting for a lighter. Toga lightly strokes the nape of my neck. I lean against the wall and stretch out my hand to light his cigarette.

He gazes down at me and plays with my hair. 'Don't be angry,' he says. 'I didn't know it would be such an issue.'

I think about how brave Jack was with Ellie. If I love Toga, then – 'I'm in love with you,' I tell him.

'No, you're not.'

'Don't be stupid. Of course I am. I've always been in love with you.'

I met Toga at a friend's house many years ago. The doorbell rang when she was busy in the kitchen so I answered it, and there stood Toga.

'It doesn't happen like that,' he replies.

'I've been in love with you since the minute I met you,' I tell him.

Toga made me feel special. In the beginning he took me for champagne cocktails and fancy meals, but recently he's made endless promises that he hasn't kept. The thing we had – it always felt so real, so full of something.

Toga listens to me, and looks amused rather than flattered. Now I'm stricken with terror that for the last few years I've had it all wrong. I've been building sandcastles in the sea.

'You told me you were happy, that you loved Rhodri.'

'I did love Rhodri very much. But you're single, and now I'm single. All I ask is that we try dating,' I add quietly. 'Let's see where it takes us.'

'We can't go from this to dating,' he says abruptly. 'It would be too weird.'

I begin to walk away from him in the direction of Albert Square. I look across at the clock on the town hall – it's almost ten. I stand gazing at the lights on the Christmas tree until he catches up with me.

My phone rings. It's Nancy so I pick up.

'Hi, darling, you having a good evening?'

'It's not quite going to plan,' I say. 'Where are you?'

'We're still in Odder on Oxford Road. Prince is here with Zelda and Sybil. Emmeline's gone to another bar. Why don't you join us?'

'I'll be with you in five minutes,' I say.

I turn to Toga. He's looming over me, smiling, which in the past has always been enough for me to agree to do anything.

'I can't do this. If you aren't going to be with me –'

'I don't love anybody and I don't love you,' he replies. He teases his fingers through my hair.

I long for him to say something different. Everything he does seems to me to be at odds with what he's saying. I could just walk to another bar with him and take him home at midnight. We could forget this conversation and carry on as we did before. 'You don't love me even a little bit?' I ask.

'I don't want it.'

What he means is that he doesn't want me. Then I think, I thought I wanted him, but now when I'm with him I feel worthless. I've felt worthless for years and I don't want to be that person any more. I don't want to spend the last two hours of my twenties with someone who only wants me for 'adult fun'. I deserve more than that. I glance at the line of black cabs at the edge of Albert Square. 'It's everything or nothing, Toga. No emails. No contact. Nothing. This has to end.' I stand on tiptoe to kiss his cheek. 'Goodbye, Toga.'

'You're going?'

'My friends are waiting for me,' I tell him.

Then I run as fast as I can across the road. I don't know what I'm doing or why: all I know is that I if I don't run from Toga now, I never will.

'Oxford Road,' I instruct the cabbie. I fasten my seat-belt. He pulls off quickly. And I'm out of there.

Epilogue

It's a hot summer's day when Zelda and I crash through the long thick weeds on my overgrown allotment. 'Look here,' I call to her. 'This is where Rhodri made the first seed-bed.'

I push back the long grass and point to the branches pegged to the ground. Rhodri grew potatoes there. I remember the day we made this seed-bed together. He had collected windfall branches from the park and dragged them onto his bicycle trailer, which he pedalled here because, of course, he wouldn't use the car. He handed me the mallet, held the wood firmly and told me to whack the peg down with all my might. It was a sunny day. I suppose the past seems brighter now that it's further away.

I fight my way from one side of the allotment to the other. At the far end I wait under the elder tree and look across the plot. I can just about see the compost heap where Rhodri and Jack peed high into the air – 'Wee accelerates the compost,' they insisted, but when I pulled my knickers down to join in they complained: 'It doesn't work if girls do it.' Everything on the allotment is tangled. I can't find what I'm looking for.

'Are you going to keep the allotment?' asks Zelda.

'The council have taken it from me – I had a letter yesterday. I didn't know it looked so bad.' I scuff my feet through the undergrowth, hoping to spot some stray onions, but it's too dense. 'I couldn't come here once Rhodri left,' I tell her. 'It's been abandoned for months.'

Back home we sit with our legs dangling out of the patio doors, drinking coffee. I gaze out over the garden, thinking of all the things I could do if I were to stay in this house. I'd grow red roses up and over the shed and plant a cherry tree by the gate. I hear a neighbour screeching and swearing at her daughter, then a loud argument breaking out with her boyfriend. Josie's dogs bark and sniff by the fence in search of the rabbits . . . They'd spent a few nights in their new hutch – and disappeared. We got down one morning to find the hutch door open and the rabbits gone.

'You won't miss this estate,' says Zelda.

'God, no.'

We roam my house looking for things I may have forgotten. Jack and I have thrown a small lifetime of belongings into bin-bags to be recycled. Carloads of junk have been deposited at the tip. What could be reused was sent to charity shops. I distributed Jack's old toys to neighbours and friends' children by the sackload. I finally emptied the attic of babywear and gave it to an expectant friend of Emmeline's.

When I had stripped our lives of possessions, I could see some truth in what Rhodri believes, that we don't need to keep accumulating new belongings. Now that we own almost nothing, I feel happier than I've ever felt. Jack said, 'Let's just go with our bags, we don't need anything else. We can start again.'

Start again. Yes, please.

Zelda turns to me. 'If you think he might change his mind when you move to London, well, he might not,' she says seriously.

'I'm not moving to London because of him, I'm moving despite him.'

Toga called me a few days ago, around midnight, drunk. He slurred, 'I've something to tell you. I'm going to be a father.' I think I heard my heart crack.

'I'm moving,' I tell Zelda, 'because ever since Damien, I've been waiting for someone to transport me and Jack to a different life. But that's never going to happen, is it? The only person who can change our lives is me.'

When Zelda finally leaves, we share a tearful farewell on the doorstep. It's early evening and the sun is low in the sky, casting long shadows across the communal gardens.

Not long now.

When Rhodri came to say goodbye, he said, 'You should use a ceramic pot to keep your food cool instead of a fridge. It's better for the environment.'

'Do *you* use a ceramic pot to keep your food cool?' I asked.

'No,' he said. 'I don't think the others would agree to it.'

Rhodri is still living in a shared vegan house. When I asked what he'd been doing, he told me he'd been on a protest at a biodiesel plant.

'But I thought biodiesel was good?' I asked.

'So did I,' he said, 'but now it's causing world food shortages.'

I know he's right. I saw pictures of children in Haiti,

stomachs swollen, eating mud cakes because crops are being grown to fuel trendy cars, disrupting food production.

In a few hours, Jack and I will leave this place for ever. Things had just started looking up: at last I'd made a mum friend at school – the photographer. One day in January, when I'd almost given up hope of befriending another mum, she invited me over to hers for coffee, and ever since then we've met up for chats about simple things, like bringing up boys and school work. Jack's first brush with love is over. On Valentine's Day he cried a small storm of tears for Ellie when she handed him back his homemade card, and now, thankfully, he's into football and not girls. And from what I've been told, Damien is making great efforts with his new family. I hope it works out for them. I do.

When we leave this house, another single mother will be moving in. She will rent the house from me. Fingers crossed, she'll have better luck here than we did. We're going to live in London with other single parents and their kids in a large old semi-detached with a big garden. We met on the Internet.

I never thought I'd say this but we've formed a communal single-parent household, which we fondly call The Big Mother House. Rhodri had more of an impact on us than I'd thought.

After my father has loaded what little we're taking to London in the car, I hold on tightly to Jack's hand as we run from room to room. 'Goodbye, bathroom,' we call. 'Goodbye, my bedroom,' I sing.

'Goodbye, my bedroom,' shouts Jack.

'Goodbye, landing.'

'Goodbye, stairs,' shouts Jack.

'Goodbye, kitchen.'

Jack groans. 'Mum, you can't love the kitchen! Come on. We're leaving it.'

I stroke the double-glazing. 'Goodbye, windows,' I tease.

'*Muuuuuuuum.*'

'Goodbye, living room,' we both call.

We run out into the hall and stand on the step and shout, '*Goodbye, house!*'

We knock on Josie's door: 'We're going now,' I say, hugging her. 'Thanks for being a good neighbour.'

'Good luck,' she says. 'I'll miss you being here.'

Then we run to Philomena's house, rap on the letterbox and wait. But she isn't there. The other day I told her husband, Alf, that we are leaving. He said, 'That's a real blow. I mean it. You were one of the good ones. We'll miss seeing you around here.'

And I thought: Why didn't you ever say that before?

'I won't see Scarlet ever again,' whispers Jack sadly. Which is true: Scarlet and Anna have been taken by Social Services and put into care. Their mother never did leave her violent boyfriend.

We dash across to Albert's house. It's almost ten o'clock. He opens his door and stumbles out in his shorts and vest. He doesn't have his teeth in and smiles a wide, gummy smile. 'Where you going?' He laughs, all broken and hoarse.

'We're leaving Albert,' I call. 'You look after yourself, yes?'

I'll miss Albert. And Josie. And Scarlet. I'll miss those three the most.

We say two more goodbyes, hop into the car and meet my dad by the garages.

'Are you ready now?' he asks.

'Yes.'

Then we pull out of the estate.

As the car picks up speed on the motorway, Jack says, 'I have the perfect song. Can I wind the window down and play it loudly?'

'Of course.'

He blasts out 'The Great Escape' from his mobile phone. At first he whistles, but then he hangs his arms and head out of the car and screams and shouts and shouts. I draw my window down too, until we're both shouting at the top of our voices.

'I never thought it would feel so good to leave that house.' I beam at Jack.

'Neither did *I*!' he bellows.

'We're going to have an adventure, Jack.'

'Yes!' he shouts, at the top of his voice.

As we drive towards our new lives, I know that everything will be okay. I can sense it. Something good is going to happen when we move to London. I'm certain of it.

Acknowledgements

Special thanks to PTCR, for making me laugh; and to Rhodri, for our crackpot romance. Also to Mum, Dad, Rufus, Eleanor and the boys, Margarets 2 and 3, Eddie and Josephine. To Pete, Zoe, Emma, Nicola and Sarah for much-needed good words and wine, *cheers*. And to Anne, RP, Morton and Toga too. Duncan, for your weekly guru tasks – send me a (very small teeny-weeny) bill.

Super thanks also to special agent Patrick, editor Katy, to Hazel for her sharp eye, Nicola and Katya.

For help during the dark years, my big thanks to the team at Refuge, plus AS, RK and Ms Lester.

And for help during the light years, SA.

Love letters?

Find someone whose words
could inspire you at
www.penguindating.co.uk

Discover your own happy ending.

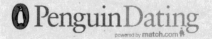